Fostering
LEARNER
INDEPENDENCE

For my parents, Ken and Linda, for instilling in me a strong sense of independence.
For my husband, Paul, for supporting and encouraging me in my independence.
For my son, Tyrel, for giving me an incredible sense of joy as I watch his independence grow.

—Roxann

For my family, who supports me with unwavering encouragement.

—Karin

And for our friend, colleague, and mentor, Darcy Bradley,
who is the reason this manuscript ever began.

Fostering
LEARNER
INDEPENDENCE

An Essential Guide
for K–6 Educators

Roxann Rose-Duckworth
Karin Ramer
Foreword by Ron Ritchhart

CORWIN PRESS
A SAGE Company

For information:

Corwin Press
A SAGE Company
2455 Teller Road
Thousand Oaks, California 91320
www.corwinpress.com

SAGE Ltd.
1 Oliver's Yard
55 City Road
London EC1Y 1SP
United Kingdom

SAGE Pvt. Ltd.
B 1/I 1 Mohan Cooperative Industrial Area
Mathura Road, New Delhi 110 044
India

SAGE Asia-Pacific Pte. Ltd.
33 Pekin Street #02-01
Far East Square
Singapore 048763

Printed in the United States of America

Library of Congress Cataloging-in-Publication Data

Rose-Duckworth, Roxann.
Fostering learner independence: An essential guide for K–6 educators/ Roxann Rose-Duckworth, Karin Ramer.
    p. cm.
Includes bibliographical references and index.
ISBN 978-1-4129-6606-1 (cloth)
ISBN 978-1-4129-6607-8 (pbk.)
    1. Active learning. 2. Elementary school teaching. 3. Motivation in education. I. Ramer, Karin. II. Title.

LB1027.23.R67 2009
372.1102—dc22   2008022904

This book is printed on acid-free paper.

08 09 10 11 12   10 9 8 7 6 5 4 3 2 1

Acquisitions Editor:	Jessica Allan
Editorial Assistant:	Joanna Coelho
Production Editor:	Veronica Stapleton
Copy Editor:	Rebecca Keever
Typesetter:	C&M Digitals (P) Ltd.
Proofreader:	Dennis W. Webb
Indexer:	Sheila Bodell
Cover Designer:	Rose Storey

Contents

Foreword

On a recent visit to a school in Australia, a colleague of mine shared with me an item that had just appeared in the education section of the local newspaper. The article, provocatively entitled, "Results back principal's return to instruction," was printed the same week scores on the state achievement tests were released. The short piece heralded the remarkable gains being achieved by one school that had recently implemented "explicit instruction in which teachers closely direct student learning." Although little was offered to explain what explicit instruction actually was, it did contrast it to the "dominant inquiry model" prevalent in most schools in Australia. In quoting a member of the Australian Council of Educational Research, the piece suggested that direct instruction was the only logical teaching method for schools since "Direct instruction and explicit teaching is two to three times more effective than is inquiry-based learning or problem-based learning." My colleague shared with me how this article had sparked considerable debate in educational circles and that there was a flurry of interest among school principals to find out the secrets of direct instruction.

I admit that the article sparked my interest as well. It certainly got me thinking. Coming at the exact time as I was reading *Fostering Learner Independence: An Essential Guide for K–6 Educators* by Roxann Rose-Duckworth and Karin Ramer, I found it quite provocative. I found the need to reconcile the straightforward, slam-dunk, tidy approach to improving education being portrayed in the article with the more nuanced and elaborated practices Rose-Duckworth and Ramer were painting for me in their own text. Furthermore, since my own work focuses on the important role of teachers in creating cultures of thinking in their classrooms that can effectively nurture students' intellectual character, I found myself at odds with an approach to education that views the teacher's role as the mere delivery agent of prescribed instructional practices.

Of course, the flurry to embrace a successful test-performance method will not be surprising to today's educators. Although the article appeared in an Australian newspaper, it could just have easily come from any town in North America. The desire to improve education for all students, to meet annual yearly progress toward that goal, and improve one's classroom, school, state, or nation's standing is widespread. And rightly so. We all want the best for students. We all want them to succeed. However, this report on direct instruction and the article's seductive suggestion that explicit teaching is the "smart move" for schools to make needs to be examined further. On first blush, it all seems clear enough, but like most simplistic solutions to educational problems, we shouldn't be so quickly seduced.

Two basic assumptions about education are implicitly being made by the advocates of direct instruction. They need addressing before any serious debate can continue: First, what is the purpose of education? This report, and many others like it, concentrates on short-term gains on narrowly focused tests while failing to take into account the broader purposes of education. Second, what is being learned about learning through the methods being proposed as a solution? As these two questions directly relate to the fundamental underpinnings of what you will encounter as a reader of *Fostering Learner Independence: An Essential Guide for K–6 Educators*, I'd like to explore these questions here as a way of introducing the text and priming your thinking for what you are about to read.

I believe one of the most important questions we need to be asking ourselves, both as a society and as professional educators, is: What is it we are teaching for? (And, yes, I know that sentence ends with a preposition.) How we answer this question ultimately provides the basis for the decisions we make about education. Are we teaching for the test so that our school bests the other schools, or are we teaching to foster the kinds of thinking and habits of mind that will develop our students intellectually? Are we teaching to develop students who are adept at playing the game of school, or are we teaching to develop the curiosity and independence that will make our students lifelong learners? Are we teaching students to be good at taking tests or good at learning new things? Are we teaching them to depend on others for evaluation or to develop their own sense of quality and a desire to do their best?

Since the way we frame a problem ultimately shapes the types of solutions we embrace, the way one answers the question, "What is it we are teaching for?" is important. Our answers will guide the kinds of solutions we seek and the types of teaching practices we embrace. While advocates of direct instruction may point to scores on tests as a "slam dunk" that their methods work, the evidence they offer is only meaningful if test performance is the ultimate end of education. For those of us wanting more from our teaching, more from our students, and more from an education, we might be skeptical of such an easy fix. However, in rejecting the easy fix, we need to be clear that we are not rejecting achievement. To be sure, we want good test scores for our students as well, but we know that providing students with a quality education means rejecting a reductionist view of education and embracing a more expansive view. It means avoiding an either-or dichotomy and instead adopting a both-and perspective. We know that good teaching can cultivate students who not only do well on tests but who also love learning.

Rose-Duckworth and Ramer provide just such a perspective here. While acknowledging the very real demands teachers face to produce student achievement, they show that this agenda is in no way incompatible with nurturing students as independent learners. This is the beauty of *Fostering Independent Learners.* In these pages you will see how teachers can achieve great and significant outcomes for their students in terms of academic achievement, while nurturing a love of learning and belief in oneself as a capable independent learner. Chapter by chapter you will be taken into classrooms, offered vignettes, and shown specific strategies to nurture independence in your students.

As these examples unfold, it would be easy to think of the book as merely a collection of invaluable classroom strategies and practices. However, Rose-Duckworth and Ramer deftly address the other fundamental question all educators need to be aware of: What is being learned about learning through the methods we choose? Teaching and learning are not nearly the straightforward practices some would suggest. It is far more than a system of well-designed instructional inputs targeted to achieve a set of desired learning outcomes as proponents of direct instruction suggest. Rather, our teaching practices telegraph a philosophy of learning. Sitting in the classroom, a student does much more than take in information; he or she also learns what it means to be a learner and subsequently finds one's place in the world of ideas. As Jules Henry (1963) noted nearly four decades ago in *Culture Against Man,* a child writing spelling words on the chalkboard is learning much more than spelling. He or she is also learning how not to make the chalk squeak, how to ignore the distraction of the other students in the room, how to focus, how to deal with evaluation and possible failure, how to respond to the authority of the teacher, and so much more.

As teachers, we send a constant stream of messages to our students about what counts and what doesn't, how learning operates, the nature of knowledge and thinking, how to deal with mistakes, the purpose and intent of school, among other things. Through these messages, students develop their own epistemology as well as their own approaches to learning. These approaches can either focus on surface learning, just memorize it and remember it long enough for the test, or on deep learning, strive to make sense of new ideas and connect them to one's other learning. Rose-Duckworth and Ramer recognize this crucial aspect of teaching by not merely presenting a collection of instructional strategies, but by situating these within the context of the teacher's beliefs about teaching. Throughout the text, they engage readers in reflecting on their own deeply held assumptions and on making sense of how these personal views about the nature of learning and teaching ultimately influence the type of classroom they create for learners. In doing so, they have created an invaluable resource for all educators who seek the highest level of learning for all their students: independence.

—Ron Ritchhart, Ed.D., Project Zero,
Harvard Graduate School of Education

References

Smith, B. (2008, May 10). Results back principal's return to instruction. *The Age.*
Henry, J. (1963). *Culture against man.* New York: Random House.

Preface

The late educational researcher John Nicholls once remarked to me that he had met a lot of administrators who "don't want to hear a buzz of excitement in classrooms—they want to hear nothing." His implication was that some teachers strive to keep tight control over students less because of their principles than because of their principals.

—Alfie Kohn (2003, *Educational Leadership*)

Several years ago, we sat around a table of educators analyzing our classrooms for evidence of learner independence. Our collective journey to uncover the role and significance of learner independence began as we dialogued with our colleagues and reflected on our practices. For three years, we met as a group of five educators once a month to discuss habits of independence and the consequences of dependent behaviors. Over time we debated the role of the learner and the educator in fostering habits of independence. Through research, reflection, and classroom experience we drew conclusions about fostering independence and formed common understandings about developing these behaviors in learners. Recognizing the power of learner independence, we decided to share our understandings with other educators. As you spend time reading and reflecting on your own practices, it is our hope that you experience a journey that melds together your current understandings with new insight found in the pages of this book.

As we researched learner independence, we found ample information on how to effectively teach learners. We also uncovered many books that claim their model will systematically train students to participate in various structures intended to develop independent learning habits. This book goes beyond a text that lays out a detailed plan or step-by-step formula of how you can develop independence in the classroom. We believe that independence is not about training students, nor is it about controlling students in more palatable ways. Independent learning is not keeping students occupied, busy, and quiet, nor does it have to do with following set routines and procedures with precision. Classrooms where management structures are used can certainly be positive learning environments where independence is valued—but we believe that it is not these models in themselves that create the lasting habits of independence. So whether you are currently using a management model such as The Daily Five (Boushey & Moser, 2006) in order to promote independence or if you are not using any particular management model, this book will challenge you to reflect on your philosophy of teaching and learning.

In *The Energy to Teach*, Donald Graves (2001) notes what many educators want for their students:

> . . . to be better readers, writers, mathematicians, historians, and artists. [They] also want them to learn to be responsible participants in a democratic society and care about justice for all people, not just themselves. The school is often the first place children learn to participate in a society beyond the home. (p. 134)

The approximations learners make toward what it means to be independent start early, and school is an ideal place to carry on this important work. Consider the impact of a teacher's efforts when the focus is on preparing students for life, not solely for classroom experiences. Dorothy Rich writes in her book, *MegaSkills* (1988):

> In the workplace, employers are alarmed. Today's graduates, they say, are only marginally prepared for job success. The problem is not just literacy. Students have trouble giving their best to their work and in having disciplined work habits. (p. 4)

We aim to help you reflect on why you do what you do by focusing on why you do things a certain way, rather than how to do them. We challenge you to make decisions that reflect your principles and choices that are manageable for you and your students. It is our goal to illustrate the impact teacher decisions can have when we focus on why we make the choices we do and stop looking for cookie-cutter approaches where we aim to duplicate procedures that are promised to encourage independence.

The chapter features of this book are designed to aid you in reflecting on what you have read. Each chapter introduction includes several questions to prompt you to reflect on your current understandings about fostering learner independence. We encourage you to revisit these questions at the end of each chapter as a way of reflecting on how your thinking may have changed as a result of what you read. Documenting your thoughts may be helpful as you sift and sort through challenges you encounter and work to formulate new understandings. In the sections titled "A Time to Reflect," we have presented activities that are intended to promote conversations and professional growth. In the final portion of each chapter, we have included a section called "A Visit to Our Classrooms" that provides a snapshot into our classrooms and reflective practice. This feature is designed to show some of the changes we have made over time and to illustrate how we continually strive to refine our practices. However you choose to utilize these chapter features, it is our desire that you access this text in a way that leads you to optimum personal learning and reflection in regards to fostering independence in your students.

In this book, we will not provide a cookbook approach where you simply follow our recipe to create independent learners. But we will help you identify key ingredients, necessary tools, and helpful tips that will assist you in creating your own process for creating student success and independence. Each classroom has a set of variables influencing the way children learn, and we recognize that your classroom is no different. We are excited to be part of your journey. We are honored to help you delve into the "whys" so that you can choose the appropriate "hows." Some of these hows we will provide as examples and some of the hows will come to you as you reflect on your understandings about what it means to be a lifelong and independent learner, both as a student and as a teacher. Alfie Kohn (1999) advocates that teachers need to move away from "doing things to" students and instead, focus on "doing things with" students. It is our hope that as you read our text, you will consider a variety of things that you can do *with* your students to help them develop as independent learners. No matter what grade level you work with, or what special needs your students have, all of your students have the potential to grow in their independence. This is the greatest gift you can give your students, and it is the greatest gift you will ever give yourself as a teacher.

Acknowledgments

We would like to express our gratitude to Darcy Bradley, Pam Pottle, and Trish McClure for their many hours of dialogue when we began this book. We thank them for their insight, expertise, and wisdom.

Thanks also to our editor, Jessica Allan, for approaching our manuscript with enthusiasm, confidence, and diligence from the beginning. We also recognize and appreciate all of the hard work by the staff at Corwin Press who continuously focused on refining our project.

Roxann would like to acknowledge these educators for their modeling and collegial discussions that have had a strong impact on her understandings about teaching and learning: Dawn Christiana, Denise DesJarlais, Roger Hasper, Ian Buchan, Chris Hoyos, Adrienne Nelson, Tom Venable, Marsha Riddle Buly, Sally Holloway, and Tauna Johnson.

Karin recognizes the role Pat Buhl has had in shaping her first as a kindergartener, and later as a teacher. With her humor, reflection, intellect, and support, Pat has taught many to read and even more to become passionate about literacy instruction. Thank you for your dedication and contribution to the field of education.

And thank you to all of the educators who influence lives today, one teaching decision at a time.

PUBLISHER'S ACKNOWLEDGMENTS

Corwin Press wishes to acknowledge the following peer reviewers for their editorial insight and guidance:

Marycay Densmore
Middle School Teacher
Mesa Verde Middle School
San Diego, CA

Sandra K. Enger
Associate Professor of Science Education
The University of Alabama in Huntsville
Institute for Science Education
Huntsville, AL

Kathleen T. Isaacs
Adjunct Instructor
Children's Literature
Towson University
Towson, MD

Renee Peoples
Fourth-Grade Teacher
Swain West Elementary
North Carolina Western Region Teacher of the Year
Bryson City, NC

Stephen G. Peters
CEO/President
The Peters Group
Orangeburg, SC

Cynthia L. Wilson
Associate Professor, Teacher Education
University of Illinois at Springfield
Springfield, IL

About the Authors

 **Roxann Rose-Duckworth** is an innovative elementary and middle school teacher, college instructor to preservice educators, and respected educational consultant. Rose-Duckworth has nearly fifteen years experience working with students in kindergarten through sixth grade in three different states. She was recognized for her creative and effective teaching strategies in 1996 when the Walt Disney Company honored her dedication to her students as one of 36 teachers chosen nationwide to be honored by Disney's American Teacher Awards. Rose-Duckworth's teaching was highlighted in *The Creative Classroom Project*, a video series by Harvard Graduate School of Education's Project Zero (1999–2004). She has presented at national conferences for both ASCD and IRA and published articles in NCTE's *Primary Voices*. In 2006, Rose-Duckworth co-authored *The Teaching Experience: An Introduction to Reflective Practice*. She enjoys preparing future teachers for tomorrow's classrooms and working with current teachers to help them reflect on and improve their teaching practices. Rose-Duckworth takes an active role in North Sound Reading Council, her local International Reading Association affiliated organization.

 **Karin Ramer** is a reflective and respected elementary school teacher and educational consultant. She has taught kindergarten through third grade, Reading Recovery®, Title I, and special education. Aside from teaching in the classroom, she has effectively worked as a mentor, literacy coach, and staff development facilitator at the elementary level. Her passion is teaching students and guiding educators as they reflect on best practices. Currently, Ramer works as an educational consultant in Oregon and Washington, aiming to enhance understandings about literacy and learner independence. Over the last ten years, she has presented for conferences sponsored by the Western Literacy & Reading Recovery®, The Learning Network®, and Washington Organization for Reading Development (WORD).

1

Learner Independence

The greatest sign of success for a teacher . . . is to be able to say, "The children are now working as if I did not exist."

—Maria Montessori (2007, online)

Like every teacher, we want what is best for our students: while academic standards are held high, we strive for all learners to feel capable, valued, and powerful. We work diligently to interact with students in a way that will bring them success in both the classroom and the real world where our teaching ultimately is intended to impact students' lives. Throughout our years of teaching, we have found that learner independence consistently contributes to student success, but facilitating learning that fosters habits of independence can be a challenge.

Although we could craft a lesson, manage a classroom, and prepare for student learning, questions about our teaching practice remained. Can learner independence be taught? When is independence an appropriate expectation? And perhaps most importantly, what is learner independence? In sifting through our experiences, we first decided what learner independence is not: learner independence is not freedom without accountability, nor is it the systematic knowledge and completion of routines and procedures. Independence is not quietly staying on task and keeping busy or finishing work without teacher support. Learner independence has more to do with the thinking behind the decisions we make and the actions we take. The behaviors that belong to a truly successful learner are more complex than just following protocol and being self-sufficient.

In order to further understand independence in the classroom, this chapter is devoted to defining learner independence, examining how it impacts student self-esteem, and analyzing the thinking habits of truly independent learners. Just as we took time to sift and sort through what we understood about learner independence, it is important that you analyze and evaluate your prior experience with respect to this topic. Reflect on the following questions and jot down some of your current understandings to support you as you read the rest of the chapter.

- What is learner independence?
- Why is the concept of independence important and to whom is it important?
- What kinds of teacher behaviors encourage students to be independent learners?
- What do I do now to encourage independent learning?

DEFINING LEARNER INDEPENDENCE

It would be an error to assume that our definition of independence matches that of our readers; therefore it is essential to clarify this term from the beginning. When we researched independence in the dictionary (Merriam-Webster Online, 2007), we found over twenty definitions. As we analyzed the myriad of descriptors that followed 'independent,' we began to see just how complex deciding upon a common definition could be. While no one definition truly supported our thinking of independent learners, we concluded that to agree upon one definition was the only way to have common grounds for our written and verbal conversations. Our working definition is as follows:

> Independent learners are internally motivated to be reflective, resourceful, and effective as they strive to accomplish worthwhile endeavors when working in isolation or with others—even when challenges arise, they persevere.

As we worked to create this definition, we aimed to keep it short and concise, making sure that this definition encapsulated all that we believe and understand about independent learners. We had many discussions about what was meant by "internally motivated," "reflective," "resourceful," "effective," and "worthwhile endeavors." These are ideas that we will clarify throughout our book.

To expand on our definition and its relevance to the classroom, let us take some time to explain some of our wording. For example, notice how we wrote that independent learners are able to accomplish worthwhile endeavors whether they work in isolation or with others. Although others do not control them, independent learners are influenced by others' thoughts, beliefs, and actions. This influence occurs once the learner has the opportunity to sift and sort information, and as a result, he formulates his own ideas, culminating in a set of core understandings and beliefs. Through the reflective process, learners ask questions of themselves and of others, and make decisions based upon a clear set of standards. Learners who are independent proceed with confidence as a direct result of seeing the consequences of their decision-making process. Independent learners look similar to students who exhibit high levels of responsibility. In order to identify independent learners, you must further analyze the students' work, words, and actions for attributes of learner independence. Students who are independent do well with intrapersonal tasks as well as with interpersonal experiences. It may be helpful to describe independent learners in further detail by breaking down specific behaviors and by explicitly identifying them as actions of independence. As you read this list in Figure 1.1, you may want to consider how these descriptions relate to students you know.

Figure 1.1   Elements of Learner Independence

Our Definition	Observable Behaviors of Independent Learners
Internally motivated	• think and plan before they act • know when to act quickly and when to give more time to decision-making • strive to do their best because they care about the quality of their work • able to answer "Why are you learning this?"
Reflective	• know how to seek and consider answers to their questions • suspend judgment of ideas, people, and concepts until they have carefully considered them • able to answer the question, "What are you learning about ____?"
Resourceful	• curious about the world around them • ask thoughtful questions of others and themselves (not the *do we have to know this for the test* type questions but those life-long questions such as *how do I solve this challenge* and *what resources will I need to do it?*)
Effective	• reflect on what they believe and how that matches (or doesn't) with how they behave and learn • exhibit critical thinking skills in a metacognitive fashion
Accomplish worthwhile endeavors	• productive decision-making capacities • aim to make connections to learning experiences • able to answer the question, "What are you doing and what will you do next?"
Work in isolation	• modify their thinking and actions based on quality evidence • make their own and observe others' mistakes and successes and learn from them • have strategies for personal problem solving
Work with others	• aware of how their actions affect others • understands and appreciates how various perspectives bring value to learning experiences

There is no magic age at which we suddenly become independent learners; we've met toddlers who exhibit many of these characteristics and adults who show limited use of most of these behaviors. Ultimately, our goal is for students of all ages to develop characteristics of independence. As you read this book, we will clarify our definition further and help you to expand upon the definition for yourself. It is our hope that you take our working definition and use it to create your own understanding of independent learning.

To aid you in creating your own definition, think about when you learned to drive. Most teenagers use their independent learning skills as they earn their driver's license. Did you make mistakes and learn from them? Did you watch others make mistakes and learn from those errors? When you made a lane change and almost hit a car driving in your blind spot, was your thinking modified? Did you check your blind spot when doing future lane changes? Are you careful not to drive in other people's blind spots? Were you curious about learning how to parallel park? Were you thinking and planning before you acted? Most likely you were using critical thinking skills, productive decision-making capabilities, and you had an incredible sense of internal motivation. It is very unlikely to hear someone in a drivers' education class ask, "Why do we have to learn this?"

Whereas driver's education is unquestionably motivating, we believe it doesn't require a topic like this to encourage independent learning skills in students. We can set up any learning environment to help students develop the critical life skill of being an independent learner. Most people are motivated to be independent learners as they learn to drive and a huge part of that is because they have an authentic purpose for learning the skills associated with driving. We believe that teachers can set up their classrooms so that students have genuine purposes for their learning. Research has shown that authentic learning experiences, rather than tasks that are void of meaning for learners, have a positive impact on learning. Duke, Purcell-Gates, Hall, and Tower (2006) monitored the authenticity of literacy activities in a variety of classrooms. They found that those teachers who included a greater number of authentic literacy activities more of the time had students who showed higher growth in both comprehension and writing. We can only conclude that incorporating genuine literacy into the classroom increases learner engagement, thus impacting student learning.

A recent article found in the National Science Teachers Association's journal, *Science and Children*, provides another example of how an authentic learning experience impacts student independence. The article (Coskie, Hornof, and Trudel, 2007) summarizes a five-week study that taught students how to write a field guide (Figure 1.2) that identified the plants in a small wooded area on their school property. By creating this authentic genre of scientific writing, students came to understand and care for the natural world in their immediate environment. They also developed important science, reading, and writing skills through purposeful work.

Once their field guides were published, the students' families were invited to a special afterschool event where students took their guests on a scavenger hunt. The authentic learning opportunity culminated when students had the opportunity to watch their guests use their class-created field guide to find each plant listed in the scavenger hunt list.

Our goal is to develop learners, and in turn, citizens who rely on an intrinsic desire to keep learning. Children are naturally curious, and we believe that tapping into this internal drive to inquire and discover can encourage habits of independence in learners. School can be a place to foster the growth of the independent learner at any grade, age, or stage of development. Success comes to those teachers who figure out how to further develop independence in themselves and in their students, while still meeting or exceeding academic standards.

Figure 1.2   Sample Field Guide Page

Scientific Name: Ranunculus Repens

Leaf: Each leaf is compound and the side parts look like hands and the top part looks like a head making the leaf look like a person. There are pin-head sized dots of light-green where each lobe meets and specks of light-green all over. There are also odd claw-like hairs growing on it. The leaves are about an inch long and an inch and one quarter wide.

Zoom H1 stem

Zoom 2. leaf

Zoom-in of the Creeping Buttercup

Did you know? These weedy species reproduce when its nodes touch the ground.

Figure 1.2 (Continued)

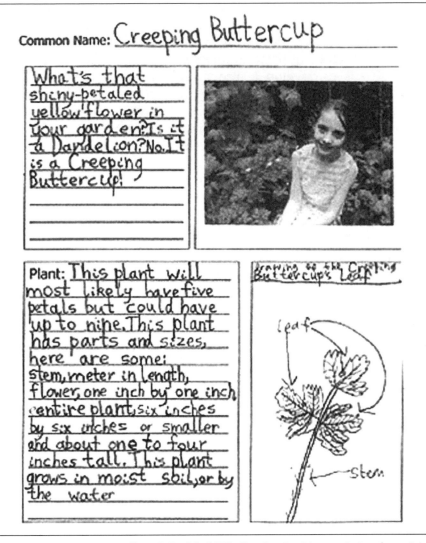

SOURCE: From Coskie, Hornoff, and Trudal (2007). Reprinted with permission from *Science & Children*, a publication for elementary level science educators published by the National Science Teachers Association (www.nsta.org).

LEARNER INDEPENDENCE ENCOURAGES SELF-ESTEEM

As adults, we have a vast repertoire of experiences, some of which resulted in success, whereas others ended in failure. Reflect on your own life and think about a specific skill that resulted in success and another that resulted in failure. Which are you more likely to continue, the activity that was "doable" or the one that was seemingly impossible to accomplish? Although there are exceptions when people have chosen to prevail over failure, as a rule people choose to continue with a specific activity when it positively contributes to their self-esteem. How many adults have you met who openly admit that they hate math because they struggled in school? What about people who choose not to read for pleasure because it was a chore growing up? The same concept can be transferred to young learners: how students feel about their own capabilities influences their ability and internal drive to learn. This does not mean that learning should be easy for students and all attempts successful. As teachers, this knowledge should drive us to set up learning experiences where students take on a challenge because they are equipped to do so. Kostelnik, Whiren, Soderman, Stein, and Gregory (2002) have identified three dimensions to self-esteem: competence, worth, and control.

- *Competence* is the belief that you can accomplish tasks and achieve goals.
- *Worth* can be viewed as the extent to which you like and value yourself.
- *Control* is the degree to which people feel they can influence the events around them.

Examining each of these qualities can help a teacher concentrate on specific ways for developing habits of learner independence while impacting self-esteem. We have chosen specific examples, not to tell you how to promote learner self-esteem but to demonstrate why each of these components is such a powerful influence in contributing to student independence.

Competence is the belief that you can accomplish tasks and achieve goals. Select from your experiences a time in which you felt encouraged to continue on a specific task, not because of your automatic mastery, but because you experienced gradual success. Your sense of competence was the fuel you needed to continue regardless of the level of challenge you faced. Figure 1.3 shows how a teacher can focus on student approximations while building learner competence by using the *I am learning to . . . I can* sheet (adapted from Campbell Hill, 2001; Graves, 1983). When this type of monitoring sheet is implemented, the teacher identifies the next learning step as she evaluates student work. As she meets with students in writing conferences, either the teacher or student records one writing goal in the "I'm learning" section of the chart. For example, Cashawn's "I'm learning" goal might be "I will capitalize people's names." Once his teacher notices that Cashawn is capitalizing proper names without adult support, she will move this skill to the "I can" section of his chart and record the date (see Figure 1.3). As Cashawn's "I can" list builds, he will feel a growing sense of competence as a writer. Focusing on one goal at a time and then seeing his writing skills and strategies grow will encourage him to continue learning and working. His sense of competence will also be increased as he is held accountable to continue applying the writing skills and strategies that are now listed in the "I can" side of the chart. Cashawn's competence is not assessed by a "one time application"; instead high and clear expectations will support him to employ the skills and strategies of an independent writer.

Figure 1.3 I'm Learning/I Can Sheet

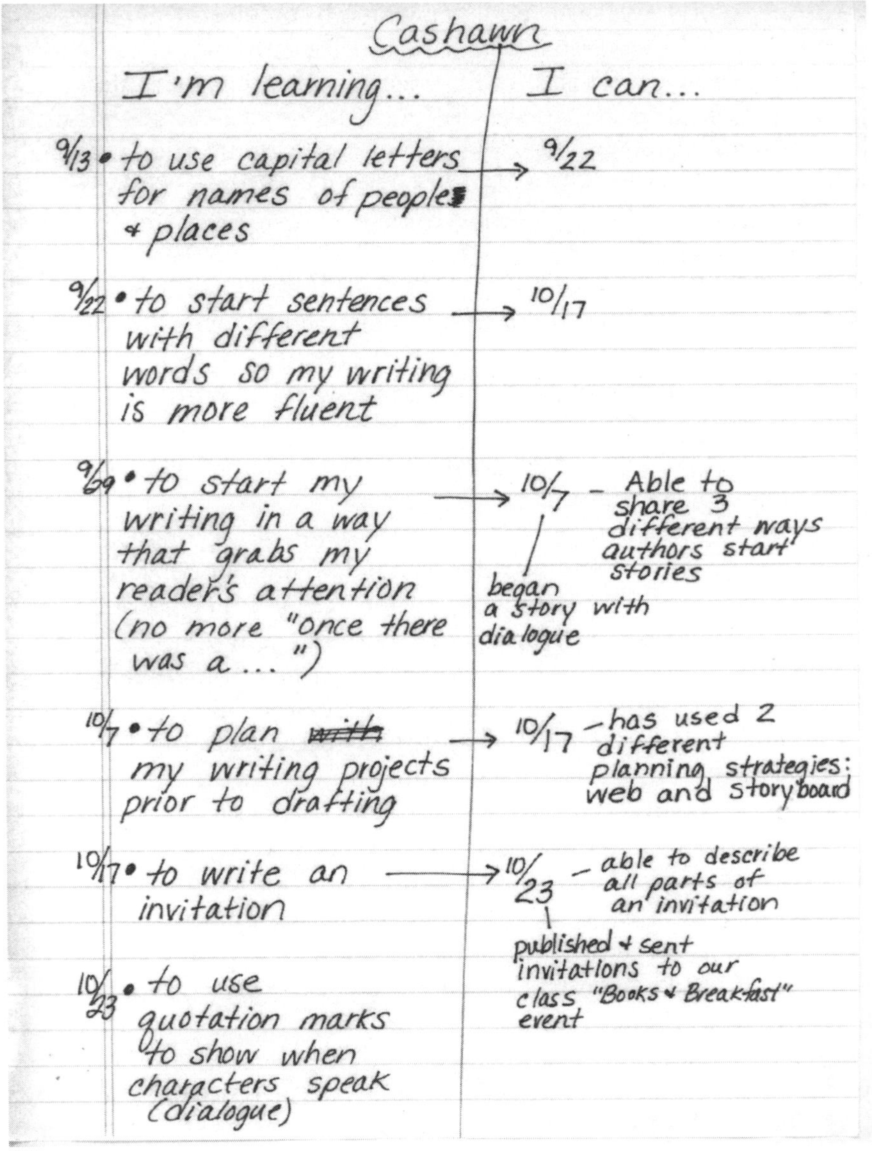
Cashawn

I'm learning...	I can...
9/13 • to use capital letters for names of people + places →	9/22
9/22 • to start sentences with different words so my writing is more fluent →	10/17
9/29 • to start my writing in a way that grabs my reader's attention (no more "once there was a ...") →	10/7 – Able to share 3 different ways authors start stories; began a story with dialogue
10/7 • to plan ~~with~~ my writing projects prior to drafting →	10/17 – has used 2 different planning strategies: web and storyboard
10/17 • to write an invitation →	10/23 – able to describe all parts of an invitation; published + sent invitations to our class "Books + Breakfast" event
10/23 • to use quotation marks to show when characters speak (dialogue)	

Worth can be viewed as the extent to which you like and value yourself. Consider how a learner's sense of worth increases when students are encouraged to focus on sharing their own lives and accomplishments. Brian Bowser, a third-grade teacher, aimed to increase his students' sense of worth by having learners use a unique text feature to write about their lives. The social studies curriculum required students to learn about timelines so Brian decided the best way to begin this study was to have students design timelines on something they have expertise in: themselves. When he explained this assignment, he encouraged learners to highlight accomplishments they were proud of achieving. Brian encouraged students to think of a wide array of successes from academic, athletic, artistic, social, spiritual, to family responsibilities. Once the timelines were complete, students shared their lives with others as they presented their final product to their peers. This example illustrates that students can demonstrate habits of independence in a teacher-chosen activity when learners see an authentic purpose for the task and are encouraged to focus on individualizing the assignment within certain guidelines. In previous years, Brian had simply used a worksheet where students looked at a timeline of Amelia Earhart's life and were asked to place certain life events in order. By changing the assignment, Brian was still helping students learn about timelines, yet in a more meaningful way; but now he was also addressing his students' sense of worth.

Control is the degree to which people feel they can influence the events around them. As adults, it is our sense of control of a situation that empowers us with a feeling of confidence. When we plan for the day, for example, we will approach specific tasks with more vigor if we make the decisions. If we have control over how we spend our time, even the tasks that are less than appealing are easier to accomplish. The same is true with the learners within a classroom when a teacher decides to offer more choices to her students during literacy time. Jillian Portly works diligently to empower her third graders to be in control of their own learning throughout the year. She structures activities so that learners receive modeled and guided instruction when beginning new learning, and then gradually releases responsibility to learners when they demonstrate readiness for independence. At the start of the year in her literacy block, Jillian may begin by structuring student learning by assigning learners specific jobs: "During our literacy block today, you need to read the book about castles and work on drafting your story about living in a castle." Although she is not giving choices about what to read or write, she is allowing students to choose which task to complete first. Afterwards, she will debrief the students about their choices. "Who read the book first? Why did you choose to do that first? How did that help you when you wrote your story? Who decided to write your story first? Why did you choose to do that first? How did that help you read and understand the book?" It is this process of reflecting on why learners made certain decisions and evaluating the consequences of such actions that allows students to gain habits of independence. In order to support learners, Jillian might begin by determining how much time is spent on each assignment by giving a cue to students when it is time to switch to their second task. "Today you'll decide whether to read or write first, just like you've been doing for the last week. But we're going to add a new responsibility today. You will decide when it's time to change to your second activity. How will you know it's time to move onto your next task?" Students will use a variety of strategies including splitting the time evenly, writing or reading for a particular amount of time and then switching tasks, and then there will be students who require or seek teacher support as they make these choices. Jillian will encourage her third graders to think about how they will decide when to switch from task one to task two and then help students reflect on those decisions at the end of that literacy block. A teacher who focuses on fostering habits of independence knows it is important for students to hear each other reflect on these decisions; these reflections will be used to help them make future decisions with regard to independently managing time. As her students become thoughtful and reflective about the order in which they work, Jillian could opt to increase the number of choices students have during the literacy block. Perhaps learners are ready to add other activities such as word sorts, spelling practice, literature circles, listening center, and partner reading to their literacy tasks. At this time, the teacher might begin to support students in selecting their own writing topics, audiences, and purposes as well as their own independent reading. Helping students manage their time within parameters gives them a sense of control. Notice that in this example, increasing behaviors of independence has nothing to do with altering the curriculum, yet everything to do with the thinking behind the decisions students are asked to make.

It is the teacher's job to not only foster academic intelligence and meet standards when working with students; it is even more essential that the teacher does everything to preserve and encourage self-esteem through interactions and endeavors within the school setting. By focusing on student competence, control, and worth a teacher promotes learner independence and creates a classroom community that is internally motivated to learn.

Within any classroom one will inevitably find children who are unique and deviate from what we might consider the average student. Perhaps this student, or group of learners, demonstrates difficulty with time management, organizing assignments, or staying engaged. At the other end of the spectrum, you may find that students are looking for more of a challenge academically and their lack of challenge is evidenced in their work and behavior by sloppy workmanship and an indifferent attitude toward the task at hand. When we aim to differentiate instruction, we can plan to provide a variety of means and support for our students' learning goals (Tomlinson, 2001). Differentiation guru, Carol Ann Tomlinson points out that no matter what you are teaching, it will be learned better if taught in a way that is responsive to the needs of all learners. We believe one aspect of this should be a focus on how we acknowledge the competence, worth, and control of the students in our classroom.

Teachers who strive to encourage independent learners do not opt to raise student self-esteem by giving them unfocused or empty praise or through the use of awards or certificates. These teachers believe self-esteem will increase when students feel competent, worthy, and in control as a result of their own successes: they have learned that these feelings and beliefs come from within. The teacher can facilitate classroom experiences that enhance competence, worth, and control—but the teacher cannot give students self-esteem. Taking time to consider the role competence, worth, and a sense of control plays in developing a learner's self-esteem will help you begin to analyze where you can increase student independence and develop a strong sense of confidence in the learning community.

INDEPENDENT LEARNING: A HABIT OF MIND

A teacher who values habits of independence is more likely to help students establish independent learning habits. Since there is evidence that independent behavior can be learned, then surely we believe that independence can be taught. Take a moment to examine Figure 1.4 for the differences between dependent and independent learner behaviors, regardless of age or stage of learner development.

As you look over this figure, consider how you encourage independence in your classroom by the questions that you entertain from your learners. What is your response to "Am I done?" Do you say, "No, because you need to finish this portion of your work" or do you respond by asking the learner to question himself, "Tell me what you would expect to see in a complete answer. How does that compare with your work here? Now answer the question yourself, are you done? Think about whom is doing the work. According to Harry K. Wong (Wong & Wong, 1998), "The person who does the work is the ONLY one who learns." If this is true, it is essential to reflect on who is thinking with respect to student work. Are you making all of the decisions in the classroom, or are you supporting students as they learn to make decisions based upon their own understandings? If we are supporting students as they make decisions, instead of making decisions for students, we are in fact moving learners along the continuum of independence.

Often times when teachers move to dialoguing with students in a way that encourages independent thinking, they are met with resistance from their students. Anne Udall and Joan Daniels write about this in their book, *Creating the Thoughtful Classroom* (1991):

> . . . students are surprised (sometimes astounded!) when asked to extend their thinking. You will notice blank stares and hear "I don't know." Do not accept "I don't know." (p. 73)

Udall and Daniels give advice for how to address the "I don't know" statement. They encourage teachers to use one of these responses:

- "If you did know, what would you say?"
- "Ask me a question that would help you understand."
- "Pretend you do know and make something up."
- "*I don't know* means you need more time to think—listen to others and I'll come back to you." (Then make sure you do.)

Respected educator and psychologist, Haim Ginott, pioneered many techniques for conversing with children. He points out that the effective teacher is one who makes himself increasingly *dispensable* to children (1965). He encourages teachers (and parents) to lead children to make their own choices and use their own powers. He points out how our conversations

Figure 1.4   Comparison of Thinking: The Dependent Versus the Independent Learner

	Dependent Learners	Independent Learners
Questions to Others	Ask functional questions that require someone else to do the thinking. • Am I done? • What do I do now? • What resources will I need to do this? • Can I go to the bathroom?	Ask questions that promote reflection and require thinking. • Will you provide me some feedback? • This part was tricky for me. Here's what I tried. What do you suggest? • Reading my essay, what do you think is the main idea?
Self-Talk	Think questions belong to others to answer or ask. • After reading aloud to a teacher, the teacher asks some comprehension questions. The student remarks, "I didn't know you were going to ask me questions about what I read. I don't know what this story is about."	Unthreatened by others' or their own questions; persistent in finding answers. • As the student reads aloud to the teacher, the student makes comments like "That title makes me wonder if someone is going to tell a lie . . .", "Oh, it's the mom who lies; I thought it was going to be the kid . . . ."
Motivation	Think learning is extrinsic or "outside" of themselves. • When asked why they are revising a piece of writing, the student replies, "Because my teacher says that I am supposed to do it."	Think learning is intrinsically rewarding. • When asked why they are revising a piece of writing, the student replies, "Because I want to capture my audience's attention."
Resources	Appear unaware of or disinterested in the variety of resources available to seek answers to questions. • *I can't find the answer.* • *What's the answer to this one?*	Know and use a variety of resources to answer questions and solve problems (Internet, other people, inside self, books, magazines, experiences, museums, libraries). • *Hmmm, the answer isn't here. I wonder if an atlas would help.*
Feedback	Wait for others to judge and evaluate their performance. • *Am I done?* • *Is this good enough?*	Identify their own challenges and strengths; seek and value feedback from others. • *I solved the problem accurately and used the work backwards strategy for the first time.* • *My classmate recommended that I add more details so I'm working on that.*
Problem Solving	Rely on others for direction in learning, problem solving; wait for others to do the work. • When the teacher notices that a student has not started an assignment that the class has been working on for 15 minutes, the student responds with "I didn't know what to do . . ." or "Sarah keeps interrupting me."	Act to solve problems appropriately, do the work needed to support themselves, see themselves as "do-ers." • When a student is confused by a task, the student asks specific questions to peers or adults. If no one is available to help, the student tries a variety of solutions while waiting.

with students indicate our belief in their capacity to make wise decisions for themselves. Ginott challenges us to avoid our inner "yes" responses when a child makes a request. Instead of giving a simple "yes" to a request, think how these statements (which Ginott refers to as *freedom phrases*) foster student independence:

- "If you want to."
- "If that is really what you would like."
- "You decide about that."
- "It is really up to you."
- "It is entirely your choice."
- "Whatever you decide is fine with me."

Ginott writes that a "yes" answer may be gratifying to children, but these *freedom phrases* give children a sense of satisfaction of making a decision and shows them that their teacher has faith in them.

Just as Ginott helped us realize how our "yes" responses can undermine student independence, author and educational consultant Barbara Coloroso has helped many teachers realize that our "no" answers can negatively affect student independence and motivation. Coloroso gives three alternatives to "no" responses (1994):

- "Yes, later."
- "Yes" with conditions as in "Yes, you may work on the computer after your math assignment is complete."
- "Give me a minute." (This gives you and the student a moment to think about the decision/problem.)
- "Convince me." (You can keep responding with "I'm not convinced" until either you are convinced, you say "yes," or the student has run out of ideas.)

The learning environment is conducive to creative, constructive, and responsible activity; all of which have a big impact on student independence. Coloroso points out that teachers should save their "no" answers for the big issues, when there is no bend, when they mean it, and when they intend to follow through with it. Coloroso writes:

> With the no they give an explanation that is meaningful. Children can then begin to develop their own internal moral structure that enables them to function responsibly and creatively in society. (p. 61)

So, consider a simple request made by a student such as "Can I use markers on this assignment?" Your inclination might be to say "yes" but consider how things change when you say, "It is really up to you." Maybe the request to use markers on a particular assignment would likely lead to you replying with "No," because you worry that the student won't make revisions on the poster she is creating because the markers are not erasable. But what if instead of quickly replying "No," you said "Yes, you may use markers after you. . . ." or maybe you would say, "Convince me why using markers is a good idea for this project."

When dealing with discipline issues, we recommend using what Jim Fay and David Funk (1995) call thinking words as demonstrated in Figure 1.5. They also recommend enforceable statements that tell students what the teacher will do or allow rather than telling students what to do. An unenforceable statement of "Stop yelling at me!" becomes an enforceable statement by saying, "I'll listen to you as soon as your voice is as calm and quiet as mine." Enforceable statements acknowledge the shared control in a classroom setting—in reality, no one can really control another person's behavior—we can only influence behavior. Enforceable statements model for students how we can care for ourselves when interacting with others. These statements set high expectations but do not require compliance of students. Enforceable statements and thinking words encourage cooperation and independence. Peter Johnston (2004) points out how the things teachers say, and don't say, have huge consequences for what their students learn and how their students think:

> Talk is the central tool of their trade. With it they mediate children's activity and experience, and help them make sense of learning, literacy, life and themselves. (p. 4)

Figure 1.5   "Thinking Words" Using Love and Logic Principles

When you ____ then you ____.	When you have your book, then you will be ready for literature circle.
Yes, you can ____ when you ____.	Yes, you can go on the computer when you have cleaned up your publishing materials.
Feel free to ____ when you ____.	Feel free to sit next to your friends during writing time when you are able to focus on your writing.
I'll know ____ when you ____.	I'll know you are ready to have me check your spelling words when you put your spelling log on top of your desk before lunch.

SOURCE: Fay and Funk, 1995.

CONCLUSION

While it is likely that our working definition of independent learners will be altered by experiences and research over time, human behaviors will not change. Independent learners will continue to be internally motivated, and they will work toward goals alone or with others. They will be reflective, resourceful, and effective as they work to accomplish particular tasks and challenge themselves to think beyond one specific assignment. Independent learners will continue to be motivated for the pure sake of learning, and students' self-esteem will be enhanced as a result of their proficiency, feeling of importance, and sense of command in their environment. It is the teacher's job to construct an environment that will develop learners who are eager to contribute to humanity beyond the classroom. In turn it will be our privilege to live in a world that is enhanced by their efforts.

As a result of challenging your beliefs and understandings about learner independence, what are you thinking now? Take some time to review the questions that we addressed at the start of the chapter.

A TIME TO REFLECT

One of the benefits of highly independent students is that responsibility is shifted from the adult to the student who is internally driven. Sometimes it is helpful to analyze particular tasks for levels of student independence and the impact this has on the teacher or other adults involved. As you are thinking about this concept, turn to Resource A where you will find a chart depicting three levels of student independence: highly independent, somewhat independent, and dependent. We encourage you to use this tool as you consider the impact learner independence has on you as the teacher.

To guide you through this activity, we have provided an example of the impact student independence has on homework. As we were completing the chart we thought of one question in particular: *How does the level of student independence impact the adults who support them?* As you apply your understandings to this chart, consider the behaviors you might encounter for a highly independent student, a somewhat independent learner, and a student who is dependent. How does each student function with respect to problem solving in math, independent reading, independent writing, and peer interactions? Perhaps you could select another aspect of the curriculum or class procedures that will help you focus on habits of independence with your learners. Take some time to analyze how instructional time and student learning is impacted by each behavior. Evaluate student performance and reflect on your role as the teacher. What did you notice about your learners? As a result of your new understandings what do you plan to do differently the next time you work with students?

A VISIT TO OUR CLASSROOMS

Grades K–3: A Primary Perspective by Karin Ramer

During my first few years of teaching I felt that students needed to be held accountable for the time I spent reading from a chapter book. I viewed reading aloud from *Charlotte's Web,* for example, as pleasurable and because of that I had a nagging sense that I was responsible to provide evidence of learning as a result of our time in the text. I adopted the practice of asking questions following the last chapter of the book and then assigning students a task that I felt would indicate their level of comprehension. Evaluating student understanding in this manner left me frustrated and wondering if reading aloud was worth students' time because I was not seeing the levels of engagement and comprehension I had hoped for. It wasn't until a few years later that I had the answer to my question: reading aloud was not only worth students' time; it was essential to their development as proficient readers.

My shift in understanding came as a result of a schoolwide focus on reading instruction. We analyzed and evaluated student data in reading, read professional literature, dialogued about explicit reading instruction, and participated in workshops and conferences aimed at improving students' reading strategies and comprehension. As I challenged my understandings and practices, I began to implement teaching practices that supported student growth and development toward skillful reading. Ellin Keene's (2008) research regarding monitoring for meaning and reading comprehension greatly influenced my thinking and in turn my instructional practices. She wrote:

> Readers must *learn* how to pause, consider the meanings in text, reflect on their understandings, and use different strategies to enhance their understanding. This process is best learned by watching proficient models 'think aloud' and gradually taking responsibility for monitoring their own comprehension as they read independently. (p. 3)

A major shift in my instruction came as I experimented with 'thinking aloud' while reading. I found that when I took time to consider the meaning of text, reflected on my understandings, and modeled a variety of reading strategies, student reading was impacted. As opposed to asking questions about character development following reading, I articulated my purpose for reading prior to opening the book each day: *"As I read today, I am searching for ways the author describes the main character."* Once this expectation was in place, I read until I had evidence of character development. At this point I paused to reflect on my understandings: *"After reading about Harvey, I think the author wants me to believe that he is a nervous dog because she wrote about his body shaking, and the way his eyes darted around the room. Instead of just telling us that he was nervous, she showed us by the way he acted."* This explicit focus on the craft of writing as seen through the eyes of a reader, supports students as they develop thinking skills that will help them comprehend text.

I no longer question the value of reading aloud nor feel that I have something to prove when I share a chapter book with students. As a result of consistent modeling and 'thinking aloud' students implement skills and strategies that enhance their comprehension of the texts they read independently. And as we stated earlier in this chapter, learner independence is not about staying busy or completing work to prove that learning has occurred: it is about the thinking behind the decisions we make such as the comprehension skills and strategies students will independently employ as a result of explicit modeling.

Grades 4–6: An Intermediate Perspective by Roxann Rose-Duckworth

For many years, I created a weekly newsletter for my students' families. I spent at least an hour each week writing about what we had accomplished as a class and what our goals were for the near future. I would remind parents of upcoming events and approaching deadlines. As I began to focus on acknowledging students' worth, competence, and control, I began to hand over this writing responsibility to my students. Each day, we would take a few moments and brainstorm anything that needed to be addressed in our classroom newsletter. For example, my students might suggest that we should include information about an upcoming field trip and a guest speaker we just had in the classroom. I could also suggest a topic such as an invitation to next week's PTA meeting. Then students could volunteer to take responsibility for that part of the newsletter. Their name would be written on the whiteboard next to the topic and they knew their deadline was Thursday so that copies could be made for Friday's newsletter. All of a sudden, my students were becoming passionate writers! Students weren't forgetting to hand the newsletter to their families, and it was obvious that parent readership grew dramatically! Supply requests that had once went unnoticed were now being responded to immediately by my students' families. And when students wrote about the need for parent volunteers, parents eagerly stepped up in a way they rarely had before. Students were proud of their newsletters, and they saw themselves as competent writers. They had control over what information was shared with their families and how it was shared. Our classroom newsletter now helped students feel competent, gave them a sense of worth, and helped them exercise a high degree of control.

This small change had a huge impact on our classroom and tremendous influence on student learning. Now the time I used to spend on creating the newsletter could be spent doing something else that had more impact on student learning. I could spend the time looking over student writing and planning writing conferences. I had to let go of perfection and be willing to have the students truly have ownership with our newsletter. This meant there were some article topics that I would not choose, some writing that wasn't as polished as I would hope, and some organization that wasn't done the way I would prefer. But I had to come to the realization that arents were buzzing about this newsletter—they were obviously reading the newsletter—which is more than I could say when I wrote and published this weekly written correspondence. It was at this time that I came to the realization that it was not only my students who benefited from becoming independent learners; I benefited as well. The more independent my students became, I noticed that my teaching energy increased and my planning, instruction, and assessment time became even more productive.

2

Structuring for Learner Independence

Student ownership is about more than making choices. It is about making sure that students take control of their own learning and make choices necessary to direct and guide it along its path. As teachers, this means moving out of the role of the person always in control of the activity, letting students gradually assume more and more responsibility. At the heart of fostering student ownership is helping students to feel that learning is not something someone does to you, but something that you do for yourself.

—Ritchhart, Moran, Blythe, & Reese (2002, *Teaching in the Creative Classroom*, p. 47)

Perhaps the single most significant factor in fostering habits of independence in learners is not the curriculum, standards, or even the classroom itself: it is the way teachers intentionally interact with learners. Over the years, we have taught students of varying developmental levels, and without question, our approach determined learner independence. As our core understandings have changed and have impacted our classroom practices, increasing levels of student independence have resulted. When we structured for learning instead of controlled classroom activities, students demonstrated the ability to function independently within the

19

classroom. Activities that required students to incorporate higher level thinking skills, such as knowing when and why to do something, resulted in students making connections and applications of new learning. And when we encouraged interdependence instead of promoting a competitive atmosphere, students were motivated to be resourceful.

We have worked with learners who represent a diverse population including students with special needs, students who are English Language Learners, students who are homeless, students who are at risk, and students with severe behavior concerns. What we have found is that there is no student who is incapable of becoming an independent learner. We refuse to say, "I've tried everything possible to help this student gain independence." When faced with a student who takes more interventions to develop independence, we say, "I haven't found what will help this student gain independence yet." We believe our words carry power and we never give up on any student. Each student we work with moves along that continuum of independence as we make changes in our practices.

The purpose of this chapter is to examine the impact of the teacher, more than any other factor, on student independence. It is how we approach teaching and learning that directly correlates to developing independence. Prior to reading this chapter, use the following questions to guide you in analyzing your experiences and understandings:

- In what kind of environment do students learn best?
- What role does the teacher play in promoting independence?
- In what ways do students depend upon one another? How does this interdependence affect learning and independence?
- In what ways is competition used in the classroom? How does this competition impact student learning and independence?

CONTROLLING VERSUS STRUCTURING FOR LEARNING

Teachers are responsible for structuring and organizing their classrooms, but how they do so plays a pivotal role in determining student independence. How teachers organize the classroom can be viewed on a continuum from controlling to structuring. The more teachers move from controlling learning to structuring learning, the more likely it is that students will move toward the characteristics of effective independent learners.

Fostering behaviors of independence has nothing to do with allowing students to decide what to learn, when to learn, and if to learn. It has everything to do with inspiring and encouraging learners to reflect on their own questions and beliefs, rather than telling them how and what to think. Consider for instance, an example from Katie Wood Ray and Lisa B. Cleaveland's book, *About the Authors: Writing Workshop With Our Youngest Writers* (2004) where they share a practice that Lisa uses in her first-grade writers' workshop (see Figure 2.1):

Our youngest writers know thousands and thousands of words and have made these words a part of their oral speech. Many of these words are not ones they would recognize in print yet in their reading, but we want them to be able to use these words in their writing. To help nudge them do to this, Lisa has developed a simple ritual for celebrating when children tackle words that are challenging to spell. A chart in the room reads "I'm not afraid of my words!" and when someone is caught being a fearless speller, the word the child tried is listed on this chart. During share time the class will look at the word and the writer will explain how he or she thought of the spelling. Then Lisa will show the children the conventional spelling, and they'll either celebrate how close the writer came or marvel at how different the spelling is from what the writer thought it would be. It's a celebration either way, because the focus is on not being afraid to try a hard word you don't know, not on getting the spelling right. (p. 70)

A spelling chart such as this communicates that spelling does matter, but getting ideas down on paper also has tremendous importance as a writer. When students consistently ask for teacher assistance in spelling, their dependency points to someone else being in control of their learning.

Figure 2.1   I'm Not Afraid of My Words! Class Poster

I am not afraid of my words!		
Student	**Kid spelling**	**Conventional spelling**
Aidan	egul	eagle
Austin	oshn	ocean
Cierra	byoudfal	beautiful
Laci	srces	circus
Parker	bisecl	bicycle

SOURCE: Adapted from Wood Ray and Cleaveland's *About the Authors: Writing Workshop With Youngest Wrtiers*, 2004.

When teachers implement structures that support learners, such as this spelling chart, they scaffold student learning and reinforce behaviors of learner independence. This chart alone is not sufficient to foster habits of literacy independence; it is one of many practices described by Wood Ray and Cleaveland that encourage students to get their ideas down on paper while using various strategies to use their best spelling skills. This example does show that when a teacher moves from controlling to structuring, student independence will be increased.

Consider another example of a simple kindergarten coloring task where the teacher starts the year instructing students on "appropriate colors" to use for activities. When the kindergarteners routinely ask permission to use a certain color, question what color they should use, and report when other students deviate from the teacher's expectation, the teacher reflects on the cause of student dependence. When she recognizes her role in their teacher-reliant behaviors, she begins to make changes in how she interacts with students as they color. To begin with, the teacher encourages learners to make their own decisions about the colors they select while reinforcing individuality. As independent decision making is practiced in the classroom, learners start to choose colors with confidence, they detour from the norm with pride, and peers begin offering words of admiration for displays of individuality. Although this example focuses on a simple coloring activity, it is clear that our daily decisions as teachers have great impact on student behaviors when we move from controlling to structuring learning in our classrooms. Take a moment to analyze Figure 2.2 and reflect on the different outcomes when learning is controlled and when it is structured. Consider the impact each has on the child as a learner, rather than on just the activity at hand.

Student independence does not happen overnight. When the focus is shifted from controlling learning to structuring for learning, continuous yet gradual growth in student independence will become evident. Teachers who grow weary of making decisions for students and tire of passing out materials will find reprieve when students make decisions independently and access materials without teacher direction. Teacher time can then be utilized for intentional teaching and focused monitoring of students. Students are supported as they accept responsibility for their own learning and develop habits of independence that will benefit them in the classroom and beyond.

FOSTERING INDEPENDENCE THROUGH STUDENT THINKING

Within all activities, there are opportunities to foster habits of independence in learners by how we encourage students to think. Activities that focus solely on teaching declarative and procedural knowledge tend to lean toward the controlling end of the spectrum. Those that focus on structuring

Figure 2.2   Controlling Learning Versus Structuring Learning

Controlling	Structuring
Second-grade students have the same list of spelling words, complete the same spelling assignment, and take the same spelling test. Some students find the list too hard, some find it just right, and others already know how to spell each word without studying.	The teacher creates an individualized spelling program where each second grader has a weekly list of spelling words depending upon the developmental stage of each student speller.
Working to meet the state requirement of reading and writing procedural texts, the teacher assigns each of her first-grade students to create a "How to Build a Snowman" book. Some of her students are interested in the task, while some are not interested at all. When the books are complete, most of the students do not read each other's books and when they do, they make value judgments between the various products.	Working to meet the state requirement of reading and writing procedural texts, the teacher assigns each of her first-grade students to create a "how-to" book. The teacher brainstorms a list of potential topics with her class, acknowledging the expertise they have in various topics from "how to make a pizza" to "how to catch a frog" to "how to get out of taking a bath." The teacher uses the topic of "how to build a snowman" as a writing demonstration to show how to write procedural text. The students are eager to write and share their expertise. Students read each other's books to find out information and to give each other feedback.
The teacher requires his sixth-grade students to create a PowerPoint presentation on a communicable disease. The teacher has created a template for the students where they are to have one slide for each of the following: • What is the disease? • What are the symptoms? • How is it transmitted? • How is it treated? • How can transmission be prevented? • Who is most affected by this disease? The teacher provides feedback to students.	The teacher informs his sixth-grade students that they will be presenting to each other on various communicable diseases. As a class, they brainstorm what information is necessary to share and how the information could be shared. The class also discusses if there are any other audiences that could benefit from the information. They decide as a class how they could share the information with those audiences. The class works to create a description of what a quality presentation will look like. Students receive feedback from peers and the teacher, all based on the criteria they set as a group.

learning place a strong emphasis on conditional knowledge, in addition to including declarative and procedural knowledge. When learners are encouraged to practice all three types of knowledge, they come away with not only meeting the standards, but also moving along the continuum of independence. Gagné, Yekovich, and Yekovich, (1993) define these three types of knowledge. The first is *declarative knowledge*, which is often described as the "what" or content of learning. Knowing a piece of information, i.e., a concept, fact, idea, or label, would be considered to be in this category. The second type of knowledge is *procedural knowledge*, which pertains to the "how" type of information that tells us rules to follow to accomplish a task. With declarative knowledge, we know about something, and with procedural knowledge, we know how to do something; then the final category of knowledge (*conditional knowledge*) relates to contexts and circumstances of using the specific procedures, addressing "when," "where," and "why" to use these skills.

A teacher working to develop independent learners focuses on encouraging students to use their conditional knowledge as well as their declarative and procedural knowledge. For example, many teachers focus instruction on what an atlas is (declarative knowledge) and how to use an atlas (procedural knowledge). If learners are not provided with opportunities to use their conditional knowledge of atlases, they are less likely to become curious, independent learners with respect to geography. Consider the difference between these two scenarios in Figure 2.3 when a classroom of fifth-grade students studies geography.

Although students who experience controlled learning still study what an atlas is and how to use it, they are not getting the opportunity to determine when to use an atlas, yet isn't that the ultimate goal? Learners who discovered the importance of using an atlas for this particular assignment used a higher level thinking skill and had the opportunity to practice habits of independence. Notice how both fifth-grade teachers facilitate the same activity, but encouraging students to decide when to use an atlas impacts independence and provides an ideal opportunity for a quick assessment.

There are many decisions teachers make in the classroom that will give students the opportunity to use conditional knowledge. Consider what happens when students determine which materials are necessary for the particular task, rather than being told to get out a ruler, scissors, and a pencil, for example. Supporting students as they make these daily decisions will build on learner resourcefulness and confidence that encourages independent behaviors.

Figure 2.3   Use of Conditional Knowledge

Teacher who does not encourage conditional knowledge (CONTROLLING)	Teacher who encourages use of conditional knowledge (STRUCTURING)
"Coral, will you please hand an atlas out to everyone? We're going to play a game where everyone will need an atlas." The fifth-grade teacher's instruction and assessment focuses on procedural knowledge—how the students use the atlas.	"We are going to play a game where we are going to make a list of states. Your goal is to make the list as long as you can. There's an important rule, however. Whatever state you start with, the next state in the list must start with the last letter in the name of the first state. For example, if you choose to begin with 'Washington,' the next state must begin with 'N.' Then if you choose Nevada as your second state, what will the third state in the list need to begin with? That's right, Tyrel, it would need to start with 'A.'" As fifth graders work on their lists in groups, the teacher watches to see what resources they use. When she sees a few students get an atlas off the resource shelf; she asks those students to share why they chose to get that resource and how that will help them accomplish the goal. The whole class benefits from this modeling and the teacher makes a note of which students used their conditional knowledge of atlases.

INTERDEPENDENCE ENCOURAGES INDEPENDENCE

Historically, within the academic setting, there is a hierarchy of achievement as evidenced in daily success or failure, grades, and scholarships. Although it is often evident who excels in school and who is a tangled learner, promoting a sense of interdependence encourages habits of independence within the classroom. When a classroom focuses on building community through interdependence, students will more likely develop habits of independence, as opposed to when competition and domination is the constant outcome. When there is always one winner, the strong will become more resilient and the floundering learners will often find their way out of competition in order to preserve their self-esteem. We strongly believe that competition should not be removed from the curriculum, as it is healthy when it is focused on individual growth, group progress, and attainable goals for individuals to strive toward. But when competition clearly focuses on isolating the best, there can only be one winner. Consider the experience of one fourth grader during a class spelling bee. Meagan Lee found spelling to be a challenge and she cringed as her teacher announced the following, "Meagan, your word is 'vacuum.' That should be easy for you because your parents own a vacuum shop." Under pressure and with few spelling strategies, Meagan couldn't remember that she needed to double the letter "u," and as a result added this failure to her growing list of disappointments. We must be careful when we set up learners for what we believe might be success because we cannot predict how students will perform under certain circumstances. Instead, when we create a safe environment where learners work together, students gain independence and benefit from the contributions they make to the group. The following year, Meagan was enrolled in Danica Austin's fifth-grade class where the teacher also used competitive spelling, but with more of an interdependent approach. Whereas spelling bees highlight those in isolation who are already strong spellers, Danica concentrated on using spelling baseball to build teamwork and students' abilities to visually focus on words. Adapted from Rebecca Sitton (1996), Danica randomly divided the class into teams and then set out to play a game of spelling baseball. When a player was up to bat, she would select a word from the following categories: "one-base words," "two-base words," or "three- base words." Lists were divided into consecutively more challenging words so that students could select a difficulty level they were comfortable with. When Meagan was first up to bat she selected a word from one-base words, the easiest of the three lists. The batter announced her word was "stain." Since spelling is a visual task, Meagan wrote the word down on a whiteboard and had the opportunity to collaborate with her team. Soon after Meagan was given her word, she heard her teammates shouting things like, "It has a similar spelling to the word, 'pain'!" "It starts the same as 'stop.'" Learners worked together for the success of their team, while still focusing on building spelling skills.

Meagan was responsible to make the final decision about how to spell "stain," but with peer coaching, she was able to focus on making an educated decision, rather than spelling out of fear as many spelling bee contestants do. Consequently Meagan spelled "stain" correctly and went to first base. The next player chose a three-base word and sent Meagan to home plate. Consider the difference in these two approaches and how spelling baseball encourages students to be reflective and resourceful, all the while building habits of strong independent learners. In a traditional spelling bee, students are focused on spelling one word correctly. In Danica's class, students are participants and observers during the construction of many words, thus strengthening their repertoire of spelling words and strategies, rather than just reciting a string of letters. Within an environment that is structured for interdependence, student independence is enhanced as learners work in a community toward a common goal.

Marshall Rosenberg (2003) describes the ideal learning environment as one where students are not only concerned about their own learning, but also equally concerned for the learning of everyone else. For students to develop independence, they need to be encouraged to be interdependent. Consider Paul Eugene, a third-grade teacher, who is expected to teach students the following genres: biographies, friendly letters, advertisements, speeches, diaries, brochures, fables, plays, essays, and narratives. Paul created a chart in his classroom where students place a slash in the designated box when they begin writing in that genre and they turn the slash into an X when they have published something in that genre (see Figure 2.4). This chart not only communicates clear expectations to students and helps Paul monitor what genres students are using and attempting to use, it also encourages students to rely on each other. If Gil is going to begin writing a friendly letter, he may look to see who has already published a friendly letter to ask for help in formatting the letter. Paul may gather Gil and other students who are in the midst of writing friendly letters to teach a mini-lesson on letter writing. Paul can then encourage these students to peer edit with each other.

When Rick needs peer feedback on his survey about tetherball rules, for example, he can look at the chart and discover that Kylee has published a survey. She is able to question Rick about the purpose of his survey and to point out that he still needs to provide instructions about when and where to turn in the survey. Rick is able to use Kylee's family reunion survey as a model and make changes in his work accordingly. Creating this class chart helps Paul plan his instruction, group students, communicate his expectations, and structure for peer coaching and feedback. Paul is cautious that this chart is not seen as a competition among writers, but instead as a tool that supports independence within a literacy block. Remember, it is not just the "how" that we need to be consumed with as educators. A teacher who only thinks about how might hear about this idea to create a genre chart and later find that students become competitive with each other, seeing who can complete all genres first. But a teacher

Figure 2.4   Status of Class Wall Chart: What Have You Written?

	Business Letter	Friendly Letter	Persuasive Piece	Editorial	Schedule	Survey	Narrative	Newspaper Report	Promotional Material	Speech	Cinquain Poem	Haiku Poem	Narrative Poem
Austin	X		/	X				X		X		X	X
Brian	/			X		/	/		/	X	/		
Cashawn	X		/		X			X			X		
Clerra						/					X	X	X
Cortanee	X	X				X			/				
Duong											X		X
Ehrin	/			X		X							
Emma	/	X							X				
Gabby	X	X	X	X		X	X	X	/	X		X	
Gary	X		/		X			X			X	X	
Gil	X	/		X	/		/				/		/
Haylee		X			/						X	X	X
James						X		/	X				
Jennifer	X	X								/		/	
Jessica			X	/		X			X				
Jessie	X		/							X		X	
Juan		X		X			X				/		
Julie	/	X		/		/	X		/				/
Kairee			X	/			X						
Kylee	X	X				X		/					
Lawrence			X		X		X				X	/	
Natalie	X		/			X		X					
Rhonda	X		X	/	X								
Rick	/	X	/	X		/							/
Thatcher		X		X				X			/		
Val							X					X	X
Yeabsira	X	X	X	X	X	X							

/ = started
X = published (shared with an audience after working through writing process)

reflecting on "why" would strive to use the chart as an informative tool for students and the teacher. Paul uses the chart to encourage students to write for a variety of purposes and points out how the chart helps learners choose what to write and how to get help with writing. The chart also allows for students to work on various genres at different points during the year, but still communicates the expectation that all genres will be addressed. Ideally, the chart provides some freedom within a structure while allowing for all students to play an "expert" role at some point. Rosenberg (2003) points out that students who participate in teaching gain a considerable awareness of the learning process and this appears to facilitate their own learning. Students who are encouraged to be interdependent develop habits of independence because they work together and view peers as resources, not competitors that must be beat at any cost.

CONCLUSION

For the reflective teacher, best practices are constantly, yet gradually, refined as a result of analyzing evidence of student progress toward independence. We note that although curriculum and standards may remain the same, learner independence develops as a result of how we structure for learning within the classroom. The daily choices we make about our interactions with students and how learners work within the academic environment result in behaviors of increased or decreased independence. A classroom that has refined habits of independence closely resembles a working or social environment that students will ultimately encounter. One supervisor summed it up best when talking about necessary technological skills for an oil refinery, "Getting along with other people is crucial to this business" (Gallagher, 2006). Consider the opportunities teachers have to influence students and the impact that habits of independence have far beyond the academic years.

We encourage you to take a moment to revisit the questions that we posed at the start of the chapter. Have your understandings about teaching and learning shifted? How will your classroom practices be impacted as a result of your new understandings?

A TIME TO REFLECT

Reflect on your teaching experience: what are two structures, procedures, or protocols that make your classroom or teaching environment unique? Perhaps it is how you take attendance, set up a class library, display student work, or how you assign special projects to learners. Jot these down and turn to Appendix B. Appendix B is set up for you to analyze these two structures, procedures, or protocols in light of teaching that is controlled and teaching that structures for learning. There are two rows for you to place what you have identified as unique to your teaching and learning environment. Take time to write down how you can create each item into a controlled activity and then how to turn the same activity into one that is structured. What do you notice? What does it look like when you work with students: Does it appear more controlled, more structured, or somewhere in the middle? How does this impact student independence?

A VISIT TO OUR CLASSROOMS

Grades K–3: A Primary Perspective by Karin Ramer

For a stretch of my teaching career, I would answer any question that came my way as long as it was appropriate. I probably did this more out of habit than anything, but as I answered all questions, I modeled that the teacher was in control of the information and decision making within the classroom: "How do you spell *school?*" "Can I go to the bathroom?" "Does this look right?" "Am I finished?" "What do I do next?" and the list goes on.

As my understanding of developing independent learners progressed, I realized that I needed to ask students to become more self-reliant on answering their own questions. Now when they ask a question that is knowledge based, such as spelling, I ask students to think about resources and prior knowledge that might support them in finding their own answer. If the learner is not yet ready to self-select a dictionary for example, I will ask him or her to write the word and see if it looks right. I will follow that with specific prompts such as, "Underline the part of the word that you know is spelled correctly." "What does it begin with?" "Do you know another word that sounds like the one you are trying to figure out?" The level of support I offer students is dependent upon a learner's level of understanding and independence; however, by encouraging students to participate in answering their own question, they gain independence.

When the question is procedural based, such as if a student can use a computer, I ask the student to reflect on the procedure we decided on as a class and then answer their own question. The conversation might go as follows:

Student: Can I use the computer to publish a piece of writing?

Teacher: Remind me about our class decision about the computers.

Student: We said that if we had a piece of writing ready to publish we could type it on the computer. First we agreed to sign up for a computer with the time next to our name and then we could work for up to one hour.

Teacher: So now, what do you think? Can you use the computer?

Student: Yes, I just need to sign up first.

Teacher: You are right. That worked well to remember our classroom procedures. Next time feel free to make that decision without consulting me.

Supporting students with this type of dialogue encourages them to think like independent learners and gain confidence in an environment that is structured for success. Ultimately I found that when student independence increased, I had more time to focus on meaningful interactions that led to student self-reliance.

When learners ask questions that have to do with quality, I ask them to reflect back on expectations that have been set by the class or by their own past performance. If a child asks, "Does it look right?" I might say, "What part looks right?" or "In order for it to look right, what does the problem need to have?" In response to "Am I finished?" I ask what a finished paper might include, possibly referring to a class-generated rubric to use as a standard. And finally, when learners ask a question that has to do with a routine, I prompt them to access a resource within the classroom such as the schedule on the board, the calendar on the wall, or the clock above the door.

I have discovered that when I support and model this type of decision making from the first day of school, and sustain students as they gain habits of independence, my role as the teacher is much more enjoyable. I am no longer peppered with questions, but I get to put the responsibility on learners who soon rejoice in their own discoveries. At first it takes continuous modeling and redirecting of student questions, but as children experience success and support one another, they become more independent and less reliant on the teacher as the giver of knowledge. Students gain control over their thinking and decisions, and I have more control over the schedule I keep so that I can spend my time interacting with students in ways that will enhance their academic, social, and emotional intelligence.

Grades 4–6: An Intermediate Perspective by Roxann Rose-Duckworth

When I first brought calculators into my classroom, I had a fear that students would misuse them. I bought a pocket chart for the calculators and let students know that I would determine when they were allowed to use calculators. Sometimes students would ask "Can we use calculators for this assignment?" or "Can we use calculators to check our work?" I would make the decision as to what was allowed and often with student disappointment.

As I began to focus on conditional knowledge, I realized that I had been stealing this opportunity away from my students. They had the declarative and procedural knowledge of calculators but I had never given the opportunity to use their conditional knowledge. I thought about how it was really important they not only know HOW to use a calculator but WHEN to use one and I began to understand that they would never learn this if I was the "calculator queen." I also knew that it would not benefit my students if I just gave them free reign without any guidance. So I gave them a homework assignment to find out when their parents use calculators, when they use mental math, and when they use pencil and paper math. We then gathered this information and created a list of expectations for how calculators would be used in our classroom. I used to think that if students were given the freedom to choose when to use a calculator, they would misuse their power—but how wrong I was! My students made wise decisions about how and when to use calculators. Were they being used more than before? Yes, but with great intention and mathematical thinking. As students talked about how they solved their mathematical problems, they would share with each other what tools and strategies they used—and sometimes a calculator was one of these. They would challenge each other if they felt the calculator had been misused. Of course, there were still some days when we would do some math tasks where I would dictate that calculators could not be used but I was very careful not to overuse this rule and I always explained why I was using this rule when I did. As I provided open use of the calculators, I also opened the use of math manipulatives and tools. I found that students gained a lot of independence and math skills as they chose what tools to use, how to use them, and when. Students who needed more visual and kinesthetic experiences benefited. I found that as I gained focus on conditional knowledge, I also differentiated my curriculum and met the needs of all of my learners. As I reflect back on my teaching, I can see that it was often my fear that made me hold onto control, which in turn made my students very dependent on me. I feared my students would misuse calculators and come to rely on calculators for computation of numbers. What I learned was that it didn't have to be a choice between me having all of the power or them having all of the power—I could choose to share the power with them. I could guide them into using the calculators independently in a wise manner . . . and they rose to the occasion not only because I trusted them but because I prepared and supported them.

3

Teaching That Promotes Independence

The most effective classes are those where the students are self-disciplined, self-motivated, and self-responsible learners.

—Harry Wong and Rosemary Wong (1998,
The First Days of School: How to Be an Effective Teacher, p. 97)

If you have ever watched a young child for some time you will notice mannerisms and phrases that are adopted from both surrounding media and loved ones. You may even glimpse students mimicking our teaching behaviors and reactions to events, even when we cringe at the thought of what they are mirroring. Young minds are like sponges—they absorb most everything, but often do not have the ability to place value on what to keep and what to discard. As children grow and mature, they are more capable of critically analyzing their influences, but it is ultimately the teacher's responsibility to be a filter in the classroom.

Students learn in spite of and also because of their teachers, but learning in spite of us is surely not our professional goal. Learners adopt attitudes, behaviors, and habits portrayed by their teachers, partly because of the substantial time we spend with students. It is a sobering thought that we as teachers play such a major role in developing young minds—far beyond the academia that is often at the forefront of our minds. Our student cohort can be compared to that of a mirror or reflection in the water—the habits we are observing could be the habits we are modeling and demonstrating on a daily basis.

Keeping this in mind, it is our goal to help you reflect on your role as the facilitator of learner independence. In this chapter, we focus on implicit and explicit teaching, discuss how constructivism promotes independence, explain Vygotsky's zone of proximal development, and examine the role of problem-based learning in the development of independent learners. It is with appropriate support that students are capable of functioning at a high cognitive level; therefore we will discuss how the gradual release of responsibility will aid you in facilitating for independence. Before you read any further, take a moment to jot down your thoughts about the following questions:

- How is learning impacted when students are aware of specific learning targets? How does this influence your practice?
- How can the required curriculum standards be balanced with student needs and interests?
- How does teacher support impact student learning? How does this impact learner independence?

IMPLICIT AND EXPLICIT TEACHING

Educators have standards that are intended to guide the teaching decisions they make on a daily basis. Making these standards, or expectations, explicit helps students attend to the most essential part of instruction. Isolating what is important to focus on helps students pay attention to a specific part of the lesson, instead of allowing students to determine the essence of the teaching. This focused attention encourages learners to acquire new skills and understandings because objectives are obvious and manageable. For example, when a first-grade teacher reads aloud to students, she may provide an implicit model for fluent and expressive reading. Some students will simply listen and generalize reading behaviors to their own reading, but many will not unless it is brought to their attention. If the same teacher reads aloud to students and "thinks aloud" to model what she understands about fluent and expressive reading, that is an explicit model. Her explicit teaching may sound like this: "As I read this next paragraph from Eve Bunting's autobiography, listen to how I make my reading sound just like I talk. I'm showing and telling you about this because it's a chance for you to notice how good readers think. Reading this way is called fluent reading and it's important because it helps us better understand what we read." This type of demonstration is helpful because it explicitly shows and tells how and why a strategy works while reading.

Teachers have an immense influence on the students they work alongside. Any actions taken and decisions made in the classroom have consequences. Teachers who value independence will use daily instruction to develop self-sufficient students who practice and apply new learning. Intentional acts of teaching have the potential to foster positive attitudes and behaviors that build habits of independence and influence cognitive understandings. Examples of these intentional acts might include:

- Picking up trash in the hallway and throwing it away while children observe, emphasizing the importance of contributing to a clean environment.
- Writing in front of students while thinking aloud about the writing process and articulating the decisions you make as a proficient writer.
- Generating a variety of solutions when problems arise and discussing each option before making a final decision.
- Prompting students with specific language to reflect on their work and revise approximations accordingly.

Explicit instruction allows teachers to focus teaching on the essential components of a lesson. When learners are aware of specific learning objectives, it is likely that they will acquire new understandings, skills, and strategies as a result of this focused attention. While not every concept requires us to be explicit, it is the act of focusing in on the most valuable teaching point in the most explicit manner that enhances student understanding. Rick Stiggins (1999), founder of the Assessment Training Institute and author of many books on assessment, reminds educators that learners can hit any target they can see and that holds still for them. When we make our learning targets explicit, it is more likely that students will walk away from a lesson with the knowledge, understandings, skills, and strategies that we specifically intended for them to acquire.

CONSTRUCTIVIST EDUCATION

Most educators aiming to develop independent learners use concepts based in constructivist education. Grounded in the developmental theories of Jean Piaget (1950) and Lev Vygotsky (1978), this approach to education is based on the notion that students process information differently depending on their stage of intellectual development. Teachers using the constructivist approach promote the idea that students build or construct their own understanding of the world through activities based on personal interests and prior experiences. As they manipulate real-world objects and interact with the people around them, students create for themselves an understanding of the world.

Perkins (1999) describes three main types of learning that take place in constructivist education. The first of these is *active learning.* In this type of learning, students engage in discussion, research topics, and become involved in tasks that stimulate them physically and intellectually. Secondly, constructivist education engages students in *social learning.* Students learn through their social interactions with peers, teachers, and other adults. Finally, students engage in *creative learning.* Rather than simply taking in new information, students actually create or recreate knowledge for themselves. It is this type of learning that encourages independence in learners and prepares them for the future. Teaching for independence focuses on implementing an education that is "a process of living and not a preparation for future living" (Dewey 1897, p. 78). Constructivists aim to make schools do both: design student-centered instruction and successfully prepare students for their adult years (Brooks & Brooks, 1999).

SUPPORTING STUDENTS: THE ZONE OF PROXIMAL DEVELOPMENT

Along with the constructivist approach, teachers aiming to promote independent learning apply the concept of the zone of proximal development, a key idea from Vygotsky's writing (Arends, 2000). Vygotsky proposed that learners have two different levels of development: the level of actual development and the level of potential development. The level of actual development is the current intellectual capability of a student; students are able to work on their own when performing at this level. The level of potential development is the level a student can perform with assistance. The zone between the learner's actual level of development and the level of potential development is referred to as the zone of proximal development, often referred to by educators as the ZPD. To ensure new learning, the teacher must appropriately plan learning opportunities that incorporate a current knowledge of students. The teacher might ask herself, "What have individual children mastered?" "What skills and strategies need to be acquired next?" and "What will help students as they become independent?" Acquiring new skills, strategies, understandings, and content requires a teacher to plan to teach children on the brink of new learning. Being aware of what skills and strategies students control allows a teacher to build upon the foundation while introducing new skills, strategies, and content knowledge. When new learning builds upon what is already mastered, the learner is able to take on new knowledge. Teachers who acutely know their students' individual strengths and needs, and then plan for learning experiences that fall on the edge of what is known, and not yet controlled, plan to teach children in the ZPD. Instructing students in the ZPD allows a teacher to foster independence in students while supporting them along their journey as learners.

According to Vygotsky (1978), the zone of proximal development is "where students can independently complete tasks by learning the ability with the help of teachers, fellow students or parents." When lessons satisfy these criteria, academic anxiety is minimized and the student is ready to learn. Educator and author, Brian Cambourne (2008), points out that it's okay for students to struggle:

> ...I make a distinction between struggling and suffering. I think it's ok to struggle in the sense of being challenged—not all good learning has to be "fun" in my opinion. However there's no excuse for "suffering" as you learn. It means your teacher or your own approach to what you're trying to learn is flawed.

As teachers of diverse students, it is our job to support students and measure growth not by what can be checked off a list of curriculum, but by the gains students show throughout the year. Evidence of developing the learner, not just student learning, looks different for each child. Taking a constructivist approach to curriculum does not mean that educational standards are ignored; but the standards become just one piece of the puzzle. Teachers taking a constructivist approach to teaching aim to balance all three of these questions (Rose & Rathjen, 2001):

1. What are the students required to learn? (standards)

2. What are the students ready to learn? (assessment, ZPD)

3. What do the students want to learn? (interests, constructivist theory)

Planning for teaching based on the answers to these questions helps to ensure that we are teaching the learner, not teaching the curriculum.

PROBLEM-BASED INSTRUCTION

Some teachers using the constructivist approach develop independent learners using the problem-based instructional strategy. Consider a third-grade teacher, Tadd Martinez, who helped his class focus on the problem of litter on their school property. His students noticed this problem and became passionate about finding a solution to keep their environment clean. They gathered information to see if they could figure out why this was happening, broke into groups, and each group proposed a solution to the problem. Following this work, students decided they needed more garbage cans on school property and the cans should be painted in a bright color. Next, these third-grade learners worked to determine how to collect and paint more garbage cans. After implementing their solution, the class analyzed the effectiveness of the solution and evaluated the problem-solving process.

Another example (Ritchhart, Moran, Blythe, & Reese, 2002) demonstrates how a teacher can apply constructivist learning while meeting curricular requirements. Joann DesLauriers, a primary school teacher, had taught data collection and analysis to her students using the traditional practice of graphing: learners would input data onto a graph about favorite colors, ways of getting home, and number of people in each family. One day while walking with her students past the school's lost and found box, her students questioned why the box was overflowing and no one was claiming their lost items. Joann recognized that inquiry as a teachable moment and considered their authentic question when structuring for mathematical learning on data collection and analysis. Students began by predicting reasons why children were not claiming their lost items. One of their predictions was that the older children were less likely to check the lost and found than were the younger ones. In order to verify this assumption, the class sorted all clothing items into sizes and graphed the results. Then they designed a survey to ask students how often they checked the lost and found. They surveyed the entire school population and graphed the results. After analyzing the data, learners concluded that their prediction about older students caring less about lost items was inaccurate. In fact, they found that all students rarely checked the lost and found. Imagine if students worked together to determine how they could reunite lost items with their owners and lower the number of items being placed in the lost and found in the future. One solution could be to set up a table with permanent markers near the office so students could label their personal belongings. In going through this process, they could not only meet curricular standards of data collection and analysis—even more importantly they could contribute to the school community. Jane Nelson, another teacher highlighted in the video and text, *Teaching in the Creative Classroom* (Ritchhart, Moran, Blythe, & Reese, 2002), writes:

> I really let go of the reins, and the students find their way home literally and figuratively. It is hard to know that I am not ever again going to be star of the classroom, but what a joy to know that the new stars will shine brightly when they leave my protection. (p. 50)

When a teacher moves to a constructivist approach to teaching, he moves from being the "sage on the stage" to the "guide on the side." This can be a difficult, yet very worthy, transition to make.

GRADUALLY RELEASING RESPONSIBILITY

Teachers who develop independent learners with a constructivist approach also use the gradual release of responsibility model (Pearson & Gallagher, 1983). For example, consider how fifth-grade teacher Jack McZee supported student learning using the gradual release of responsibility. Jack taught in a school that bought a new supplemental math textbook series

(Levine, Beck, Naylor, & Rose, 2006) that used mathematical crossword puzzles to reinforce math skills. When implementing the curriculum, he noticed that students struggled with completing the crossword puzzle assignments, mostly due to the fact that learners did not completely understand the genre of crossword puzzles. Jack planned to gradually release responsibility to students by explicitly presenting crossword strategies and then gradually supporting learners through modeling and guided instruction. First, he modeled the strategies used in figuring out a crossword puzzle and then Jack demonstrated the reading, writing, and mathematical problem solving behind crossword puzzles. During this process he allowed fifth graders to observe how a proficient reader tackled a crossword puzzle as he explicitly thought aloud during his modeled demonstration. He showed learners how to use classroom tools (e.g., glossaries, dictionaries, calculators, rulers) and prior knowledge to solve the puzzles. In addition, Jack modeled what to do when faced with a clue that was not easy to solve. This modeling happened over a series of lessons because he knew that just one demonstration was not enough; it is better to have many short examples rather than one long lesson. Next, he supported students as they solved crossword puzzles as a shared class endeavor. As students worked together, he encouraged them to talk about their thinking behind their recommendations. He still participated in the problem solving and completion of the puzzle by providing direction and support. When his students showed they were capable of further independence with crossword puzzles, Jack broke learners into small groups and stepped back from direct participation. He monitored students and then used the assessment data he gathered to determine whether further instruction was needed. Jack encouraged fifth graders who excelled at figuring out the mathematical crossword puzzles to "think aloud" as they shared their answers and strategies. Finally, when learners demonstrated competence, they were assigned to work on crossword puzzles independently. In the beginning, students worked independently in the classroom and then, after repeated success, students took their crossword puzzle skills home as homework. Even with this gradual release of responsibility, Jack continued to assess his students as they worked on their crossword puzzle skills. In this example, the teacher shifted from taking primary responsibility, to sharing responsibility with students, to monitoring student performance, to encouraging students working independently on crossword puzzles. It is this gradual release of responsibility that fosters independence and success in students.

CONCLUSION

In this chapter, we discussed specific teaching behaviors that promote learner independence. When teachers draw attention to specific learning targets, students are more capable of taking on new skills and understandings as opposed to expecting students to discern the importance of a lesson without support. While students are actively, socially, and creatively engaged in academics, they are able to process information based on personal interests and prior experiences. And learners who engage in problem-based learning are incorporating conditional knowledge, which supports the development of independent thinking. It is through our continuous interactions with learners that we create the dance of independence: As we lead students each step of the way toward habits of independence, learners follow with movements that will gradually have them dancing gracefully with others.

At the start of this chapter, we posed questions that were intended to help you analyze your current practices. By looking at the questions again, we hope that you have an opportunity to analyze how your understandings may have changed or been supported as a result of your research and self-reflection in this chapter.

A TIME TO REFLECT

Explicit teaching is focused, concise, and timely, yet often in the interest of time or of adhering to set curriculum, we teach many concepts in one lesson. In the end, we have consolidated our teaching points into a half-hour lesson that could be broken up into three ten-minute blocks over time. Student attention would be more focused and our teaching more direct if we in fact used brief snippets of time to focus on explicit teaching. As a result, student learning would be more evident as learner independence is enhanced.

If you are currently teaching, take some time to reflect on a recent lesson you have implemented. Otherwise, consider a lesson you have taken part in as a student. Use the following questions to facilitate an internal dialogue or to guide a conversation you can have with a colleague:

1. What was the primary teaching point? Were there others?

2. Can students articulate the focus and purpose of the lesson?

3. Is there evidence of the specific teaching point(s) in student work or response?

As a result of your conversation, challenge yourself to make one change in your instructional practice. Perhaps it will be articulating the lesson objective more clearly to students, limiting your teaching points, using explicit language, or interviewing students following instruction as a quick assessment measure of your teaching. We encourage you to make one change at a time and reflect on how that one modification can impact learners.

A VISIT TO OUR CLASSROOMS

Grades K–3: A Primary Perspective by Karin Ramer

When I began teaching, I spent a substantial amount of time planning instruction that would satisfy state, district, and grade-level expectations. Each lesson was carefully designed to incorporate instruction that would enhance student understanding of concepts, skills, or strategies. But instead of focusing instruction on one objective, my lessons included more than one teaching point at a time. If the objective was letter writing, for example, I included everything from planning to drafting to revising within one lesson. Even when my letter was brief, my students were drained and unable to grasp the essential nugget of my instruction. I was frustrated by students' lack of engagement, and ultimately my instruction did little to impact student writing.

As I began to reflect on my teaching and challenge my instructional practices, I asked my literacy coach to observe me during a writing demonstration with third graders. She documented my instruction and found that during my thirty-minute writing lesson, I included no fewer than five teaching points, none of which were specific. After reflecting on this data and dialoguing with my coach, I set out to keep all writing demonstration to ten minutes or fewer and to focus on only one teaching point per lesson.

To begin with, I selected a teaching point based on student approximations in their daily writing. At the start of the writing demonstration, I articulated my teaching point and wrote it at the top of the writing pad as a reminder to stay focused during instruction. Then I set a timer for ten minutes and began instruction. The first few lessons felt too brief, but I began to notice that students were still engaged at the end of the lesson. In addition, my instruction was becoming more explicit and focused and as a result, I was able to look for evidence of my teaching in daily student writing. For example, when I noticed that students needed help grabbing their reader's attention from the first sentence on the page, I chose this as a teaching point for my writing demonstration. At the top of my chart paper, I wrote "Effective writing starts with a sentence that will grab the reader's attention and make him want to read on." Prior to the students' arrival that day, I had drafted a plan for my writing, including essential ideas and specific details for my story. When students gathered around the writing easel, I began instruction with talking about the purpose of grabbing the reader's attention from the first sentence. Then I brainstormed a few ways that I could start my story: a question, conversation, an action, or by describing the setting. As I talked about each option, I reflected on my story and articulated my thinking about each idea. I jotted down a couple of draft sentences in the planning portion of my writing, and ultimately selected a "*crash*" sound as the attention grabber, followed by "As silence followed that horrible sound, I knew my little brother was in trouble." As I put the pen down, I reflected on the purpose of grabbing the reader's attention from the beginning of a story and challenged students to spend a few minutes on crafting the first sentence of their writing sometime during the literacy block that day. Once I excused students to begin writing, I was able to monitor their work with a specific purpose: What impact did my instruction have on student writing? Who was able to craft a first sentence that grabbed the reader's attention? Which learners needed more support to write an attention-grabbing first sentence? Would learners benefit from reading a variety of attention-grabbing sentences in published books? Gathering these data allowed me to evaluate my instruction and plan for future teaching that not only satisfied state, district, and grade-level expectations, but that also supported learners on their journey to becoming independent writers. Over time, I have realized that incorporating explicit instruction in place of marathon lessons fosters habits of learner independence.

Grades 4–6: An Intermediate Perspective by Roxann Rose-Duckworth

As I began to be more explicit of my expectations with students, I also began to move from implicitness to explicitness when it came to adults who volunteered or worked in our classroom. The way I used parent and community volunteers, para-educators and college students in my classroom changed as I worked to develop independence in my students. One thing I found extremely beneficial to my students and to my adult volunteers and educational support staff was to give training for a specific task. For example, I had two parents who came into the classroom to work with children on their independent spelling lists; one came in twice a week and one came in once a week. I spent about 45 minutes at the beginning of the year training the parents on how I wanted them to assist children with word sorts and practice exercises. I also provided them with some background information to help them understand why students had individual spelling lists and how I developed these lists. I found that when parents felt that what they were doing was crucial to student learning, they were more likely to stay committed to their volunteer time. I used the training time as a way to make expectations clear such as to how to let me know if they weren't going to be able to help on a particular day and what to do with behavior concerns. Another way I used parents to encourage independence was by having them available in the hallway as a test audience. This was helpful when the class was working on recitals, speeches, or special projects that required oral presentations. Students could sign up to go into the hallway, and the adult would offer feedback using the rubric or checklist that we created as a class. The adult would record the feedback given so I was able to monitor student progress as well. I also took part in online discussion boards where parents could be participants in online literature discussions. The Web site was password protected and allowed students to have literature discussions with students from another school, and parents also took part in these discussions. This volunteer opportunity was nice because it allowed parents to go online at any time and they were not required to come into the school; this allowed for a lot of flexibility with parents' busy schedules. Parents also helped students with their publishing (I taught parents a variety of ways to bind and publish written works), reading fluency (I trained parents on what is meant by reading fluency and how to help children with their fluency), math facts (I taught parents strategies for encouraging mental math), and penmanship (I taught parents how to type out spelling words using a font that matches the penmanship model we use so they are able to develop individualized penmanship/spelling practice worksheets for kids). The most important thing is to find out what kind of task the parent wants to do. I interviewed interested parents to find out if they wanted to work with kids, work on a computer, or do work from home. I always tried to ask myself, "What is this parent doing that is having a positive impact on student learning?" If I couldn't answer that question, then I was not using that parent in a very effective way. In a school where family participation in school volunteer opportunities was quite low, I was able to have a large number of parent volunteers in my classroom. I feel that the constructivist, problem-based, explicit approach that I used with both students and parents contributed to this success.

4

Expectations and Communication That Support Independence

> *Have we forgotten what it was like when we were learning? I didn't want to infuse negatives into my classroom. I wanted kids to feel good about learning. . . . I had to establish an expectation that I would give them the opportunity to do their best, rather than make them do their best.*
>
> —David Funk (1995, *Teaching With Love and Logic,* p. 209)

Just like educators everywhere, we experience days when we are ready to throw in the towel. Our management techniques seem ineffective, our students act squirrelly, and to top it off, there appears to be no evidence of real learning that occurred during the entire day. Instead of viewing such days as meaningless, we considered what we could learn when we analyzed the day for elements of teaching and learning.

Chances are that if you walked through a school you would see evidence of a variety of teaching styles. Students of the same grade level, yet in different classrooms, would appear to be involved in diverse tasks, although learning from the same curriculum. Since each teacher creates a learning environment according to his understanding of student learning and curricular expectations, all classrooms look different. It is easy to judge a teacher based on what you see happening at a glance, but we caution you not to jump to conclusions too quickly. Some rooms may appear to be full of independent learners when observing student behavior, yet when probing further, you recognize that students are working under teacher directive. Other classrooms may appear void of order and purpose, but when examining the setting further, you realize that each student is thoroughly engaged. While there is no set script for appropriate behavior management techniques, there are things to be mindful of when working to foster habits of independence in learners.

Regardless if you have had a day where you question your passion for teaching or a day where everything seemed successful, reflecting on management techniques will improve your teaching practice. To support you in this reflection process, Chapter 4 is designed to help you examine the benefits of a well-managed classroom, along with the purpose of setting expectations with students. In addition, we will address communication with students and how to promote decision making and problem solving, both interpersonally and intrapersonally. Prior to reading further, take some time to jot down your thoughts about the questions that follow. The answers you provide will guide you in confirming or reshaping how you approach classroom management.

- Considering the teacher and student roles, what does a well-managed classroom look like and sound like?
- How can expectations be set to encourage independence?
- What kinds of conversations promote independence?
- How can decision making and problem solving help students practice habits of independence?

BENEFITS OF A WELL-MANAGED CLASSROOM

In a classroom that plans for learner independence, the teacher makes many decisions that promote student success. Consider Kirsten Michelson's classroom during literacy: While she is conducting a small group writing lesson, other second graders are working throughout the room. They are lying on the floor reading, propped up against pillows sharing books, sitting at tables writing, practicing spelling with magnetic letters, or working on the computer. Each child is engaged and although students interact with peers, the conversations are relevant to the tasks at hand. The tone of the room is peaceful with a low murmur coming from learners who seek peer advice; even then students are quick to get back to their reading following their conversation. Students are engaged in learning that is pertinent to their individual goals, and are driven with an intense curiosity for answering their own questions and pursuing their own interests. Second graders who need to leave the room sign out on the appropriate chart, take a hall pass, and return promptly from the trip to the bathroom, library, or office to mail a letter. Kirsten is freed up to manage small groups, conduct appropriate assessments, challenge students academically, and monitor behavior. Both the teacher and students know their role within the classroom. When students are able to manage themselves and the teacher is allowed to facilitate learning, the entire learning community benefits as a result of independent behaviors.

If we had visited Kirsten's second-grade class a few years earlier, we would have seen a much different scenario. Traveling back in our "time machine," we are able to observe Kirsten as she is working at a table with a small reading group. When she first begins instruction, the classroom is at an appropriate level of volume so that all students are able to work quietly. Once she settles in the small group lesson, the volume begins to rise and children become more active. After a few minutes, the volume of the reading group has gotten louder in order to compete with the rest of the classroom, and children begin to report to Kirsten that it is too loud to work. Kirsten excuses herself from the small group lesson in order to remind the class to work quietly and the consequences if they are not able to do so. She redirects them to the list of assignments on the board and reminds learners where to place the work when it is finished, along with what to do when they have completed all of the assignments. On her way back to the small group, she answers two more questions that seem to clarify misunderstandings. When she finally sits down, she reviews where the group was reading prior to her leaving and begins small group instruction again. Within the ten minutes remaining of the lesson, she is peppered with questions from children outside of her small group about using the bathroom, spelling a word, when snack will happen, and how much longer before lunch. She hears reports of students not completing the tasks in order, and of other children being off task. These interruptions not only increase the duration of her small group lesson, but they also leave Kirsten feeling frustrated with the dependency students demonstrate toward her. In this classroom, Kirsten is responsible for many of the decisions throughout the entire academic year. At the end of the year, some students will still be asking what to do next, complaining about the volume of the room, and they may even find it challenging to work without teacher supervision, input, and approval. Students are on task as a result of clear instruction until a need arises: the spelling of a word, the desire for teacher approval, the need to go to the bathroom, or the completion of a task. Within a teacher-reliant learning environment, the teacher is fully responsible for decisions made within the confines of the classroom. Much of her energy is spent managing all aspects of the classroom, and little time is left for uninterrupted teaching. As we examine the impact this teacher-dependent classroom had on Kirsten's instructional practices, it is no wonder that she worked to make changes that would influence students' self-reliant behaviors.

When comparing these two learning environments, it is probable that the students in both settings learn the same curriculum and meet state and grade-level standards. It is also possible that if similar tests were given, the results would be analogous. The difference is that in one example, the classroom is structured for independence, and in the other example, the classroom is managed by teacher control. In a classroom where behavior management strategies support independent learning, students are responsible for many choices that are made throughout the day, within the parameters of classroom procedures and protocols. Yet when a teacher makes many of the decisions, learners do not have the opportunity to make choices and experience the consequences of their decisions. Not only are these dependent behaviors taxing on the teacher, they do nothing to promote habits of independence. Students may learn identical content and curriculum in each of the classrooms, yet the behavior management style that focuses on developing habits of independence works to enhance learners beyond just knowledge, skills, and strategies.

Teachers and students benefit when the goal of fostering habits of independence permeates both the curriculum and classroom management. Working within an atmosphere where expectations are clear allows students to focus on their own learning goals. In addition, they gain confidence as they make decisions based on clear expectations, seek resources that are available in the real world, and practice problem solving in a secure environment. The teacher is at an advantage in this environment because once expectations and routines are established, she can focus on small group and individual attention, along with assessing learners in an independent learning environment, and monitoring student learning and behavior. Students are accountable for adhering to the responsibilities, routines, and procedures once the responsibility is placed on them, and the teacher is freed up to truly facilitate learning, not just manage learners.

SETTING EXPECTATIONS

A well-managed classroom that promotes behaviors of independence is based on clear and explicit expectations. These expectations may be referred to as rules, norms, standards, or any other term that reflects a common goal for the classroom regarding behavior and academics. In order for students to adhere to these classroom standards, expectations need to be established as a class with student input and not as a result of teacher dictatorship. Once these classroom standards are established, they need to be published, posted, and revisited as many times as is necessary: daily at the beginning of the year, following any major absence from school, or when behavior issues develop. As the classroom dynamics change, the expectations need to be modified in order to reflect the qualities of the classroom cohort.

When expectations are established within a classroom, it is essential for these standards to reflect responsibilities and roles of everyone involved in the educational structure. Students may demonstrate the need for varying levels of support in creating appropriate standards depending on their age and stage of development, while the teacher remains as the facilitator of knowledge. There are many ways to discuss and publish teacher and student roles, procedures, and expectations for a classroom. Perhaps the most explicit way is to examine what the teacher role looks like and sounds like, along with that of the learner, and to use positive statements that encourage appropriate behaviors. Ron Ritchhart (2002), a research associate at Harvard's Project Zero, reminds us that the beginning of a new academic year is often the prime time for students to envision a new world inside the walls of the classroom. In his book, *Intellectual Character*, he writes:

> Amidst all this newness, anything could happen; one could even become a whole new person. . . . Nestled within and closely associated with these feelings of newness and anxiety lay a sense of expectation: What will this class be like? What is to come? What will be required here? In opening the classroom door each fall, these questions all teachers must answer in the first days of school. Indeed, all teachers provide answers to these questions, whether they know it or not. They answer these questions in their introductions to the class through the routines they establish, and in the way they allocate classroom time. Often, teachers answer these questions as much by what they leave unsaid and unattended to as by what they deliberately try to convey. (p. 56)

Establishing clear and appropriate expectations, routines, and procedures as a group allows for students to contribute ideas and institute a sense of ownership within the classroom. The teacher must guide students and work to identify behaviors with positive language in order to support learners on their way to independence. Acting as the note taker, the teacher can facilitate student discussion as they agree on appropriate expectations for the teacher and students. The teacher can prompt learners to consider what they can do independently and what should be expected from each member of their learning community. (See Figures 4.1 through 4.11 for examples of clear expectations that are posted on classroom walls.)

When classroom management is exhausting or a lesson was not as successful as you might have expected, first analyze what you asked of learners, evaluate your role in the lesson, and then look to critique student behavior. Chances are that the lesson broke down when agreed upon expectations were not realized.

Ruth Charney in her widely acclaimed book, *Teaching Children to Care: Management in the Responsive Classroom* (1991) shows the thoughtful reflection she gives to her student-created rules:

> I do not want my rules to legislate every action. I want them to encourage reasoned thinking and discussion. I want rules that we "like," not because they give license or permission, but because they help us construct a community that is orderly and safe. And

(Text continues on page 55)

Figure 4.1   Classroom Expectations: Example A

Classroom expectations can be created for students AND teachers.

SOURCE: From Linda Lee and Mary Haymond's classroom in Spokane, WA.

Figure 4.2   Classroom Expectations: Example B

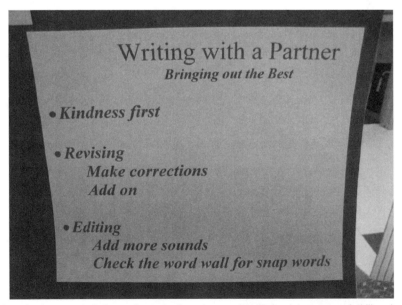

This anchor chart supports independence by focusing on developing interpersonal skills, along with developing the writer.

SOURCE: From Linda Lee and Mary Haymond's primary classroom in Spokane, WA.

Figure 4.3   Classroom Expectations: Example C

Launching the Writing Workshop
What writers do . . .
1. Think about what they know and do.

2. Tell someone the story.

3. Plan their story with sketches and label the

   important parts.

4. Write their story.

This list can grow throughout the year as students gain independence in writing.

SOURCE: From Linda Lee and Mary Haymond's classroom in Spokane, WA.

Figure 4.4   Classroom Expectations: Example D

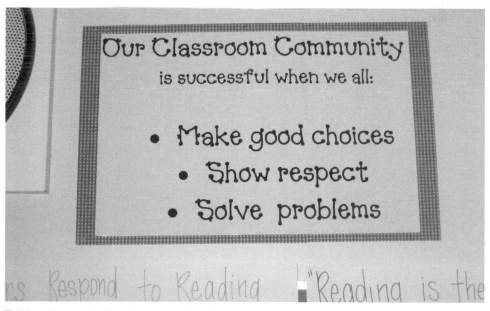

Our Classroom Community
is successful when we all:

- Make good choices
- Show respect
- Solve problems

This heading emphasizes the purpose for rules.

SOURCE: From Deanna Smith's classroom in Spokane, WA.

Figure 4.5   Classroom Expectations: Example E

This rules poster is signed by students, increasing ownership and a sense of community.

SOURCE: From Dawn Christiana's classroom in Bellingham, WA.

Figure 4.6   Classroom Expectations: Example F

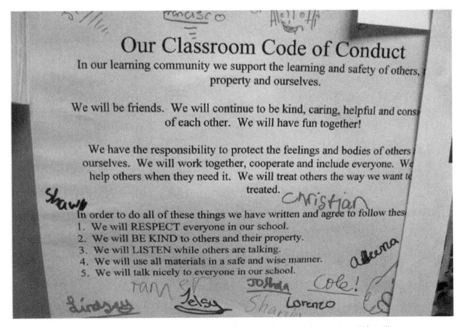

A classroom code of conduct can be signed and copies can be sent home to all families.

SOURCE: From Dawn Christiana's classroom in Bellingham, WA.

Figure 4.7   Classroom Expectations: Example G

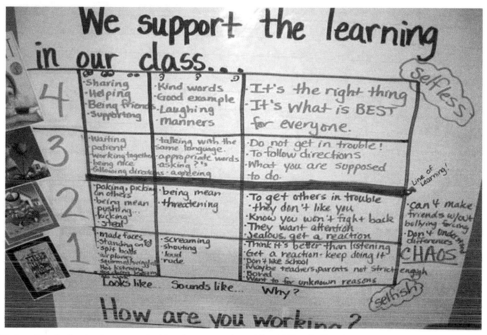

Notice how behavior is connected to characters found in children's literature. Book covers are posted on the left to identify various levels of behavior.

SOURCE: From Dawn Christiana's classroom in Bellingham, WA.

Figure 4.8   Classroom Expectations: Example H

This poster eliminates the need for teacher reminders as the text and graphics serve as a point of reference for students.

SOURCE: From Dawn Christiana's classroom in Bellingham, WA.

Figure 4.9   Classroom Expectations: Example I (Noise Chart)

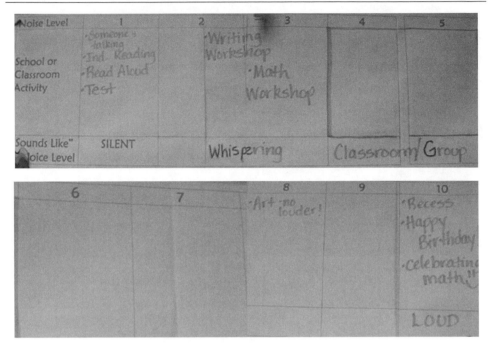

Noise Level	1	2	3	4	5
School or Classroom Activity	•Someone talking •Ind. Reading •Read Aloud •Test		Writing Workshop •Math Workshop		
Sounds Like" Voice Level	SILENT		Whispering	Classroom	Group

6	7	8	9	10
		•Art "no louder!"		•Recess •Happy Birthday •celebrating math."
				LOUD

Students created a voice continuum to determine appropriate volume levels for various tasks.

SOURCE: From Dawn Christiana's classroom in Bellingham, WA.

Figure 4.10   Classroom Expectations: Example J (Clear Expectations Communicated to Toddlers in an Early Childhood Setting)

Using photographs of "before" and "after" helps set clear expectations.

SOURCE: Used with permission of Janet Meddick.

Figure 4.11   Classroom Expectations: Example K (Clear Expectations
Communicated to Toddlers in an Early Childhood Setting)

Step-by-step visual and text instructions encourage students to be independent.

SOURCE: Used with permission of Janet Meddick.

> I want rules that have meaningful applications to concrete behaviors, which require not just passive submission but active participation. (p. 51)

Charney (1991, p. 64) goes on to give these guidelines for rules: rules provide positive directions (what you do, not what you don't do), rules serve a purpose such as making the school a safe place to be, rules need to be specific and concrete, rules should be limited to those that are essential, and rules should be posted and easy to read. She gives an example of a set of rules developed by her students (p. 63):

- We are all workers in school.
- We value our work and our work place.
- Good workers need to take care of their tools.

- Good workers need to keep their work site safe.
- Good workers are helpful, friendly, and respectful of one another.
- Good workers make mistakes.
- Good workers don't laugh at their own or others' mistakes.

Allison Fisher, a first-grade teacher, views goal setting as a way to foster habits of independence. At the end of each literacy block, the class spends time evaluating how things went and what goals they need to set for things to go even better tomorrow. Each day, they set one class goal that is recorded on the whiteboard. Some examples of daily goals related to noise level were

- We will keep the noise level down so everyone can think and work.
- We will find a place to work that is appropriate for the task we are completing.
- We will let classmates know when they are being too loud, and we will quiet down when asked to do so by our classmates.
- We will speak in soft voices when working on peer editing.

Prior to the start of each literacy block, students review the goal from the previous day, discuss the significance of the objective, and plan how to specifically accomplish that goal. At the end of literacy block, students evaluate whether or not they met the goal. If they did, they add three minutes onto their time bank. If they did not meet the goal, they talk about what needs to happen so they could meet this goal and leave it to focus on for the next day. They leave goals written until they are accomplished, and students are sure to have only one goal each day. As they save minutes in their time bank, they use their class meeting times to discuss how to use that time. The time is often used for class parties that most classes would have anyway. For example, Allison's class voted to use 45 minutes for a Valentine's Day party. They created rules for the party (e.g., if you bring Valentine cards, you need to bring one for everyone in the class) and they decided who would do what for the party. Another time the students decided to save three hours for a field trip where they took a city bus to a nature conservation area in town and then hiked and enjoyed a picnic lunch. For this field trip, they had to read a city bus schedule, figure out a budget, write a letter home to recruit parent help and support, create and gather permission forms, order school lunches, and inform school specialists who would be impacted by them leaving for a half day. There were other weeks when students just opted to spend their time earned in an extra recess. The important part of this was the responsibility they took for writing the goals and working to meet them. These goals helped make expectations clear to students and anyone else in the classroom including parents, para-educators, administrators and substitute teachers, while at the same time increasing levels of independence.

One way that teachers can help students develop habits of independence is to put structures in place that will support learners in becoming more self-reliant. To help his students become disciplined, motivated, and responsible, Andy Holland created a pocket chart that hung on the classroom wall (see Figure 4.12). When his third graders need teacher support, they place their name cards into the appropriate chart pocket. Andy checks the pockets during monitoring times (see typical schedule in Figure 4.13)

Figure 4.12   Pocket Chart

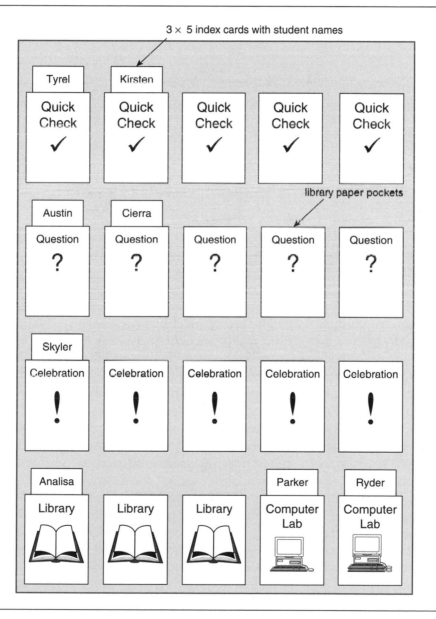

Figure 4.13   Andy Holland's Literacy Block Schedule

8:45–9:15	Hot Topics (oral speaking, student ownership)
9:15–9:30	Writing Demonstration—Whole Group
9:30–9:45	Students begin individual work time, monitor
9:45–10:00	Students continue individual work time, meet with one group
10:00–10:15	Students continue individual work time, monitor
10:15–10:30	Students continue individual work time, meet with one group
10:30–10:45	Recess
10:45–11:00	Reading Demonstration—Whole Group
11:00–11:15	Students continue individual work time, monitor
11:15–11:30	Students continue individual work time, meet with one group
11:30–11:45	Students continue individual work time, monitor
11:45–12:00	Students continue individual work time, meet with one group
12:00–12:15	Students continue individual work time, monitor
12:15–12:20	Clean-up
12:20–12:30	Debriefing, goal setting, individual accountability

and removes student nametags before meeting with those particular individuals. When he introduced this protocol, Andy had to focus on being consistent with this procedure and not be distracted by students verbally asking for his help. Once Andy articulated the purpose and procedure for the pocket chart, adults working in the room could utilize this system for helping learners. Perhaps one reason students use this chart regularly is because Andy created this system with their input. For example, students came up with the idea of "celebration" because they wanted a way to talk with their teacher about something they were excited about such as finishing a writing task, loving a particular book, or mastering a specific literacy skill. Providing for celebrations allowed Andy time to reinforce valuable learning experiences and to offer encouragement to learners. This chart helps make expectations clear and reassures students that they will get undivided teacher time at the end of Mr. Holland's small group instruction.

Another way to guide students as they become independent learners is to support their time management and decision-making skills during a literacy block. In order to do this, Andy uses a learning plan that consists of a file folder with traditional library book pockets (see Figure 4.14).

Andy's students use 3 × 5 cards as choice cards: each card has four options, depending on how students place the card into the pocket—see Figure 4.15. The "have-to" choices are on a different color of card and those cards must be used first: any "have to" card left incomplete becomes first priority during the next literacy block. Students use an "I'm done" card that addresses choices for when their work is done. At the start of the year,

Figure 4.14 Learning Plan

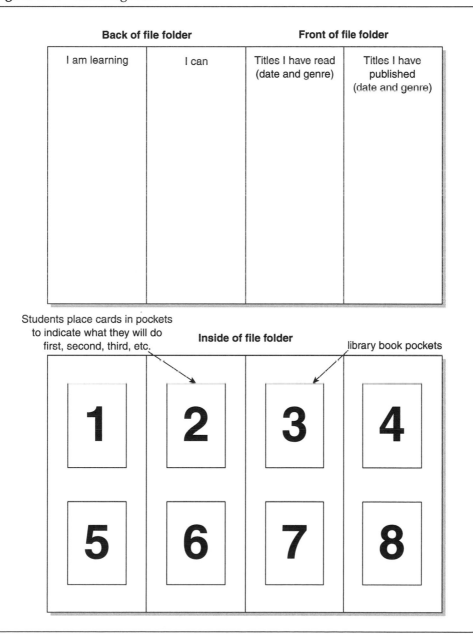

Figure 4.15 Learning Plan Choice Cards

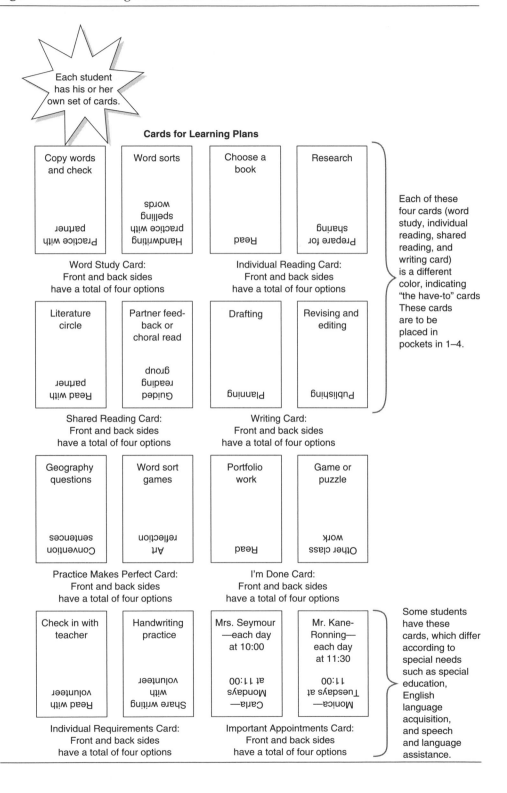

Andy asked his learners to use just one card, and then individuals added cards to their choices as they gained independence and success. These choices vary throughout the year and with individual students, allowing for differentiation. For example, not all students have an "important appointments" or "individual requirements" card. One of the choices students have when their work is done is to select work for their portfolio. Systematically, Andy lists portfolio requirements for the week or month. For example, if his class was working on a poetry unit, he might expect his students to put at least one poetry experience into their portfolio.

When walking into Andy's classroom, people often comment on how engaged and intent his students are. As students manage their own time, there are some students who chose to work alone, some with partners, and some with small groups depending on their goals and tasks. As a class, they identified parts of the room for partner and group work and parts of the room that are strictly for quiet individual work. Since students keep their learning plan with them, Andy is able to monitor students by looking at their learning plans and see that students' actions match their plans. When Andy has some students who are not yet successful at using their time wisely, he provides extra support for them. This might entail frequent check-ins with the teacher or another adult, or it could include sticky notes with times placed in their learning plan that make it clear when students are to move onto another task. It is this type of teacher involvement that increases levels of student independence.

COMMUNICATING WITH STUDENTS

The manner in which we choose to communicate with students is a direct result of our philosophy of learner independence. If we shout directives, reprimands, and reminders from our desk at the back of the room, or we give the infamous "teacher stare," we are working to be in control of our students. When we prompt students to reflect on, analyze, and evaluate their own thinking, behaviors, and decisions, we are focusing on structuring opportunities for students to gain levels of independence. If we affirm students' behaviors with phrases such as, "I like the way you put your materials away," or, "Thank you, that was a thorough answer," we are inadvertently telling students it is important to please the teacher. When we draw attention to their behavior differently, we are able to focus on their progression toward independence. "When you revised your science hypothesis so that it makes more sense, I can see where you were thinking like a scientist. It must feel good to write so clearly!" Each time we talk with students, we have an opportunity to further them toward skills and habits of independence by encouraging behaviors that we desire to build within the classroom community.

In her book, *Peaceful Parents, Peaceful Kids* (2000), Naomi Drew shares roadblocks of communication. Although she writes about effective communication between parents and children, we found a direct link to working with students. To share Naomi Drew's seven roadblocks to communication, we will use the example of a sixth-grade student turning in a book report and uttering, "My book report is awful." Would you be inclined to reply with any of these roadblocks?

- Criticizing: "You always put yourself down!"
- Opinion giving: "I think it's really good."
- Preaching: "If you would have planned better . . ."
- Fixing: "If you give more details about the characters . . ."
- Comparing: "Yours is probably the best in the class."
- Denial: "You know you don't mean that."
- Making it about yourself: "I used to feel that way about my school work."

Consider what kinds of responses would encourage student ownership and independence: "What are you not satisfied with?" or "What would do differently if you had the opportunity to do it again?" Perhaps if we sense the student was not in the mood to reflect, we might just emphasize with his feelings. "Ugh, it's hard to turn in work you aren't satisfied with." Then later, at a more appropriate time, we could talk with the student to determine why he wasn't happy with his book report. During this conversation, we would aim to talk *with* rather than talk *to* the student. This type of interaction helps shape subsequent student successes by developing skills and strategies that can be implemented on future projects.

Any communication with and about learners needs to be selective, because words can directly influence learner independence. Think about how instructions are delivered: Do your instructions show trust in your students? Do they imply that you have high expectations of your students? Consider the difference between these two statements: "If you complete this assignment, then you can. . . ." as compared to "When you complete this assignment, then you can . . ." In addition, how we view students can impact the interactions we have with them. Consider the difference between these two teacher thoughts: "Clifford won't do any writing!" in contrast to "Clifford hasn't done any writing yet!" One statement focuses on the negativity, while the other pays attention to the ultimate goal: to have Clifford writing. Our communication with and about learners has a great impact on the level of independence students acquire. Teachers who nurture independence in their students constantly reflect on their communication and make changes accordingly.

LANGUAGE OF THE CLASSROOM

As teachers we clearly are responsible for our students. Often times it is easy to translate this responsibility to a sense of ownership such as "my classroom," "my materials," and "my students." The message we send is that everything is about the teacher's classroom and students are a part of that configuration. If we intend to encourage students to operate within the classroom as equal members of a cohort, we need to change the language we use with respect to the classroom, materials, and students. It is not only what we say to students; it is also how we say it that defines the teacher and student roles within the classroom.

When building a community where independence is valued, it is important to consider how students are welcomed into the classroom. Think about the following signs and labels and consider what message they convey: "Welcome to my classroom," "Mr. Brown's fourth-grade artists," "Boys," "Girls," "Open up your mind and let the knowledge pour in." Any one of these either identifies the teacher as the owner of the classroom, the separation of boys and girls, or that the teacher is the dispenser of knowledge. None of these messages speaks to student independence, classroom community, or the role students play in their own learning. Think about how each of these messages subtly reminds students of the teacher's authority, and consider alternatives that enhance community and independence. Janet Alexander, a third-grade teacher, made a shift away from traditional thinking as she created the welcome sign for the classroom door the first day that students arrived. During her shared writing lesson, she modeled how to write a simple poem using the acrostic poetry format where the first each letter of a word is used to write a line in the poem. Then students participated in selecting essential words that would describe their learning community (Figure 4.16). The result was a greeting that hung beside the door as students entered the classroom, and spoke to learners about their role in the community. Instead of hanging a sign that said, "Welcome to Mrs. Alexander's Fourth- and Fifth-Grade Classroom," she focused on building a community that valued all members as contributors of the classroom. There are many ways to welcome learners without isolating the teacher as the owner of the classroom. It is within this type of learning environment that students will enhance their levels of independence as they are explicitly accepted as an equal member of the group.

In addition to the written display around the school, consider how we express ownership as we go about our day. When we are looking for the stapler do we say, "Who has my stapler?" or do we say, "Where is the class stapler?" Do we monitor student behavior by saying, "I expect you to walk down the hallway without talking," or do we encourage learner behavior by saying, "Who can remind me how we walk through the hallway when other classes are learning?" The subtle things we say to students consistently remind them of how we view ownership within the classroom. We cannot expect students to respect their environment as their own unless they develop a sense of ownership. It is with a sense of ownership that individuals are prompted to care for their surroundings as a result of an internal drive.

Figure 4.16   Messages That Encourage Teacher Ownership as Compared to Student Ownership

Messages That Imply the Teacher Ownership	Alternative Messages That Encourage a Sense of Student Ownership
Welcome to Mrs. Alexander's Classroom or Welcome to My Classroom	**W**hen you **E**nter this **L**ively room **C**onsider yourself **O**ne **M**ember of an **E**xciting learning community!
Mr. Brown's Fourth-Grade Artists	The Fourth-Grade Artists From Room 16
Boys and Girls	First-Grade Learners
Open up your mind and let the knowledge pour in.	Welcome. . . . We can't wait to hear what you have to say!

PEER COMMUNICATION

Within any learning community, conflict will arise and decisions will need to be made. If we are intent on encouraging independent behavior, it is important to approach conflicts as opportunities to practice habits of independence. When the teacher is always intercepting differences and presenting appropriate solutions, learners do not get the opportunity to experience the consequences of their actions and decisions. When we take away the chance to practice working through a conflict, learners will consistently rely on adults to solve problems they encounter.

During disagreements, students may need support as they work through problems, but this does not mean that learners need to handle each conflict our way. By providing students with acceptable strategies for problem solving, teachers support learner independence more than providing solutions that are palatable to the adult in the classroom. Perhaps students need a mediator who asks questions to get at the root of the problem, "Let's each take a turn to talk about the problem at hand. While one person is talking it is important for the other person to listen. Both of you will get an equal opportunity to share and then we will think of a solution together." With this approach, students are encouraged to take ownership for problem solving and will likely gain skills and strategies to use when future conflicts arise. Knowing how to approach problem solving and drawing from a variety of strategies is much more effective than mimicking adults through the problem-solving process in order to fix one conflict.

Kim Howe's fourth graders use class meetings to resolve issues. Students are encouraged to identify items of concern on an agenda, and these issues are brought up at the meetings. After one class meeting, students decided to create different volume zones in their classroom: some of the zones did not allow talking, some permitted quiet talk that focused on learning, and the co-op zone allowed louder talking that focused on learning. Students determined that the co-op zone would be a small room across the hall supervised by a para-educator or parent volunteer. This process of students identifying issues regarding their learning environment illustrates how, with appropriate support, students can become aware of their own learning and practice habits of independence.

CONCLUSION

The purpose of this chapter is to examine the benefits of a classroom that implements expectations and communication with the intent of fostering habits of independence. Student effectiveness is increased when clear expectations are set and students are supported in meeting these standards. Keep in mind that when we communicate with learners and coach them in making decisions and solving problems, our focus should be on continuously moving students closer to independence, not fixing the dilemma students face. Whenever we encounter obstacles to successful behavior management, it is essential to analyze how our actions affect students and cause their reactions. We have all said, "That will never work. You don't know my students. If you knew 'my little Marvin,' you would thank your lucky stars to even get everyone at the circle listening to a story." Every teacher we have ever met has had the opportunity to work with their own Marvin, all the while learning about varying levels of support for that one student. Some classrooms even have many of these students that make teaching decisions, transitions, and education in general quite challenging. Each group of learners from year to year is different and within any group of students, there is a broad range of skills, abilities, and behaviors. If you are reading this book and feeling like the idea of your students becoming independent learners would take a miracle, consider if you are wearing what Parker Palmer (1998) refers to as the "armor of cynicism." In his book, *The Courage to Teach*, he writes:

> It is the cynicism that comes when the high hopes one once had for teaching have been dashed by experience—or by the failure to interpret one's experience accurately. . . . Perhaps those hopes can be rekindled, because the intensity is still there: rightly understood, this sort of cynicism may contain the seeds of its own renewal. (p. 48)

Take a few minutes to reconsider the questions at the start of this chapter. How has your thinking been reaffirmed or changed?

A TIME TO REFLECT

Throughout the day teachers have many opportunities to respond to students and support them as they refine their thinking about learning, behaviors, and relationships. While we hope to be encouraging, it is our goal to support learner independence during these brief opportunities. Turn to Resource C and you will find a chart that details examples of how a student might solicit feedback from you as the teacher. Consider what you might say in response that will not simply affirm the learner, but also encourage independence. Can you think of another example in which students seek your approval where you can enhance independence by encouraging students to reflect on their behaviors?

A VISIT TO OUR CLASSROOMS

Grades K–3: A Primary Perspective by Karin Ramer

As I reflect upon my early years of teaching, I recall the confidence I had as a result of graduating and becoming employed, yet as I remember, it wasn't long before I encountered a healthy dose of reality. I had spent years thinking and dreaming about what teaching would be like, yet I had not truly experienced the human factor. When I did discover the role students play in instruction, I experienced the authentic need to differentiate learning for the individuals I taught. I first learned this when I had to coax a crying child out from under a table while still managing a classroom of kindergarteners under the curious eye of nervous parents. I learned a bit more when my best friend narrowly escaped a flying desk that had been thrown at her by a first grader, or when I had to chase down an angry six-year-old wielding scissors before he trampled other students working in centers. Perhaps I became more realistic when I realized that I was not only an educator, but also a counselor for those who had just lost a pet or the only attentive audience a child might find during the day.

The real teacher education happens when you are in the midst of implementing the curriculum you so carefully planned for while managing the twenty-six children who came to you, maybe not all ready to learn. While it is lovely to have an ideal picture of what a classroom might look like in our heads, we must also give ourselves latitude to make adjustments as we work with children. For me, this means that not everyone gets to decide where he will sit for a particular activity. Based on past performance, a child may need me to make decisions about seating until he can demonstrate more control in a particular setting. It is not my job to make everything equal or fair; it is my job to know each child and provide the level of support needed for his success.

As a result of experience, I now have confidence when I differentiate for learners. For the child who comes to me at the start of the academic year who refuses to speak aloud in front of her kindergarten peers, I focus on the conversations that she has in the kitchen center. I take on a role as a member of the household so that I too will be included in the world where she feels confident to use her voice. It is eight months into the academic year when she finally decides to share with the whole group, but her progress is no less important than the child who comes to school ready for public speaking 101. I have learned that for the student who has a history of a behavior disorder on his school record, I need to provide ample support so that he will experience success. Maybe I prompt him toward independence by limiting the choices he needs to make, "Last time you sat near me at reading group and I noticed how you paid very close attention to the story we read. Would you like to do that again, or do you think you would like to choose another seat where you can pay careful attention? Why don't you take a moment to think about where you will best learn and let me know what you decide." I know that regardless of where a student starts at the beginning of the school year, he will move along the continuum of independence as a result of the conversations we have, the support I am able to provide, and the reflection that he does with respect to his own work, behavior, and attitudes. Since students are on their own journey to independence, it is this personal growth that we really should celebrate as progress. And it is when we start looking at our learners as individuals that we are able to find and celebrate their successes toward independence.

Grades 4–6: An Intermediate Perspective by Roxann Rose-Duckworth

My first few years of teaching, I came up with the classroom rules. Then for quite a few years, I had students brainstorm the list of rules we should use in our classroom—what I found was basically the students regurgitated rules they had in previous years—but there didn't seem to a real sense of "buy-in" with these rules. Then I started using a different method. The first day of school, students were given a piece of paper divided into four quadrants. The paper heading was "In the Ideal Classroom," and the four areas to brainstorm were:

- Students would . . .
- Students would not . . .
- The teacher would . . .
- The teacher would not . . .

This was their first homework assignment. They were to brainstorm what students and teachers would do and not do in an ideal classroom environment. They were asked to get their family's input. The second day of class, students got into groups and shared their lists. I had them copy each idea represented in their group onto a sticky note (repetitive ideas could be represented on one sticky note). Then they worked on categorizing the sticky notes. Then we would list the various categories on the board. They might look something like this:

- The way we treat each other
- The way we organize our classroom
- The way we solve problems
- The way we work

Then we worked as a class to write one general expectation for each category and smaller bullets underneath each general rule that helped to clarify the expectations. Then each group would be in charge of creating a poster for each general expectation. These posters would be displayed in our room as a reference throughout the year. We would also type out a smaller version of the expectations and send them home to families and thank them for the input. I found that this process really got students thinking about what they wanted their classroom to be like, not just regurgitating the rules they have heard before. I found that when students went through a thoughtful process and genuinely felt heard, they were much more likely to abide to our class expectations.

In addition to changing how I approached class rules, my approach to classroom chores has also changed over the years. When I began teaching, I created class chores for my students. I believed this was a way to increase student ownership in our classroom but I found that students most often forgot to do their chores. After some discussion with students and some time to reflect, I came up with some changes to our classroom chores that had a lasting impact on student independence.

Each year, we would brainstorm jobs that were necessary to keep our classroom running smoothly. I found that if each student had a chore, they were more likely to remember to do their chore. As the year progressed, we would make changes to our chore chart—adding chores that became apparent to us when the need arose. For example, we added the chore of "hallway checker" when we realized that some of our students who worked in the hallway with teaching assistants or parent volunteers would periodically leave a bit of a mess. Many of chores included checking on supplies such as the "calculator checker" made sure that calculators were always returned to their designated places in the pocket chart. The supply shelf checker made sure that all materials were returned to the supply shelf. Another chore was our greeter, who was in charge of greeting any visitors to our room; this included new students. Visitors to our room were always so impressed with how a student would greet them at the door quietly, help them find a place to sit, and help them about our room as necessary. The photographer was in charge of taking photos of presentations and projects that could not fit into student portfolios; this way we had documentation of all student products. The videographer took video of student presentations. Each student had a video portfolio, which allowed students to share their presentations with family members and to do self-assessment. The vacuum operator vacuumed our classroom at the end of the day using the battery-charged wall-mounted vacuum cleaner I brought in from home. The custodian appreciated the responsibility our students were taking in our classroom; he only needed to vacuum our room once a week rather than daily. The chore list went on like this. Each year we had similar chores but in no year was the list identical—it was always based on our current needs and ideas.

I'll never forget a college student being shocked as she helped with an art project in our classroom. Some students were using glitter and a student said to her "Be careful with that glitter; it's really hard to vacuum up!" Other students echoed, "Yeah, we don't want to get any glitter on the floor." I shared with the college student how years before, I would have been stressed out about students getting glitter on the carpet and the students would not have given it much thought. This is an example why student independence is a gift to both the teacher and student!

5

Aligning Understandings and the Environment for Independence

In a real sense all life is interrelated. All [people] are caught in an inescapable network of mutuality, tied by a single garment of destiny.

—Martin Luther King, Jr. (1961)

Consider the hundreds of decisions a teacher must make in preparation to teach; each and every element of the classroom will either promote dependent or independent habits of mind. Due to the influence we have on learners, it is vital to base these decisions on our beliefs about teaching and learning, not simply follow trends or patterns in education or rely on habits and tradition. While we recognize that it is easy to follow the pendulum of the teaching season and just as easy to get drawn into the traditional paradigms of education, we caution you to think independently.

Throughout the early years of her teaching, kindergarten teacher Leslie Martin focused on creating a classroom that looked ready for parents, students, and colleagues alike. Since she loved vibrant colors, fanciful arrangements, and eye-catching designs, her classroom reflected these passions. She justified the time it took to hang window details, the money it required to create a visually appealing décor, and the creativity that was vital to making the classroom resemble something out of a teaching

71

catalogue, all because she spent a significant amount of time within the classroom walls. While her efforts were not in vain, she soon realized that she truly missed the mark on how to prepare a classroom for learners. It is not the matching lamps or fun rugs that contribute to educating children, nor is it the well-designed bulletin board outside the classroom. Planning for learner independence mandates more than what is visually evident: it requires us to think about constructing an environment that meets our goal of fostering learner independence.

Time spent creating an environment to support students should be focused on matching the environment with our core beliefs and understandings about learner independence. Instead of devoting time to the interior design of the classroom, Leslie has learned to concentrate on how the physical arrangement could best support both herself and her students. While walls could wait for student work, she now spends time before students arrive reflecting on her practices and deciding on which routines and procedures to establish in order to foster habits of independence. She arranges the furniture to match her beliefs about teaching and learning, and places materials and resources to ensure that student independence is encouraged. Over time, her focus has changed as a result of her growing understandings about learner independence. And where she once spent the majority of her time on the physical décor of the classroom, now she limits her effort to just what is basic. Still the classroom is visually appealing, yet not all consuming. Her focus is on the art of teaching and planning for student independence rather than the art of interior design.

To further understand how the environment can support learner independence, Chapter 5 is devoted to discussing the role of the environment. We will address the benefits of a well-planned environment, the impact of a teacher's understandings on the creation of the environment, the significance of analyzing the physical environment prior to making decisions, and finally we will address the role of the teacher in an environment that promotes independence.

Whether you are looking to reevaluate an established learning environment or are setting up a classroom for the first time, reflect on these questions prior to reading Chapter 5:

- What are your core understandings about learner independence within an environment? How can the physical environment align with your beliefs?
- Which decisions do you make based on your understandings about learning?
- How can you plan for the physical environment prior to setting foot within a classroom?
- Are there elements of the physical environment drawn from tradition, habit, or trend?
- What advantages and challenges does the physical space offer?

BENEFITS OF A WELL-PLANNED ENVIRONMENT

With each new cohort of students, we have an opportunity to reflect on our teaching practices, and more specifically the environment within which we aim to cultivate learning. As the facilitator of learning, a teacher has the sole responsibility to make decisions regarding the physical environment of the classroom even before meeting learners for the first time. Oftentimes the decisions we make reflect our understandings about teaching and learning, but other times we make choices based on other factors that do not reflect our understandings of how students learn best. In order to intentionally cultivate habits of independence, the physical environment must be given much consideration before any physical labor begins. When a physical environment is created with the intent to support learner independence, students work within a laboratory of sorts where they experiment with problem solving, make learning decisions, set goals, and work alongside peers. Under adult supervision and guidance, students receive varying levels of support which allow them to test theories, beliefs, and understandings in a safe learning environment, and in turn to experience the consequences of their actions. These experiences directly shape student thinking and future decision-making processes, thus contributing to learner competence as independent members of the classroom.

Concentrating on aligning the physical environment with goals for student independence will encourage the teacher to take a proactive rather than a reactive approach to behavior management. Marzano, Marzano, and Pickering (2003) found that effective teachers spend time focusing on the physical environment at the start of the school year. They acknowledge that the physical learning environment must "support effective classroom management" and must be preventative in nature. An environment that promotes habits of independence is organized so that learners have access to materials and resources independent from the teacher. And a physical environment that is corrective in nature has elements in place, such as a teacher who monitors students and guides children through decisions in order to work effectively. It is not the element of teacher control that promotes positive behavior among students; rather it is working within an environment where independence is valued, encouraged, and supported.

Another factor to consider when educators reflect on the correlation between the physical environment and student behavior is what researcher and educator William Glasser addresses as basic needs. Glasser advocates that when a learner's basic needs are met, the likelihood of student engagement increases. He identifies the five basic needs as survival, belonging, power, fun, and freedom (Glasser, 1986) and discourages teachers from blaming outside events for student behavior. Instead, when a student does not meet our expectations, we must examine whether or not we appropriately set up an environment that considers student needs (see Figure 5.1). This is often a new way of looking at student behavior for many educators;

Figure 5.1   The Physical Environment and Independence

Student Needs	Examples of How the Physical Environment Can Encourage Independence	Examples of How the Physical Environment Can Discourage Independence
Belonging	There are photos of students around the room	Everything on the walls is commercially or teacher created
Power	Students choose which work they want to display on classroom walls	The teacher chooses which student work to display on the classroom wall
Fun	Student interests are represented in classroom decorations (e.g. skateboarding, personal hobbies and collections, and favorite authors)	Everything on the wall is informative, but nothing seems to evoke a smile from students
Freedom	Students choose where to sit or provide input regarding seating assignment and/or have flexibility to choose work spaces	Students have assigned seating that rarely changes

however, we can learn much about our teaching when we indeed examine the impact and effects our practices have on learners. Within an environment where basic needs are accounted for and the teacher provides for learner independence, student behavior tends to reflect these expectations.

On the other hand, when basic needs are not accounted for within the learning environment, students may feel alienated and controlled. As we write this book, there is a Web site (www.school-survival.net) that is geared toward students who voice their disdain for school. As educators, it behooves us to examine how some students interpret the purpose and effect of schooling. Consider this quote found on the Web site:

> They say school is for learning? Well, being bored is hardly any way to learn anything! No wonder most people don't remember what they were forced to memorize at school. School isn't about learning, it's about training people to be obedient to those with authority over them.

The unfortunate experience of this learner can benefit a reflective teacher who is willing to examine her own teaching practice in light of providing for learners' basic needs and setting up for learner independence. When we analyze our teaching practices and decisions with respect to the impact they will have on student behaviors, we have more influence over what occurs within the classroom. And when we plan specifically to increase student independence, the environment becomes a place of growth for all learners. Students are appropriately engaged and they are no longer fighting for control—they are freed up to learn and the teacher is empowered to educate.

AN ENVIRONMENT THAT MIRRORS A TEACHER'S UNDERSTANDINGS

A physical environment that reflects a teacher's understandings about student learning will be constructed with a different set of criteria compared to those that are fashioned out of trend or solely visual appeal. When a classroom's design reflects a teacher's understanding of how students best learn, decisions about setting up a classroom go beyond color-coordinated accessories, eye-catching bulletin boards, traditional arrangement of student seating, and even the placement of the teacher's desk. A classroom that is intent on fostering learner independence can be designed so that it is pleasing to the eye while at the same time enhancing habits of independence. The difference is in the thinking that goes beyond the details in the environment. For example, instead of designing bulletin boards out of consistent color and border styles that might reflect a teacher's preferences, consider soliciting student input and assistance in hanging bulletin boards that will be accessible and engaging for learners. The latter experience will build on learner strengths and help students practice behaviors of independence. Although the manual labor is often what takes so much time when setting up a classroom, if a teacher focuses on the "why" before the "how," the environment will be an asset when working toward student behaviors of independence.

When a physical environment emulates an educator's core understanding about teaching and learning, the classroom will act as a tool in building habits of independence in learners. Let's take a moment to examine how this might look in a classroom.

Consider Connie Paige, a first-grade teacher who establishes a learning environment based on what she believes about developing independence in young learners. She has arranged the classroom to meet students' basic needs and to support her instruction. When you look around the classroom, you will find a post office center, a reading corner, math manipulatives arranged on simple shelving in the middle of the room, a science center crawling with stick bugs a student brought in, handmade posters hanging from the ceiling, a computer station aligning a row of windows, a teacher desk, in a corner of the room, that serves as a vertical surface for magnetic letters, and a round table where Connie pulls small groups for instruction. Student seating is dispersed throughout the room in varying configurations, and the group meeting area borders a whiteboard. Although Connie purchased her materials at yard sales or received them as hand-me-downs, the room is not wanting for anything. The classroom is arranged to match Connie's beliefs about teaching, learning, and fostering habits of independence. In this example, the teacher is the facilitator of knowledge, and with support, students are responsible to research, inquire, interact, and to be physically and mentally engaged throughout the day.

The belief that first graders are independent learners permeates the classroom. When Connie teaches a whole group lesson, students gather at the carpet where the teacher has access to the whiteboard, a writing easel, a variety of writing utensils, and an overhead projector. Once the short, focused lesson is complete and students are given time to reflect on the lesson and ask questions, Connie excuses them to work around the room. As learners become engaged, Connie monitors their transition and reinforces behaviors that will further independence. This is a time for her to redirect and encourage learners so that not only can she work uninterrupted but her students are also practicing habits of independence. After students are engaged, Connie gathers five learners for a short, small group math lesson on problem solving. Because the class has spent essential time talking about classroom procedures and protocols, students can be seen signing out of class if they need to leave the room, printing documents, and utilizing materials and resources within the classroom. At this time, if students who are not involved in the small group lesson have questions, they write their inquiries on note cards or sticky notes in order to communicate with the teacher. Connie addresses each note following instruction and then monitors student progress and behavior prior to gathering another small group of learners.

As you may deduce from this illustration, fostering habits of independence begins when a teacher examines how she can support learners to meet their own needs instead of relying on the teacher for decision making, information, or affirmation. One example of a change Connie has made in the classroom is the arrangement of student desks. In previous years, Connie had all student desks facing the front of the classroom. With some reflection, she realized what this communicated to students—this was a "sit and get" classroom. Now her desks are arranged in pods of four and are positioned so that students' sides face the front of the room; this way they can turn their head to look to the front, but they are facing each other. Now she finds that students are more willing to collaborate and learn from one another. As you can see from Connie's classroom, independence has more to do with the ability to be resourceful and reflective than with the ability to follow clear instructions and routines without bothering others. Connie is intentional about decisions that are made regarding the environment because she understands that teacher expectations, whether intentional or not, encourage positive student behavior.

ANALYZING THE PHYSICAL ENVIRONMENT

Prior to planning your physical environment, analyze the potential learning space with fresh eyes by asking yourself questions about the environment. When you walk into a classroom, what do you observe? Are there windows, and if so what goes on outside? If you face the playground, be mindful of the recess schedule and consider placing group learning away from this distraction. If the windows border the parking lot, is this a potential diversion for learners? Within the classroom, where will the foot traffic most likely be? If there is an interior and exterior door, visualize a clear path for walking from one door to the next. Is there any fixed furniture within the environment? If so, how can it be used to support learners? Can a built-in bookshelf be used for community supplies, reading materials, or other learning resources?

Take time to sit and reflect in the physical space; carefully analyze the classroom while predicting a day with students. Make a list of elements within the environment that will promote independence, and of other aspects to downplay so as to support students as they focus their learning. Consider where you will conduct group learning and potential distractions such as outside windows, interior doorways, or fixed furniture that would prevent students from comfortably attending to learning. Think about where you will have small group lessons. While you are working with a limited amount of students, what are others doing? Most likely you will want to work away from the sink, computers, and classroom materials and supplies that students may need to access while you are focusing on a small group of learners. Do you need to see the interior door in order to monitor who enters and exits the classroom? While you are analyzing the environment, be mindful of how your flexibility and organization can support learners as they work to develop skills of independence. You may even want to get down to the eye level of your students. How will the classroom look if you kneel down and scoot around the room? Get at the height of your students and notice how things look much different from that perspective. Once you have surveyed the physical space of the learning environment, it is time to begin applying your core understandings about teaching and learning to the construction of the environment.

Whereas there are times when you are assigned to a classroom that seems to be bursting with things to offer, there are also those times when you may be assigned to an environment that appears less than ideal for learning. Let's take a look at how one teacher influenced his environment to encourage independence. Mark Shelby is a special education teacher who was provided with an old supply room for his very first classroom. Mark often worked in his students' regular education classrooms to offer the appropriate support, but other times it was in the student's best interest to be pulled out of the core classroom for service. When students worked in this converted supply room, they were given many opportunities to practice habits of independence. Upon first entering the classroom, students turned in their homework and set their goal for the day at a check-in counter. Possible goals might be to complete work on time, check math for accuracy, pay attention during reading group, find a book to read independently, organize materials for learning, and the list can go on with respect to learning, study skills, or behaviors that students hope to modify with the help of their teacher. When they worked within the classroom, students found a variety of places to study, research, and conference with the teacher: the classroom looked more like a coffee shop with cozy chairs, a couple of tables, a few desks, and a row of computers. In addition, the books were arranged by reading level for student access, the supplies such as paper and pencils resembled an office supply store, and the math manipulatives were organized by purpose and use. Mark used the old shelves and a built-in countertop to his advantage as he based the organizational system on his belief that learners could and should access their own learning environment. Even though Mark groaned at first about the prospect of teaching in an old, dusty supply room, the organization he created reflected his flexibility as a teacher and reiterated that he was determined to build a classroom that would enhance habits of independence.

Keep in mind that creating a physical space for learning is not about replicating clever arrangements, buying the right lamp, or designing the perfect décor. In the end, the physical environment should represent what you believe about teaching and learning and when it does, the classroom will support your work toward developing habits of independence in all learners.

ROLE OF THE TEACHER

When crafting an environment that promotes and provides for student ownership and independence, it is important to examine the role of the teacher within the learning community. Glasser (1993) writes that an educator's teaching style directly impacts independence and motivation since a teacher may choose to lead or boss students. A lead teacher tries to identify and meet student needs while aligning these to curricular requirements. He understands that motivation is internal and the physical environment is structured so that materials are easily accessible to students. A lead teacher encourages this sense of independence, within reasonable parameters that create a learning environment aimed at meeting students' needs. At the other end of the spectrum is a boss teacher who does just that: controls learners by making decisions for students. A boss teacher believes that motivation is external, so he is constantly crafting ways to motivate learners. Materials and resources have clear guidelines, and the teacher is in control of when and how these items will be used. Although the boss teacher and lead teacher may teach identical content, the educator who leads students teaches them how to make decisions and develop skills of independence that go far beyond the content of the curriculum. He is also freed to teach, monitor, and guide individuals instead of controlling events within the classroom.

Let's take a look at what a lead teacher looks like within the classroom learning community. John Baker is a lead teacher who understands that motivation is internal. His kindergartners work within a physical environment that is structured for independence. Materials, such as math manipulatives, are easily accessible to students: a variety of math tools are labeled with words and pictures so as to support students at varying levels of literacy, in turn increasing independence. Students are encouraged and supported in deciding which manipulatives to use and when to use them. When John teaches number sense, he models a variety of ways to arrive at an answer. Learners are encouraged to use manipulatives, calculators, paper and pencil, and strategies for mental math. In Martha Appleton's sixth-grade history class, she leads her class by introducing a concept in history and conducting students in a discussion that helps learners formulate questions to which they want to seek answers. She guides her sixth graders as they research their curiosities, and aids them as they synthesize their findings. The sixth graders have access to a variety of research tools including atlases, almanacs, nonfiction books, biographies, and the Internet. These kindergarteners and sixth graders are naturally inquisitive. As their teachers lead them to new understandings, students not only learn required curriculum, but also gain an ability to learn and think independently as they access their learning environment.

In contrast to John Baker and Martha Appleton, there are boss teachers who control learning by making choices for learners and problem-solving issues when they arise. A teacher who aims to control student learning may teach number sense much differently than John. She may believe that there is only one way to arrive at an answer and when a student deviates from using a set strategy, she says, "I can see how you got that answer, but let's stick to this strategy so that everyone can follow along." Calculators are used when the curriculum suggests their use, manipulatives are used during free choice, and student work is graded based on how closely learners demonstrate understanding of the teacher's instruction. As opposed to Martha's sixth-grade class, a boss teacher may incorporate history much differently by lecturing his learners. Students might take notes during class and be given pop quizzes weekly, along with Friday tests that assess students' knowledge of the most current material. With consistent assessment practices, the teacher may feel that he is checking for understanding and keeping students accountable. Although teachers who control student learning may excel in teaching academia, their students often demonstrate high levels of dependence with regard to thinking, routines, procedures, and protocols.

While lead teachers and boss teachers may satisfy district and state curriculum requirements, take a moment to analyze the difference between the instructional approaches in these examples. How do teachers who choose to be the "guide on the side" differ from those who perform as a "sage on the stage"? Which role is more conducive to fostering learner independence? Educators are consistently faced with choices about how to engage learners, and it is the decisions we make that directly influence learner independence within the classroom and beyond.

CONCLUSION

When the focus is on leading learners, providing for their basic needs, and creating an environment that supports positive management practices, independent thinkers and learners will emerge. Fountas and Pinnell (1996) summarize the impact of an independent learning environment:

> The setting is safe and supportive and enables all learners to develop confidence, take risks, learn to work independently, and develop social skills. In short, an organized and well-designed classroom enables the teacher to observe, support, and meet the learning needs of each child. (p. 43)

As you have spent time analyzing the complex task of planning for the physical environment, what ideas have been confirmed for you and which are you rethinking now? Take some time to reflect on the questions that we posed to you at the beginning of the chapter.

A TIME TO REFLECT

Take some time to analyze and evaluate the physical environment for an element where students heavily rely on your support. What is one challenge that you face consistently or which element of the environment troubles you? Perhaps you are constantly receiving feedback about the seating chart from students and parents alike. Maybe materials, resources, and supplies are not cared for properly and you are consistently needing to intervene and support students in locating misplaced items. Possibly you are just tired of making many of the daily decisions that have little to do with the lessons carefully planned for throughout the year.

Select this one element of the physical environment and begin writing down your core beliefs about the issue. Perhaps students are consistently asking to use the stapler and misplacing it once they use it. First, examine your core philosophy about the stapler in the classroom. Now analyze your question further: What would the use of the stapler look like in a classroom that is structured for learning, what would it look like in a classroom where learning is controlled, and what does it currently look like? If you are looking for a change in how the stapler is accessed and cared for, what is one thing you might try to enhance habits of independence? It is our goal that this exercise helps you to reflect on your teaching practice and encourages you to refine the physical environment to support independence.

A VISIT TO OUR CLASSROOMS

Grades K–3: A Primary Perspective by Karin Ramer

Experience is a powerful teacher—especially when you learn in front of colleagues and parents. When I was fresh out of college, without children at home to entertain and care for, the classroom was my life. When I wasn't trading resources with colleagues, attending workshops, or planning for teaching, I was embellishing the classroom. You name it, I had my fingers on it—carefully printed labels, vibrantly colored bulletin boards, neatly arranged materials, and sophisticated organization that changed as often as the wind. I was intent on finding what worked the best, looked the best, and felt like it would be successful. And you guessed it—I was always searching. I still remember one winter when I spent over four hours constructing a glitter covered mural that would decorate the classroom door, just so that my kindergartens' painted animals would have a colorful place to rest. The décor was so important to me that student independence took a back seat.

I can still remember the moment I saw things differently. My best friend and I attended a workshop where the speaker talked about increasing student ownership in the classroom by encouraging students to contribute to the classroom wall space. Naturally it took awhile to let go of the urge to express myself artistically, but over time, I began to ask myself if students would benefit more by doing the work themselves.

Five years later, the start of the school looks vastly different from anything in my past. Desks and tables are void of pretty name tags and walls are hung with splashes of color but little more. The classroom never looks as ready as parents might expect, but it is my job to communicate my intentions with families at the start of the year—to foster habits of independence in all learners. I explain that this is "our" room and that we will be creating bulletin boards together, hanging important information that our classroom community deems necessary, and learners will label their own work because they can. Students practice habits of independence as they choose daily where to sit, decide what information is useful to hang on the wall, select which work to display for others to enjoy, and write labels for their belongings in their own personal font. Literally, I have found hours of time that I used to spend on tasks that actually furthered learner dependence instead of fostering habits of independence. Walls are no longer covered with stagnant information and students no longer walk into "my" classroom . . . they enter a world where they are motivated to be reflective and resourceful while accomplishing worthwhile endeavors.

Grades 4–6: An Intermediate Perspective by Roxann Rose-Duckworth

A small change my students and I made in our classroom had a big impact on student independence. We created a supply zone where students could be guaranteed to find the supplies they needed while also ensuring that students knew where to return supplies when finished. We covered the top of a low bookshelf with contact paper. We then set the three-hole puncher, three pairs of adult scissors, two staplers, one staple remover, one single-hole puncher, two roles of masking tape, two transparent tape dispensers, and a container of paper clips on top of the contact paper. We arranged it carefully, then we traced each item with a permanent marker. Now when a pair of scissors was being used, it was clear where the scissors needed to be returned. No longer were we searching for the pair of scissors or the stapler. These visual reminders held all of us accountable to return our supplies to their designated location.

On the bookshelf below, we added some plastic organizers with small drawers. These drawers held other school supplies we shared such as liquid glue containers, glue sticks, markers, crayons, rulers, colored pencils, and string. Each drawer was labeled with a word and a picture. Visitors to our classroom really appreciated this organization. I was amazed at how such a seemingly insignificant change could make such an impact on student independence.

When students were borrowing "my" supplies from the teachers' desk, they did not have a sense of ownership and I was disappointed with the level of responsibility they took for caring for these items. In contrast, when these materials became community property with a designated home (see Figure 5.2), students took full responsibility for caring for these items. They used the items with care and demonstrated independence. I never had to worry again about missing materials, and students were able to accomplish their learning tasks without being distracted by looking for necessary materials.

Figure 5.2   An Example of Adapting the Community Supply Idea for the Classroom

SOURCE: Used with permission of Nancy Pates-Riches.

6

Setting Up for Independence

In factory-like schools, you will often hear words like "performance" and "achievement," but rarely words like "discovery" or "exploration" or "curiosity."

—Alfie Kohn (1997, *Education Week*, online)

What would you do if you were given a boiler room in an elementary school to base your special education program out of, or an old phone closet for teaching reading? Would you teach differently if you were given a classroom overlooking the ocean with a coat closet larger than the supply room? Surprisingly it is a common expectation that teachers set up a learning environment regardless of what physical space, furniture, materials, and supplies are available. Each of us can think of a time when someone we know went in search of tables, books, or paper just to get the year started. Then there are times when a friend orders new tables or his room has all of the modern conveniences. Regardless of what we have to work with, the outcome needs to be the same: educating young minds. But how is this done regardless of our space and without spending a fortune?

Setting up the classroom for learning can be overwhelming and exhilarating all at the same time. A fresh start is promising and full of possibilities; yet setting up the classroom can be a vast undertaking. When the environment is arranged based on a solid understanding of teaching and learning, the work you invest before the students arrive will support your teaching long after the start of the school year.

In this chapter, we will discuss the mechanics of organizing a classroom, based on building an environment for independent learners. We provide reflective questions to aid you in arranging the environment, and deciding the feasibility of the materials, while allocating resources and wall space. Whether you are setting up a learning space for the first time or creating a classroom for the twentieth, consider the impact the physical environment has on teaching, learning, and student independence by asking yourself these questions:

- What physical space, furniture, resources, and materials do you have to work with?
- What do you believe and understand about student seating?
- What work is appropriate for you to accomplish prior to students' arrival, and what should wait for students?
- With respect to the classroom, what are procedures and routines that need to be in place to foster learner independence?

ARRANGING THE PHYSICAL ENVIRONMENT

Once you have taken time to inventory the environment where you will facilitate learning, you are ready to begin the actual physical labor. Some teachers find it useful to create a map of the environment, or a paper model with moveable features, before they begin hauling around furniture. Others can envision the environment after careful analysis of the physical space. However you go about arranging the classroom, continue to ask yourself the most essential question: How does the placement of this item help to foster learner independence?

In this section, we will address some features that are common to many classrooms. You may find that they are reflective of your teaching situation or foreign from what you know. The goal is not to dictate that each teaching environment must have particular elements, but to share the process of arranging a classroom for fostering habits of independence. As you reflect on your understandings about the physical environment, refer to Figure 6.1 to help focus your thinking and guide you as you design the interior of the classroom.

WHOLE GROUP

The organization of whole group instruction looks different from one classroom to the next depending upon how the teacher arranges students for learning. Some classrooms are organized so that all whole group instruction

Figure 6.1   Essential Considerations for the Physical Environment

Whole Group Learning	• What are my goals for whole group learning? • How can I establish a physical space to reflect those goals? • Where is the most effective place for the whole group learning area? • Are there potential distractions to avoid? • What does the physical space need in order to support whole group instruction and learning? • What materials and resources need to be available for instruction? • What does the seating configuration look like? Is it fixed or flexible?
Small Group Learning	• What are my goals for small group learning? • How can I establish a physical space to reflect those goals? • Where is the most effective place to meet for small group instruction? • Are there certain distractions to avoid? • Can the entire classroom be monitored from the small group area? • What materials and resources need to be available for instruction? • Does the seating configuration support students as learners?
Collaborative Work	• What are my goals for collaborative work? • Does my physical space reflect those goals? • Where are there opportunities for peer collaboration? • How does the environment encourage students to seek peers for collaboration? • Are there places around the room for peer work that is set apart from students who work in isolation?
Independent Work	• What are my goals for independent student work? • Does my physical space reflect those goals? • Are there a variety of places where learners can work alone? • Do students have the opportunity to move away from peers during work time if they need fewer distractions? • How does the environment support students who desire to work alone?
Materials, Supplies, and Resources	• Does the organization of materials and resources support learner independence? • Do students have independent access to everything they need? • What items require adult permission? • What are the routines and procedures for using materials, supplies, and resources? • Does the organization of the classroom support these routines and procedures?
Safety	• Are there places in the room where students could hide and play? • Are all heavy and tall fixtures firmly secured? • Is there a clear pathway to all doors and windows? • Is there a flow to my room to promote basic student safety? • Are there safety procedures in place?

(Continued)

(Continued)

Wall Space	• Whose interest, talents, and learning are reflected on the walls? • When are bulletin boards hung? • Who decides what goes on each bulletin board? • How long does information stay up on the wall? • Does the work hung on the wall support learning? • Are students encouraged to access information that is posted? • Does posted information enhance independence by providing information for children to access without adult assistance (responsibilities, daily schedule, due dates, changes, etc.)?
Easel/White-board/Chalk-board	• If using an easel for instruction, is it placed appropriately so children can see teacher work? • Does text and graphic information on the board enhance independence by providing information for learners to access without adult assistance (quality work criteria, modeled writings, and problem solving)? • Is information legible and neatly organized for independent access? • Do children partake in writing information on the board?
Student Desks and Tables	• What are my goals for student seating? • Does my physical space reflect those goals? • Where do students store their supplies and materials? • Do students sit according to a particular seating assignment? • Are desks/tables labeled as "personal property" or are they shared space? • Do students have nametags affixed to the desks? • Do students use nametags for guest teachers? • Do the desks or tables promote cooperative work? • Is there a clear path between desks/tables?
Teacher Desk	• What is the purpose of the teacher's desk? • Where are the teacher's professional materials? • How is the teacher's desk used throughout the day?
Bookshelves	• What kinds of books are placed on the bookshelves? • Are the books displayed in an inviting and accessible manner? • Does the placement of book shelves and arrangement of books promote student independence?

can take place with the teacher at the front of the classroom while students are seated at their desks. Other teachers gather students on the floor in a whole group learning area where learners sit together facing the teacher. And still other educators use a mix of these organizational methods throughout the day depending on the task at hand. Teaching from the front of the classroom does not require designating a portion of the classroom for whole group instruction, so in this next section, we will focus on setting up a whole group learning area that is specifically for gathering learners.

When determining a place for whole group learning, there are three factors to consider: the appropriate place for instruction, which materials and resources are needed for teaching and learning, and how students will organize themselves for learning. As you reflect on the environment, take time to analyze where students would be most engaged during instruction. Evaluate potential distractions to avoid such as windows, doors, shelves of materials, and other things that might take students' attention away from your teaching. Be certain to reserve a space that accommodates learners: keep in mind that kindergarten students will need substantially less room than will a classroom of sixth-grade learners merely because of their size. Second, analyze which materials and resources are helpful for instruction. Will your instruction require a place for you to write such as a whiteboard, easel, computer, or other piece of technology? In order to support your daily instruction, be certain to stock your whole group instruction area with plenty of pens, paper, books, resources, and teaching tools. Finally, think about what the student-seating configuration will look like. Do learners have a choice regarding where to sit and if they sit on the floor, chair, or pillows? Are there students who need a designated space for learning so they can remain engaged in the lesson? In kindergarten you might use a rug with blocks of color or Velcro to establish personal spaces. In fourth grade, students may have the opportunity to sit on pillows or a couch as they gather around the writing easel for instruction. For sixth-grade students, the group learning may look different. Students may gather around a table to watch a scientific experiment, sit in cozy chairs in order to observe a writing demonstration, or recline on fancy throw pillows while watching peers perform a play. The benefit of gathering students in close proximity for whole group learning is that with the entire class facing you during instruction, student attention can be focused more aptly and learners are more likely engaged as a result of immediacy to the teacher.

SMALL GROUP

Separate from the whole group learning space you will want to think about where to conduct small group lessons where groups of up to eight learners gather for shared or guided instruction. Providing this type of instruction will support learners in gaining understandings, skills, and strategies that will increase levels of independence. When you search for this location, reflect on where you will be able to best monitor students not involved in the small group. Set yourself away from distractions such as students at the drinking fountain, learners gathering supplies, and others who browse titles at the bookshelf.

As you plan for small group learning, consider placing a table for small group instruction near a shelf of materials and possibly an easel or whiteboard. When you carefully plan for small group instruction and prepare the space appropriately, you will increase the likelihood of meeting with small groups and supporting students appropriately as they work toward habits of independence.

STUDENT SEATING

After you have identified a place for whole group and small group instruction, analyze the physical space for student seating. Where you place classroom furniture will directly influence the flow of the physical environment and how students interact with one another. Consider the display of desks or tables and how a seating arrangement might support or detract from the goal of independence. If desks are arranged in groups or pods, peer collaboration is encouraged as opposed to isolating student desks throughout the room or facing all desks toward the teacher. Positioning desks or tables in groups so that students face their peers will encourage students to use others as a resource. Learners will have the opportunity to interact with peers and gain experience in learning how to problem solve and manage their time while in close proximity to others. In addition, students will be actively engaged in practicing habits of independence as they learn to work within and contribute to a community.

Another factor to consider when setting up student seating is the diversity you will find within one cohort of students. How many times has a classroom had identical desks or tables, all of the same height, along with chairs that fit one size? And for each of these classrooms, how many cohorts of children are similar in shape and size? If the aim is to create a classroom that is comfortable for all learners, strive to include tall and short desks, traditional four-legged chairs along with large exercise balls that are available to students who constantly need to be exercising large motor skills. A classroom that plans for diversity looks much different from the traditional classroom where rows of desks face the front of the classroom. According to Fountas and Pinnell (2001, p. 89),

> Your classroom should convey a warm, welcoming ambiance in which students feel they belong. Creating an inviting classroom means reflecting comfort and productivity throughout the daily routine. Your physical environment should be comfortable for all students, who will vary in both height and size. It should accommodate both large- and small-group activities as well as the individual's need for quiet, solitary activity.

Once you have arranged desks and tables for student seating, consider creating extra seating options for learners beyond just assigned seats. This might mean that learners can move to another table or a corner in the classroom when they need solitude, or it may look like a rug on the carpet where students can gather for a group project. Perhaps there are a couple of single desks bordering one wall, a table with very short legs so students can work together close to the ground, a comfortable chair or couch where students can read in comfort, a table that promotes the use of technology with peers, and corners found throughout the room where children work in partnership on a common goal. Allowing for this type of flexible seating encourages students to take responsibility for their own learning, empowers students to practice behaviors of independence, and provides students with a learning lab of sorts within which they can experiment with where they best learn.

STUDENT SEATING: THE FREEDOM TO CHOOSE

Take a moment to challenge the tradition of assigned seating as you contemplate the idea of free choice seating throughout the day. If children have a place within the classroom where their personal learning tools are stored, we as learning facilitators have more options as to what we can do with seating. What would it look like to allow children to sit wherever they would like to work within the school day? When students are encouraged to choose where to sit, it is the teacher's job to slowly release responsibility to learners and teach them how to choose a seat appropriately. On the first day of school, a teacher might encourage children to sit in a place where they feel comfortable, but inform them that this is not a permanent seating assignment. Throughout the day, while students are getting used to flexible seating, the teacher would prompt learners to switch seats during transitions. In order to focus on developing habits of independence, help students decide where to sit based on where they will learn best according to each particular activity. With this guided practice, students will gradually become capable of selecting where to sit based on where they will do their best work and the dynamics of the classroom will begin to exhibit habits of independence. Keep in mind that this is not a game of musical chairs. As learners become accustomed to selecting where to sit based on their understanding of where they best learn, you will find that some students remain in the same place throughout most of the year, others truly move seats based on the task at hand, and still others continue to need support to find the best place to learn. Learners will develop a sense of security as they test and experiment with choice seating when the social and emotional environment is supportive. When the teacher releases responsibility for selecting a seat with the intention of learning, student sense of ownership and independence is strengthened. The teacher is no longer in charge of assigning and rotating seats on a regular basis while accounting for the human complexities that are often difficult to predict. In addition, students are supported in experimenting with their own learning as the teacher prompts them with questions that promote self-reflection: "How did your choice of where you sat contribute to or detract from your learning today?" "Where will you sit next time during reading? Is that different from where you will sit for math or science?" Prompting learners with reflection questions will soon lead to students who make choices independently, not based on friendships but on learning decisions. A room where students self-select their workspace throughout the day allows learners to begin to understand how they learn best, when they profit from working independently, and when to work with peers in order to enhance learning.

THE TEACHER'S DESK

Once you have organized for whole group, small group, and student seating, the next step is to focus on where to place the teachers' desk. First, consider the teacher's desk: how can the teacher's desk be utilized to impact student independence? In some classrooms, the teacher's desk is placed at the forefront of the classroom where students can be kept under a watchful eye while working at their desks. The teacher remains at her own desk correcting papers, answering questions when students approach her, and shouting directives or praises accordingly. With this system in place, learners follow protocol and may demonstrate habits of responsibility, but true independence is not practiced. Now consider how Carrie Strawn, a kindergarten teacher, supports student independence: the teacher desk is placed at the back of the room, bordering a bookshelf full of professional literature. Students are encouraged to sit at the desk when they need to work in isolation since the only time Carrie sits at her desk is when students are not in the classroom. Carrie is careful to keep confidential information concealed and teaching materials organized so that her professionalism is not interrupted. Students follow clear guidelines about the use of the teacher desk, and Carrie finds that this is a highly motivational workspace as evidenced by a constant sign-up sheet to work there. While both classrooms make use of a teacher's desk, the purpose behind each desk is vastly different: one supports teacher control and the other provides a structure for students learning habits of independence. Whether or not you choose to include a teacher's desk in the physical environment, consider the purpose behind this piece of furniture and reflect on how you might use it to best increase student independence.

LEARNING CENTERS, MATERIALS, SUPPLIES, AND RESOURCES

Once the majority of the learning environment is set aside for instruction and seating, consider where learning centers, materials, and resources should be arranged for ease of student accessibility. Account for where students enter and exit the room, and be certain to maintain a flow to the classroom so that individuals can maneuver easily from one end of the classroom to the other. Each teaching assignment dictates different needs and how teachers organize their classrooms varies considerably. But whatever decisions you make regarding these details, continuously reflect on why you are making certain decisions and how they will impact levels of student independence.

Depending upon your teaching assignment, you might want to incorporate one or more of the following centers: reading, writing, listening, mathematics, science, social studies, technology, foreign language, and art. Some of these centers might be a permanent part of the classroom, while others rotate depending upon the current topic of study or student interest. Most classrooms offer a library that incorporates an element of comfort, such as a couch or throw pillows and an end table with lamp, along with a surplus of well-organized and easily accessible books. While the reading center takes up a corner of the classroom, perhaps the math center is constructed by lining the teacher's desk with two bookshelves and scattered with a few short stools and benches for learners to use when working close to the ground with manipulatives. Maybe the listening center is an overstuffed chair or desk where a couple of students can listen to a story together. Possibly the top of the fixed bookshelf serves as the space for the social studies and science centers that alternate throughout the year depending on the current topic of study. There is much flexibility when it comes to accommodating a variety of learning centers within the classroom, and focusing on creating a gentle flow to the classroom will provide for an ease that will encourage students to access centers independently.

In addition to setting aside space for learning centers, another vital aspect to fostering learner independence is providing student access to materials, supplies, and resources. Keep in mind that the arrangement of materials and resources within a learning community clearly states if there is a dictated or democratic approach to teaching and learning. In a classroom where students are expected to manage both themselves and materials, learners will have access to necessary learning supplies. This is a physical environment that promotes behaviors of independence.

Ownership and the Environment

Prior to physically arranging your classroom, you should be aware of what level of accessibility you feel comfortable handing over to students. Do you feel responsible for handing students everything they need for a lesson and telling them what materials to use for a particular project? Or do students know how to responsibly access the room and make decisions about which materials they will need for a certain assignment? The message we send to students with each approach is clear: either that you will do the thinking for them, or that you expect learners to make decisions about their own learning.

When we focus on building independence in learners, we need to ask, "What are students capable of doing?" "What do they need to know to be successful?" "What kind of support do I need to provide for students to experience success?" and "Do I need to support students differently?" If you believe that students should have direct access to the paper supply, for example, they will need to know how to replenish the paper when only a few sheets are remaining. Perhaps addressing the issue of conservation and careful use of paper is also necessary as students learn to respect the class-room supplies. In a classroom where learners use the computer as a resource throughout the day, they must know when computer access is allowed and what protocol to follow. When independence is valued, students may initiate a computer sign-up list so that computer time is used judiciously. Do learners need to check with the teacher prior to printing, or is there a class-created checklist to follow that will help individuals know if they are ready to print? In a classroom where learners are encouraged to access the room independently, the physical environment will include a clear organizational system, explicit demonstrations, and guided practice that will build skills of independence in all learners. The classroom will be structured so that all learners, regardless of their levels of independence, will work continuously toward developing characteristics of independent learners. The key to building independence is neither learner responsibility nor the ability to function without teacher presence. There are classrooms where students know each and every assignment and routine regardless of whether the teacher is present or not, yet when asked what they would like to do when they finish a particular task, learners are unable to make a deci-sion. Truly independent learners consider their interests and passions and become engaged in tasks due to an internal drive for further knowledge and understanding. This independent behavior manifests itself in the free-dom students express in accessing materials, supplies, and resources as determined not by teacher directive, but by individual need.

When learners make decisions based upon their own learning, they are moving toward independence. Reflect on how books can be used in a variety of classrooms to promote independent thinking and learning. In order to support children as they work toward independence, L. M. Morrow wrote about the importance of creating a classroom library that encourages and promotes literacy (Allington & Cunningham, 1996). She stated that children surrounded by an attractive display of books (accessible in quan-tity, readability, and variety) read 50 percent more books than do students in classrooms not possessing an enticing library. Providing a wide selection of literature will not only encourage students to be readers, it will also moti-vate children to access a library independently or with varying levels of support. Consider what would happen to a student who was enrolled in a sixth-grade woodshop class who claimed that he wasn't a reader. What if he was encouraged to use wood working texts as a resource to problem solve attaching a difficult hinge? What about the fifth-grade musician who was interested in reading about Mozart, yet claimed to hate school because of the reading? Consider the impact books could have on all learners if texts are organized as a tempting, yet accessible, display of high interest topics. Imagine the learning that would ensue independent from teacher instruc-tion, solely as a result of an environment that supported curiosity. Fifth-grade teacher Dawn Christiana created a poster and book display area that was titled "Book or Movie: Which is Better?" Knowing that many reluctant readers are avid TV and movie watchers, she used this area to display books related to current and recent movies and television shows. She encouraged students to consider which was better: the movie or the book? This oftentimes led to the writing of critiques, comparison and contrast papers, and sometimes led to some lively class discussions. She made sure to have a wide array of reading difficulties and genres represented in this section. The display was updated regularly, depending on which movies and TV shows were popular at that time.

Many times teachers experience difficulty instilling a sense of ownership in learners. In order for students to demonstrate responsibility, they need to know that they are a part of the community, and that all of their actions and behaviors have consequences. In a classroom where the teacher is the sole authority figure, all pressure for success falls on the teacher. Consider the responsibility a teacher has when he initiates control over classroom supplies, resources, and materials. Leaving classroom organization to the end of the day seems overwhelming, so he tries to get students involved by ordering them about in a way that gets the job done according to his measure of success. His nagging and constant reminders are evidence of students' lack of ownership; this is common in a teacher-controlled environment. In contrast, Juan Salvage works with his second graders to share in the responsibility. His students each partake in caring for the classroom: someone is in charge of the paper supply; a student is in charge of sharpening a bin of extra pencils; another child is responsible for organizing the math manipulatives at the end of the day and making certain all materials are returned; one child turns off the computers at the end of the day; and another uses a small hand-held vacuum so as to maintain a clean classroom. The list of classroom responsibilities is a result of student input and much brainstorming about what it takes to care for a classroom. While students clean the classroom, Juan notices the sense of ownership and pride as students take responsibility for caring for their classroom. During math, he will often overhear students making comments about keeping materials in the correct bin because of the extra time it takes to reorganize materials. This type of ownership and responsibility did not occur overnight, but as a result of continuous conversations about the role students have in maintaining a classroom environment. Classroom chores and guidelines are set and posted so that they are a reminder, just like a list might help you keep track of household duties for a family. It is within this type of learning environment that students develop habits of independence that will carry over into their everyday practices outside of the classroom.

Another example of a teacher who approached the organization and distribution of class materials with the goal of enhancing student independence is second-grade teacher Laci Mae. She placed a box next to the classroom entry door and labeled it "The Copy Box." When she had items to photocopy, she placed the master copy in this box, along with a sticky note detailing copy instructions. Students were encouraged to also place items in the copy box. For example, students might want a copy of a piece of writing for their portfolio or a copy to take home since their writing notebooks were always kept at school. Perhaps they might want a copy of a page from a book, or copies of their writing for publication purposes. For example, a group of learners created a survey to distribute to classmates, and another student published a flyer on bicycle safety intended to educate younger children in the school. As a class, Laci and her students established guidelines for ordering copies. These protocols were then posted above the copy box in order to honor students' independence and to support students with this responsibility. When a student misused the copy box, Laci would support the individual by checking all his work identified for the copy box until he could earn back the freedom to make copy decisions independently.

Also consider fourth-grade teacher Pamela Paterno, who was frustrated by students' lack of preparation for learning. For example, her students often couldn't find a pencil when it was time to write so she found herself constantly waiting for students to find something to write with. She decided to buy five dozen pencils, sharpen them, and put them in a bin on a supply table. The next day she let her students know that when they couldn't find a pencil, they could use one of her pencils and then just put the pencil back when they found their own pencil. This solution seemed to work for Pamela until six weeks later when she noticed that there were only a few pencils left in the bin. She complained to a fellow teacher. This teacher told her, "Oh, that's an easy problem to solve. I have a solution that works for me and I bet it will work for you." This veteran teacher explained to Pamela that if she kept the pencils on her desk and asked students to give up a shoe anytime they want to borrow a pencil, she'd never lose another pencil. Now, it is true that if Pamela implements this solution, she may never lose another pencil; but will she really be encouraging her students to develop independence?

Pamela won't be increasing her students' levels of independence if she only concentrates on "how to" make pencils available to her students instead of thinking about these important "why" questions: Why do I want students to be prepared as learners? Why is this an issue in our classroom? Why am I making this *my* problem? Her answers have more to do with helping her students develop independent working skills than just helping them prepare for a particular lesson. When Pamela began to focus on how she could encourage independence with her students rather than just focusing on her depleted pencil tin, she got to the real solution. When she began to consider her beliefs about independence, she came to realize that her students would be ready with learning tools if they took ownership of the problem. Pamela decided to share this problem with the class, and they identified not only what the problem was, but also why it was a concern. The class decided to restock the pencil tin; each student brought three pencils for what was now referred to as the "emergency pencil bin." They also talked about how they could keep better track of their own pencils. They talked about how important it is to stay organized with their learning tools, and they shared some real-life situations to make the point. Think if a police officer couldn't find her tablet to give out speeding tickets, if a chef couldn't find his knife, if a judge couldn't find her gavel, if a barber couldn't find his scissors. They decided to interview people they knew to find out how they keep from losing important items. At the end of the week, they shared some of those strategies and they decided as a class which ones they would implement. Some of these strategies included having a special container to keep their pencils, pens, and scissors in so the pencils were not easily lost in their desks. They also looked at the organization of their desks and realized that if they categorized items into separate areas of their desks, it helped them find their books, math tools, writing utensils, and art supplies more quickly. They also decided to label pencils with their names using tape flags. Now when pencils were misplaced, they were easy to return to their owner.

If Pamela was only consumed with the "how," she would have implemented the "trade a shoe for a pencil" method and she would have found that her pencil problem was solved. By doing this, she may have missed out on accomplishing a goal she had for her students—the goal to be independent learners. In fact the "trade a shoe" advice would likely discourage her students from being independent by implying to them that they weren't trustworthy. Her tactic of involving students in the problem-solving process not only solved the problem but also acted as a model for how to solve problems as a community. Pamela's students are likely to become even more independent as she helps them focus on the "whys" rather than on just the "hows" of how to solve the depleting pencil problem.

WALL SPACE

Traditionally, classrooms are viewed ready for student learning when they resemble a page from a teaching catalog or when each wall is complete with artwork, fanciful designs, and vibrant colors. But if learners enter a classroom where everything is complete on the first day of school, how can they establish a sense of ownership in this environment? Consider the message when a learning environment is filled with large spaces of empty, yet colorful, butcher paper and splashed with prompts that stimulate student thinking? We recall talking with one teacher who tells the story of a student complaining about the lack of visual appeal within the classroom at an Open House held the day before school started. Much to the teacher's surprise, the mother replied, "Don't worry honey; the class will be ready tomorrow. Your teacher still has a few hours to finish the room." It was this comment that made the teacher realize that in order for families to support her goal of fostering learner independence, she needed to clearly communicate her intentions. As a result, she began to include a brief paragraph about student independence in the monthly newsletter that reflected her core understandings and common practices that led to habits of independence. Topics varied each month, but the ultimate goal was to inform parents about the significance of learner self-reliance and of ways to begin establishing behaviors of independence. This teacher noticed that as she was explicit about her intentions, parental support increased and their misconceptions about learner independence were dispelled.

There is a fine balance between preparing an inviting environment and structuring an environment that encourages independence, even with respect to the wall space. Although it is easy to spend too much time on a bulletin board, consider how students can contribute to the classroom even on the first day of school. When a teacher has prepared the wall space even before students' arrival, hours of time may be represented by the clever display of butcher paper, borders, posters, and odds and ends that allude to what students will learn throughout the year. But how does this enhance student ownership? We like to keep in mind that if there are twenty-five students in a classroom, only 1/26th of the wall space belongs to the teacher: students are responsible for the rest (Mooney, 2000). Once children have begun to operate in the learning environment, evidence of student learning should fill the room and the once-bare walls will be alive with evidence of student learning, thinking, and experiences. This student work will demonstrate learning that takes place within the classroom along with student interests instead of ideas determined by the teacher. There will be student-established procedures, rules, routines, and rubrics published on the walls, and the wall space will be covered with elements that enhance student learning and independence.

Examine the focus of sixth-grade teacher Juanita Carr as she works to incorporate more than just current events into her instruction. She helps children acquire lifelong thinking skills throughout the day. When entering her room, you would notice a student-created world map bordered by student-chosen newspaper articles reflecting a variety of local, national, and international topics. Political cartoons, reflecting a variety of opinions, are also on display. The cartoons and articles are connected to the world map with pieces of yarn indicating where the current events are impacting people around the globe. Upon closer inspection, you would notice that these articles and cartoons are updated on a regular basis as students share and discuss the latest relevant current events. Off to the right, you would notice a poster listing the different types of current events. This class-brainstormed anchor chart has been revised as students have formed new understandings regarding this particular genre. As students enter the room, they browse through a variety of periodicals spread out on the back table. Some students choose *Time for Kids*, some the local newspaper, some *USA Today*, while others find articles online. Students decide where to sit based on who they can collaborate with on a particular topic. Juanita monitors students as they work, engaging them in conversation in order to assess student understandings, skills, and strategies. Since students are engaged and working collaboratively, she is able to work with small groups and individuals, building on their strengths and needs, while providing specific and timely feedback. Students are prepared for this Thursday routine, getting right to work upon entering the classroom, and often come to class with current events, maps, and other relevant resources from home. At the end of this work session, students share their summaries, insights, connections, and opinions as they develop critical thinking skills. Juanita aims to mesh required curriculum, needs, and interest within a classroom environment where students collaborate to form new understandings. It is evident that Juanita sees herself as a coordinator of knowledge, skills, and strategies. The learning goals for her students go beyond the four walls of her classroom or just filling students with knowledge. She is working to foster independence as her students acquire lifelong skills.

Although Juanita focused on using the environment to enhance learner independence, there are classrooms where teacher-created bulletin boards stay stagnant throughout the year. When wall space is used for current events, for example, yet not referred to on a regular basis, consider the purpose of displaying this information. Let the comparison of these two classrooms help you to reflect on how you use wall space to enhance student learning. Now consider how your classroom's wall space promotes learner independence.

A FINAL TOUCH

When you focus on constructing an environment that fosters independent habits, paying attention to philosophy and function should dictate the arrangement of the physical space. Although a significant amount of time is spent considering how to plan an environment for learner independence, the cosmetic nature is still something to be taken into account. Author and middle school teacher Nancie Atwell shares the importance of setting up the physical environment in her book *In the Middle* (1998):

> Getting the room ready for writing and reading means rethinking its physical arrangement. When students walk through the door the first day, I want them to enter a working environment . . . the easel, overhead projector, and my footstool and rocker are at one end of the room (there is no teacher's desk). I've supplied a rug or . . . pillows . . . for students to sit on when they gather in the circle. Quotes about writing, reading, literature, and life . . . are displayed everywhere. The publication center is ready and available to writers anxious to see their names in print. The low bookcases are packed with supplies and resources. Paperbacks and collections of poetry line a wall; computer stations line two others. The center of the room is filled with desks or small tables . . . to make it easy for me to move among them when I confer with writers. (p. 103)

As you put the final touches on the learning environment, reflect on what you know about teaching and learning, along with incorporating visual appeal where appropriate. You will spend a significant amount of time within this learning environment, as will a group of students, and it is essential that comfort, safety, and a sense of composure reflect your desire for the room. Visiting other classrooms might provide ideas and inspirations as to how you might arrange the learning environment, but be certain that any and all decisions you make align with your central knowledge about teaching, learning, and independence.

ROUTINES AND PROCEDURES

Along with setting up the physical environment to support independence, learners need to be confident and competent with regard to consistent routines and procedures. When setting out to create an environment that will enhance and support behaviors of independence, the teacher must consider many elements of the environment: the placement of a teacher desk, classroom books, technology, resources, manipulatives, and other learning tools. It is how students function within this physical environment that will determine their levels of independence. Dependent students will ask: "Where is the paper?" "Can I go to the bathroom?" or "I am ready to use the cubes now." And isn't the sight of an independent child one of the greatest gifts: turning in work without handing it to you first, signing out to go to the bathroom, retrieving and returning calculators that were used in a project, researching molecules simply because of personal interest. It is learner independence that helps teachers allocate the critical time for small group and individualized instruction. While whole group teaching is essential, small group and individual work allows teachers to assess, evaluate, observe, teach, reteach, and interact with students in order to make the most of their learning. When we work to provide freedom and independence to our students, they reciprocate in kind by becoming engaged in their own learning.

As with anything else, establishing routines of independence takes time, but dividends are high. The teacher needs to devote a significant period of time for children to learn how to access an age-appropriate room. For example, students should know what to do when supplies are low so that the teacher does not constantly need to manage these minute decisions that add up to wasted teaching time, planning time, or time spent outside of the school day. Consider entrusting students with the tasks that you expect they would be capable of doing at home. We have visited many early childhood educational settings that prove that even the youngest students will rise to the occasion when expectations are clear and the release of responsibility is appropriate. Consider the two following kindergartens that approach snack time from two different philosophies. At the first center, the children approach the table to find their plates of food already dished up and their drinks served in sippy cups with lids. The second classroom serves the snack family style where students dish up their own food, asking each other to pass food, and making decisions about what to put on their plate and how much. Their drinks are served in small pitchers that they pour into open cups, and students help to set and clear the table. Consider what snacktime communicates to the students—and how this impacts not only mealtime but also the whole learning environment. We must consider our expectations for how students are to function within the learning community and provide appropriate routines and procedures that will support them as they develop habits of independence.

Now take some time to analyze how a fourth-grade teacher relies on routines and procedures during science. Emalie Marcum's focus is to support her students as they research chemical reactions by establishing clear guidelines at the start of the year. Instead of the entire class conducting one specific scientific experiment as directed by the curriculum, Emalie uses this experiment for her modeled demonstration. In supporting learner independence she asks herself, "What are students capable of doing?" As a result of systematic assessment practices, Emalie believes that with varying levels of support, students are capable of conducting independent scientific experiments. When she asks the question, "What do learners need to know to be successful?" Emalie determines that students need to know what a chemical reaction is and how to research appropriate scientific experiments to conduct in class. In looking at the kind of support learners need, Emalie consistently monitors and observes students as they research and then sift and sort through information as they select an appropriate scientific experiment. Throughout the research process, she provides varying levels of support, even to the extent of pulling a small group for instruction on finding experiments in books, online, and via other suitable resources. Instead of mimicking one scientific procedure, Emalie builds on learner independence, as students are resourceful and work in isolation or with others to accomplish personally significant scientific research.

Since Emalie was not in control of all decisions students made, she needed to have specific routines and procedures in place for student safety, especially when working with chemical reactions. At the start of the year, she facilitated a class discussion that focused on designing guidelines so that students would develop a sense of ownership and pride when working in the lab, along with following safety protocols. Some of the routines and procedures students came up with were as follows:

- Always have scientific research approved prior to conducting experiment.
- Wear protective gear, including goggles, when in the experimentation lab.
- Follow safety guidelines when selecting materials and chemicals to work with.

- Respect other learners' research and experiments.
- Always conduct a project with at least one other lab partner who is acutely familiar with your research.
- Document all research following the scientific process.

As a result of appropriate teacher support and clearly detailed routines and procedures, students gained a sense of ownership and pride in their work, along with practicing habits of independence in the lab.

We have found that when students help to establish rules, routines, and protocols, they monitor their own behavior instead of relying on the teacher to police activities throughout the day. In this environment, the teacher no longer fights for control of the classroom; instead she carefully facilitates learning. As with anything else, establishing routines of independence takes time, but as stated earlier, dividends are high. There are many decisions we make with regard to our physical environment that we give very little thought to—we simply make these decisions based on habit or models. We encourage you to analyze each decision you make with regard to the physical setup of your classroom. These decisions have a huge impact, whether we intend so or not.

Bobbi Fisher clearly identifies the purpose of forming habits of independence within the learning environment: "Materials are easily accessible so the children can be as independent as possible and so I can spend my time talking with them about what they are learning" (Fisher, 1995, p. 95). After all, isn't this our real purpose as teachers? And when children continually ask permission to access materials, tools, and supplies in the classroom, this is a clear indication that they are temporary tenants in their environment. Students who have a sense of ownership in a classroom will have easy access to materials and can make independent learning decisions based on their common understandings of how the learning community operates. They will act in accordance with what they believe independent learners do to benefit themselves and others in the body of learners.

CHANGE OVER TIME

As understandings about teaching for independence develops over time, the physical environment will inevitably reflect these changes. The classroom reflects a teacher's core beliefs about students and their role in the learning process along with representing a snapshot of her teaching philosophy. It is only natural that as teacher understandings grow and develop over time, teaching practices change to reflect new learning. When working to create an independent learning environment, it is essential to create a classroom that supports goals for independence rather than one that looks right or works for someone else. Too many times educators rush to use ideas from workshops, books, or other teachers without considering first how these align with or support their own teaching goals and beliefs.

Consider for a moment the danger of attending an inservice and adopting a practice or procedure because it worked for another teacher, not because it aligned with your beliefs and understandings. This is exactly what happened when a third-grade teacher returned from a workshop that emphasized students publishing their writing. The teacher was excited to increase the opportunities for her students to share their writing so she set up a publishing center in her classroom, complete with a sewing machine and comb binder for binding books. In the publishing center, she had many examples on display that showed a variety of ways to publish books. Three months later, the teacher was discouraged—hardly any students had been using the publishing center. After reflecting on the changes she had initially made to the physical space, she realized that she did not make the most important change of all. She had neglected to implement essential elements into her writing program that would in fact support students in their daily writing and desire to publish. She realized that she needed to model the entire writing process and identify genuine purposes for writing so that students would be eager to share their writing with others. In talking with a colleague, she also recognized that bookbinding is just one way for students to publish and that she needed to help her students brainstorm a variety of ways they can share their writing with an audience. Although the book binding corner was an appealing idea, the concept was much bigger than just setting up a corner in the classroom. It wasn't until she focused on the purpose of publishing writing that her students independently initiated use of the bookbinding corner and other materials that helped them publish their work.

Oftentimes we gather ideas from colleagues or other educators but fail to address the basic need we are seeking to fill. We need to go deeper than just emulating ideas we see in other educator's classrooms. In order to experience success, we need to understand what those educators are doing, why they are doing it, how they are supporting the learning of their students. It is when we implement ideas that align with our goals and match our learners' needs that we are able to move students along the continuum of independence.

As you are constantly sifting and sorting through ideas and understandings, recognize that your teaching profile will change over time. One way to ensure that these changes will support student growth toward independence is to first consider the "why" before the "how." You will not use the physical environment to its fullest potential until it is designed to support your goals and understandings about student independence. Know that over time, as your beliefs and core understandings shift with experience, your environment will reflect these changes. It is within an environment that matches our philosophy that student learning and independence increase. As educators work to foster habits of independence within all learners, it is imperative to focus on setting up an environment that matches our intent.

CONCLUSION

Wherever you are in your teaching experience, it is our goal to guide you through the assembly of the classroom. We hope that this chapter encourages you regardless of whether you work with limited materials or have been collecting things for years. Both situations beg us to reflect on how the physical space can best be utilized for optimum student learning. We anticipate that as a result of reading this chapter, your focus for organizing materials and resources is driven by the purpose of developing learner independence. Asking yourself questions about why you make certain decisions will aid in the development of learner independence. Take time to revisit the questions that we posed at the start of the chapter and reflect on how your responses may have changed.

A TIME TO REFLECT

Constructing a physical environment based on increasing student independence takes much thought and consideration. Although you may design a physical space that directly aligns with your teaching philosophy, unless others are aware of your understandings and values, confusion will often ensue. We once heard of a teacher dragging a couch out of her classroom following a parent conference where a misunderstanding obviously occurred. The mother felt that when students were given the opportunity to sit at a couch, they socialized instead of remaining engaged. Instead of communicating about the role of the couch in the learning environment and discussing student accountability, the teacher gave in and felt unnecessarily defeated for the rest of the year.

A situation like this could have been averted had the teacher articulated her beliefs about student independence. Although you cannot predict what will worry a parent, colleague, or supervisor, it is essential to be clear about why you do what you do. Think about a construct within the classroom that has been designed based on a sound foundation of understandings about teaching and learning. Perhaps you wait to create bulletin boards until students can contribute their work, learning, and ideas. Maybe you have decided to allow students to choose where to sit and therefore do not have names taped on the desks when parents first see the classroom. Possibly students share supplies once they are brought into the classroom. Whatever element you decide upon, jot down three to five reasons this decision impacts learner independence. Consider communicating these benefits in a short newsletter or a brief note. You will find that when decisions vary from the norm, parents feel more confident about a teacher's choices when they are communicated clearly and when they illustrate the benefits to student learning.

A VISIT TO OUR CLASSROOMS

Grades K–3: A Primary Perspective by Karin Ramer

I began my teaching career just as I had learned through experience and during teacher education—assigning students to a particular seating arrangement based upon my interpretation of where students work best. I spent time predicting where students would best be engaged and consequently created a seating chart in order to alleviate problems that students might face during work time. Students sat in their assigned seats and I was solely responsible for deciding when and how to change the seating arrangement. Little student input was gathered and considered with regard to student seating; I made all the decisions about where students would spend time learning.

Over time, I became weary with the responsibility of deciding where to seat students and when to change the configuration. With papers to grade, lessons to plan, parents to contact, and other responsibilities, changing the desks around was just one more thing to do. In addition, I would often receive input in the form of complaints from learners, and occasionally from parents. "I haven't gotten to sit with Keisha yet, and you never put me with my friends." "Can you please make sure Harold doesn't sit beside Larry? At home Harold complains that Larry talks all day and doesn't allow him to finish his work." Even when I tried to accommodate student input, there were too many factors to think about in order to please everyone with a perfect seating arrangement. Considering all of the extra time it took to plan for assigned seating, I decided that sometimes learners did need an opportunity to choose where to sit. I continued creating a seating chart, but decided that students needed extra seating opportunities for when they desired to work alone or in small groups away from classmates. When a learner expressed difficulty working at his assigned seat, he was encouraged to move to one of the extra tables or desks around the room to work alone, or to another place in the room to work on a project with a friend. Allowing students to independently move to another location in order to remain engaged took time to implement. As a class, we spent time discussing the purpose of the extra seating, along with the expected behaviors that accompanied the privilege of choosing where to sit. Over the first few weeks of implementing independent seating, it was my job to monitor for student engagement and support learners as they reflected upon their choice of seating and their levels of engagement. Within a month, students started the beginning of the day in their desks, and after an hour into the literacy block, only a handful of learners remained at their assigned seats—they were actively engaged throughout the room.

After reflecting on the success students had with choosing their own seating arrangement, I removed nametags from desks and tables so that they could choose where to sit from the start of the day. Knowing that there would be critics who challenged this idea of free choice seating, I analyzed the purpose for assigned seating. After much thought I realized that I had been assigning permanent seats based on three reasons: to provide a sense of student belonging, to have control over where students worked, and to know student names at the start of the year or when we had a guest teacher. With respect to providing a sense of belonging, students chose a cubby space to store their supplies, books, and unfinished work. In addition, we continuously worked to establish an environment where students developed a sense of belonging. When evaluating whether or not I would loose control in the classroom, I realized that I would indeed be able to manage learners within the classroom. Once students were supported in choosing where to sit, if they did not follow classroom expectations, it was my responsibility to provide them with more support until they were again ready to make an independent choice. I discovered that when learners independently choose where to sit, they remained more focused since they appreciated the independence they were provided. In order to learn student names at the start of the year and to support guest teachers, I gathered supplies and taught students to make their own name stickers when a guest teacher came in the room, even if I was not present. I found that encouraging students to sit where they best learn transferred this responsibility from me to the learners, thus providing a daily opportunity for students to practice habits of independence.

As I shifted my thinking about student independence, and released responsibility to students for selecting where to learn, the configuration of the classroom environment changed too. I shifted from making decisions based on my prior experiences and what I had seen modeled to making decisions that honored what I truly believed about teaching and learning. At the start of my teaching career, I relied solely on how to design student seating and placement. As my understandings about student independence developed over time, I began considering the why along with the how. I asked other teachers how they provided for independence in student seating and experimented with a variety of solutions until I found one that worked. As a result of student choice seating, learners became aware of their own learning needs and felt more ownership and control within the classroom. And as for me, I benefit from increased student engagement and more time to focus and reflect on the strengths and needs of my students.

Grades 4–6: An Intermediate Perspective by Roxann Rose-Duckworth

What do rain gutters have to do with encouraging independent reading? A lot in my experience! When I first began teaching, my class library had books on a shelf with the spines arranged in a neat order of book height. Students could browse through books by looking at the book spines or by pulling books out one by one. As I visited other classrooms and paid attention to how books were displayed to readers in bookstores and libraries, I began to see that our classroom library was not one that would encourage readers to browse through books, which is something that independent readers do! I attached some gutters (normally used on the outside of buildings to gather rain water) to the wall and set books up in the gutter so the covers faced out. I also began to place books into baskets based on categories (see Figures 6.2 and 6.3).

Figure 6.2   Book Organization

SOURCE: From Dawn Christiana's classroom in Bellingham, WA.

Figure 6.3   Book Bins

SOURCE: From Dawn Christiana's classroom in Bellingham, WA.

This new arrangement of books had a big impact on the level of independence my students took on as readers. Suddenly books that had not been touched in years were being devoured by my students. This is why rethinking my paradigm of how a classroom library should look was one of the best decisions I ever made in my teaching career!

$$7$$

Assessment That Fosters Independence

We must change from a model that picks winners to one that will create winners.

—Harold Hodgkinson
(1989, "Michigan and Its Education System")

Assessment is something educators are consumed with on a daily basis. The idea that assessment needs to be ongoing and varied is probably nothing new to you as an educator. But have you considered the difference between assessment *of* learning and assessment *for* learning? Although each phrase is nearly identical, the differing outcomes are worlds apart. While teachers often find that the assessment of learning provides them with numerical data, many educators have found that assessment for learning encourages independence in their students (Black & Wiliam, 1998; Chappius & Stiggins, 2002; Stiggins, 2002).

Chapter 7 is designed to help you clarify the difference between assessment of learning and assessment for learning. We will provide examples such as reading fluency and examine how rubrics can enhance learner independence. You are encouraged to analyze how you incorporate assessment into your classroom and reflect on how you are enhancing student independence through assessment. Before you delve into reading, take some time to jot down answers to the following questions. They are intended to guide you as you reflect on your current understandings and practices.

- What is my definition of assessment?
- What do you do with assessment data once it is collected?
- What is the purpose of a rubric?
- When should a rubric be developed? Who should develop it?
- How can assessment practices encourage learner independence?

A COMPARISON OF ASSESSMENTS

Assessment for learning and assessment of learning both play a role in education; but it's the assessment for learning that will help your students become independent learners who strive to do their best. Asking yourself the following questions can help you analyze which type of assessment you use most. If you tend to use mostly assessment of learning, you will answer "yes" to the following questions:

- Am I measuring student growth for the purpose of assigning a score or grade to their work?
- Am I assessing my students to submit scores to an administrator, parent, district, or state office?
- Are my students consumed with "what they got" for a grade or score?
- Do my students receive feedback only after their work is complete?
- Am I the only person in the classroom who provides feedback to my students?
- Do students generally have to wait a while before receiving feedback on their work?
- Do students ever complete work for which they never receive any feedback?

If you answered "yes" to most or all of the questions, this chapter will challenge you to consider ways you can move toward assessing for learning. Regardless of your answers to these questions, we invite you to use this chapter to rethink some of your current assessment practices as a way of encouraging student independence.

Assessment for learning leads to developing assessment tools that will support student growth. You will aim to inform students about themselves as learners, not so much informing others about your students. Students will be encouraged to understand what they do well and why that's important. In addition, they will be able to clearly articulate what they are learning and why that's important to them.

Referring to Figure 7.1, you can read about assessment of spelling, pointing out the differences between assessment for learning and assessment of learning. The purpose for including this descriptive chart is not so that you strive to emulate the practice of providing individual spelling lists in your classroom, although some readers may be inspired to do so. We aim to illustrate the difference between assessment of learning and assessment for learning by analyzing the common classroom practice of weekly spelling tests. There are many approaches to teaching and assessing spelling, many of which can use an assessment for learning concept. Looking at the two spelling assessment examples given in Figure 7.1, one can see that students are encouraged to be independent learners when assessment for learning is the focus. Students see more accountability for learning and applying spelling skills when their assessment is focused on helping them learn. Accountability needs to be more than a score. When students have an authentic need and purpose to learn something—that is the highest form of accountability and motivation you can find.

Here's another example of how assessment changes when the teacher focuses on assessment for learning rather than on the traditional assessment of learning. Many teachers today assess students on reading fluency: rate, expression, phrasing, and accuracy are each a part of a fluency score. The teacher who completes assessment of learning will assess students one to three times a year on fluency and most likely will not share the results with students. Scores will be reported to parents and/or administrators, and the teacher will be relieved when this assessment task is completed. Assessment results will have little impact on reading instruction in the classroom.

Now change this scenario to the teacher who uses assessment for instruction by testing for reading fluency throughout the year. The teacher may still formally gather data on reading fluency one to three times a year, but she gathers anecdotal information on a regular basis and uses checklists to monitor reading fluency systematically. These checklists might include, but are not limited to, the following: reading behaviors such as self-corrections, expression with character dialogue, and notice to punctuation. Students understand the behaviors of a fluent reader and how these aid understanding of the text because the teacher gives feedback to students on a regular basis. She might say, "The expression you used when you read that part aloud really helped me picture that character in my mind," or "Try reading that part aloud again, but this time, pay attention to the punctuation. Consider how those commas and periods will affect how you read and understand that text." The teacher demonstrates how to give feedback to one another by prompting students: "We've been talking about how a fluent reader uses proper rate, phrasing and expression when reading aloud. Listen to your partner read one of the paragraphs and tell your partner one thing he did well on reading fluency and one thing he should do differently the next time he reads that paragraph aloud." A skillful teacher helps students learn how to assess their own fluency with coaching such as, "Listen to the recording of your reading and evaluate how you did as a fluent reader using the checklist we created in class." When the focus is on assessment for learning, the teacher is helping the

Figure 7.1   Assessment OF Learning/Assessment FOR Learning

	Assessment OF Learning	Assessment FOR Learning
Where do the spelling lists originate?	• List comes from a curriculum guide • Each student in the class receives the same list	• Each student has an individualized spelling list • Words come from misspelled/approximated words made in their writing • Words are chosen by the teacher based on close approximations, developmental appropriateness, associated word families, and high frequency word lists
Why do students study the words?	• To perform well on the test (often, these words that are spelled correctly on a test are misspelled in the students' written work after the test) • Focus is on a score or grade	• To learn and apply the correct spelling in order to enhance written communication • Student knows that if he spells the word incorrectly again in his writing, the word will show up again on his spelling list, he becomes motivated to proofread his own writing carefully • Students are shown how to generalize spelling words so learning to spell one word can often help them spell other words
What happens if a student misspells a word on the test?	• Word is marked wrong and the score reflects the number missed	• Word is moved to the next week's list • Teacher may help the child learn the spelling by adding other words from the same word family or by teaching a spelling strategy or rule • Word stays on the student's list until the word is spelled correctly • Teacher adjusts, either up or down, the number and types of words chosen for each student, based on understandings and needs of each learner
How are students challenged?	• Students may either already know how to spell the words on the list or find the list overwhelming	• Each student has an individualized spelling list derived from authentic writing • If a child rarely misspells any words in her writing, the teacher might encourage the use of a thesaurus in order to use more interesting words in daily writing and as spelling words • Proficient spellers may partner with the teacher to choose words based on special interests and topics • There may be some students where spelling lists are not used on a regular basis
How are students tested?	• All students are tested at once • Words are read aloud by the teacher; students write the words down • Some students find that the words are given too slowly while others may feel that the test is given too quickly	• Each student is assessed one-on-one; some students are given tests by their peers, some by adult volunteers, and others by the classroom teacher • The test is given at the pace appropriate for that student • Students take their tests on a schedule; a handful of students may be tested each day or students may choose what day they are ready to be tested • This spelling assessment may be referred to as a spelling check, a test, or perhaps a spelling conference

	Assessment OF Learning	Assessment FOR Learning
How do students receive feedback on their test?	• Test papers are either corrected by peers in class the same day (leaving some students humiliated) or are corrected by the teacher and returned 1–2 days later • Students get checkmarks next to words that are misspelled and a score is written on the top of the test paper • Results are sometimes public on a wall chart or through the use of rewards, creating a competitive environment	• Each student has a spelling notebook where his spelling words are recorded • Students get feedback as soon as they spell the word • If the word is misspelled, the word is moved to the next week's list • If the word is spelled correctly, it is expected to be spelled correctly in future writing • No scores are given • Immediate instruction can be given following a spelling error
What kind of information does the teacher gather on the student?	• Teacher has a list of spelling test scores that he/she can average for an overall spelling grade	• Teacher can refer to each student's spelling word lists and distinguish where the child's spelling skills are developmentally • Teacher takes anecdotal notes on spelling errors and successes and is able to notice patterns and stages of spelling development of students
What messages about spelling are being given?	• Spelling is separate from writing • Learning to spell is all about memorization • Spelling is about competitiveness and natural gifts	• Spelling is a tool for writing; we need to spell accurately to help us communicate with an audience • "When I learn how to spell one word, I can apply some of those same strategies to other words."
How are students held accountable to their learning?	• Class takes a spelling test each week • Tests are scored and recorded by the teacher • Students often don't apply correct spellings of these words in their own writing	• The student is tested once during the week; the student decides when he/she is ready for the test • Many opportunities for practice are given prior to the test • Once the child spells the word correctly on the test, he/she is expected to spell the word correctly in his/her writing from then on, if the child does not spell the word correctly on the test, or if the word is misspelled in his/her writing again, it will become a spelling word on a future list • Written work could be handed back to the student if he/she submits the work with misspelled words that he/she has spelled correctly on tests previously, once the spelling errors are corrected, the work will be accepted again
What do students see as the purpose of the assessment?	• To spell the words correctly on the test and receive a high score • Sometimes rewards are associated with these scores	• To learn how to spell these words to help him/her become a better writer • To learn spelling strategies that can be applied to other words • Student is learning to be an effective proofreader, communicator, and problem solver

(Continued)

(Continued)

	Assessment OF Learning	Assessment FOR Learning
How many words are on the spelling test?	• Usually, students are tested on about 20 words each week • Some students are exempt from the test due to a perfect score on the pre-test while others are unintentionally spotlighted as a result of having to take Friday's test	• Usually students study 5–10 words per week
How are spelling lists geared to individual needs?	• Students take a pre-test to determine which words they don't know • If a student doesn't misspell any words on the pre-test, he/she is excused from the spelling test • If a student misspells any of the words on the pre-test, he/she needs to study all of the words for the test	• Teachers choose spelling words based on students' spelling errors in their own writing • If spelling errors are not found, the teacher may encourage the student to expand his/her word choice in his/her writing, choosing some of the more difficult words as spelling words for the week (or no list may be given for that week) • If lots of spelling errors are found, the teacher will focus on the words that are close approximations of the correct spelling and words that are frequently used

student hit a clear learning target. The students receive feedback along the way, helping them to focus their learning. When the teacher only addresses assessment of learning, the teacher ends up finding out how far or how close the student is to the target—but her instruction is not impacted by this data. The information is just reported but it is not used for any real learning purpose. When the focus is on assessment for learning, teachers tend to get energized by observing their students' progress rather than feeling burned out by completing assessment tasks. Assessment for learning benefits not only students' learning, but also teacher morale and motivation.

THE LINK BETWEEN RUBRICS AND INDEPENDENCE

Rubrics are a common tool used to assess student work in many classrooms and may intentionally enhance independence if used adeptly. A rubric is a scoring tool that lists the quality criteria for a piece of work; it also articulates gradation of quality for each criterion. Although rubrics are used in classrooms throughout the United States, they are not without their critics. Paul Bodmer of the National Council of Teachers of English (NCTE) stated, "The problem is that they oversimplify a complex process . . . kind of like paint-by-number kits . . ." (as cited in Mathews, 2000). In the same *Washington Post* article, Thomas Newkirk points out "Rubrics promote mechanical instruction in writing that bypasses the human act of composing and the human gesture of response." The truth is that rubrics can be a powerful tool to encourage independence and promote creativity while keeping students focused on clear performance targets. Just as we pointed out at the beginning of the book, effective educators not only focus on *what* to do, but also on *why*. We believe that educators who implement the use of rubrics without carefully considering why and how they use rubrics risk the encouragement of "paint by number" student performance, which ultimately leads to learner dependence. Even if you do not use rubrics in your classroom, we aim to help you reflect on the assessment tools you use and highlight how it's not so much what we use as teachers, but how and why we use it that really matters.

The common educational tool of a rubric changes when the focus is on assessment for learning, rather than assessment of learning (see Figure 7.2). Rubrics can be used to encourage independent learning in the form of assessment for learning. For example, in Roxann Rose-Duckworth's fourth- and fifth- grade multiage classroom, the class contributed a weekly article to the local newspaper (see Figure 7.3). The "Pet of the Week" articles focused on a pet available for adoption at the local Humane Society. Each week, two students visited the animal shelter with a parent volunteer where their photo was taken with a "difficult to adopt" animal. Learners took notes on the breed, personality, appearance, background, and skills of the pet and over the course of the next few days at school, they composed a persuasive piece of writing to encourage community members to either adopt the animal or visit the Humane Society. As students worked, they practiced habits of independence by referring to a class-generated rubric that can be seen in Figure 7.4.

Figure 7.2   Assessing With Rubrics

Using a Rubric for Assessment OF Learning	Using a Rubric for Assessment FOR Learning
• The teacher develops the rubric	• Class develops the rubric by discussing what a quality product or performance looks like • Examples and non-examples are used to encourage dialogue
• Purpose of the rubric is to give a score or a grade • Student does not see the rubric until the teacher uses the rubric for scoring	• Purpose of the rubric is to help students meet the learning goals • Rubric helps the learner throughout the learning process
• Rubric is written for teachers, parents, and administrators to understand	• Rubric is written in student-friendly language • Language used in the rubric is commonly used in classroom discussions
• Rubric is only used by the teacher	• Rubric is used to help the teacher and student assess progress in collaboration • Students use the rubric for self-assessment and peer assessment

When designing the rubric, learners asked themselves "What is a quality Pet of the Week article?" and they examined samples of persuasive writing in order to establish standards for their own writing. It was important to clarify who their audience was and the purpose for their writing. Once they established that the majority of their readers were adults living in their community and the purpose was to persuade them to adopt this or another pet from the Humane Society, it became easier for learners to figure out what was important to consider for this piece of writing. As the year progressed and the students became more proficient writers, the rubric was modified to meet their new understandings as writers. For example, the criterion of fluency was not something the class initially had on their rubric. Roxann noticed that fluency was lacking in many students'

Figure 7.3   Published Pet of the Week Article Examples

▼ PET OF THE WEEK

Spaniel just had puppies

Hi, we're Tim and Lieu and we'd like to tell you about our new friend named Alley.

Alley is a black-and-white spaniel. She just had puppies. She would be good in a home with children if they're not too young.

Alley has a docked tail and very sleek fur. When you call Alley, she usually comes and she barely barks at all.

Alley has dark brown eyes and weighs about 36 pounds. She is about 2½ years old and very playful.

We hope that Alley finds a home soon. If you are interested, please call the Humane Society.

The Herald's pet-of-the-week column is written by students from Alderwood Elementary School. To inquire about pets, contact the Bellingham-Whatcom County Humane So-

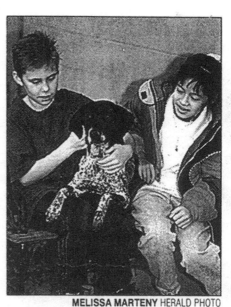

MELISSA MARTENY HERALD PHOTO

NEW FRIENDS: Alderwood Elementary School students Tim Bovat (left) and Lieu Phan hold Alley the spaniel.

ciety, 3710 Williamson Way, 733-2080 or 334-3056. If the featured pet already has been adopted, the shelter has other pets awaiting owners.

Pet of the Week

A DOG NAMED OREO: Slavic Donets (left) and Tam Phan pose with Oreo, the dog they named. Oreo is up for adoption at the Bellingham Humane Society.

Our names are Slavic Donets and Tom Phan. We go to Alderwood School. We are in fifth grade. We are doing an article about a pit bull terrier. It's not mean, it's really nice. It's black with a white chest. His name is Oreo. He won't run away if you put him outside and don't put him on a leash. It's a boy. He doesn't bark. We hope you adopt him.

SOURCE: Reprinted with permission from *Bellingham Herald*, Bellingham, WA.

writing so she began to incorporate that teaching point in her writing demonstrations and in writing minilessons. Her students then initiated the revision of the Pet of the Week rubric to include their new understanding about effective writing. As they discussed the rubric throughout the year, they would talk about why each criterion was important. For example, Roxann asked, "We have determined that a quality article uses varied sentence beginnings and lengths. Why is that important?" As learners discussed this, they focused on their audience. As a result, the rubric helped writers clearly communicate with their readers. These students became independent learners because they had a clear purpose in what they were doing and received feedback on their performance along the way.

As students worked on their articles, they kept the rubric next to them as a reference throughout the writing process. When they asked peers to give them feedback, their peers used the rubric. These things did not happen naturally at first. When Roxann noticed that students were not using

Figure 7.4   Pet of the Week Rubric

Area of Performance (Criteria)	Degrees of Performance (Quality)		
	Does Not Meet Standards	Meets Standards	Exceeds Standards
Conventions	Frequent errors in conventions interfere with readability	1–2 errors with conventions	Correct spelling, punctuation, capitalization, and grammar
Organization	Difficult for reader to get main point	Introduction and conclusion used	Introduction and conclusion, flows smoothly with transitions
Persuasion	The reporter does not appear to persuade the reader to adopt the animal	Recommends adopting the pet	Clear statement for adoption recommendation with supporting details
Word Choice	Limited vocabulary and redundant words	Adequate and functional words	Specific, accurate, natural, and effective language
Fluency	Incomplete or run-on sentences, choppy sentences	Varied sentence beginnings	Varied sentences beginnings and lengths
Score Figuring	____ × 2 =	____ × 3 =	____ × 4 =

Total of points above: _____ ÷ 5 = _____

3.5–4 = Exceeds standards

2.8–3.5 = Meets standards

2.7 and below = Does not meet standards

rubrics to help them with their writing, she had to think about why that was so. She realized that she had not modeled how a writer might use a rubric throughout the writing process. In addition, she realized that peer feedback was important so she provided demonstrations of how peers can use a rubric to give feedback to one another. She continued to reflect on her teaching: Were the rubrics easily accessible? Were discussions related to the rubric focused on the quality of the writing (assessment for learning), rather than on the score for the writing (assessment of learning)? Were students clear on what a rubric was and how it could help them as learners? Roxann found that as a result of ownership, students became more willing to make the needed revisions even if it meant totally revamping their writing. As Donald Graves and Penny Kittle wrote in *Inside Writing* (2005, p. 109): "Revision always requires faith that messing it up will make it better."

When students turned their articles in for teacher revision, Roxann looked at their work and used the rubric to begin the assessment process, but her assessment did not end with the rubric. Figure 7.5 shows a draft from two students and what follows is how Roxann used the rubric to plan the next learning steps for the students. When Roxann used the rubric, she noted this work exceeded the standards in conventions and persuasion. The writing met the standards in organization and word choice. The sentence fluency did not meet the standard because so many sentences began with "he." Although this rubric focused on this one piece of writing, Roxann's focus was to develop the writers, not so much develop this particular piece of writing. Therefore, when Roxann assessed their work, she thought not only about what they did with this piece of writing but how she could help them grow as writers. Roxann knew that if she taught them to rewrite sentences to change word order, they would not only improve this piece of writing but they would become more proficient writers. In fact, she encouraged these students to look at other pieces of their writing as well. They discussed how sentence fluency had impacted their writing effectiveness overall. What mattered was that her students learned why sentence fluency is important, how to create fluent pieces of writing, and how to incorporate this strategy into their repertoire of writing. That was the focus of her assessment. Her focus was not on giving a score, although in the end a score was given. Roxann focused not on just this piece of writing, although in the end this piece of writing benefited from this assessment and it was published in the local newspaper. Her focus was not even on just these students. When she realized their challenge with sentence fluency, she considered whether this was a common challenge for other writers in her classroom. She created a checklist where she looked at students' writing with a focus on fluency. As she did this, she asked herself the following questions: "What will I find when I look at the entire class? How can other students' writing be used as a model for sentence fluency? What are they reading as a class? Do the authors of the texts they are reading model fluency? How can I help my students see this?"

Figure 7.5   Draft Writing of Pet of the Week

Hi, our names are Jennifer and Steven. We are from Alderwood Elementary School and we chose a cat and named him Teddy. He is 3 years old and he has long hair is very intelligent.

He would be a good pet for an older couple. He needs to be brushed daily, likes attention and loves to sit on laps. He is a bit playful and needs lots of love and a good home.

He is also very quiet and is very annoyed by dogs. In fact, he despises large dogs. Teddy can fit into small spaces, is very calm around people and loves kitty treats. He also can be stubborn at times.

Teddy is a tabby and is beautiful, but can be very lazy. He is fluffy and soft like a teddy bear, and would be suitable for a home with other cats. Just remember, if you are looking for a cat, look for Teddy.

When teachers challenge themselves to use assessment for learning, they become more reflective about their assessment practices. And when teachers are reflective about both their assessment and instructional practices, students tend to be more reflective and independent. Roxann rarely needed to remind a student to work on this writing task—students were motivated to work through the writing process not because of the score, but because they were aiming to become accomplished writers for an authentic purpose and a genuine audience. They were so successful in adopting out needy pets, students insisted on creating a summer schedule during which they continued this writing endeavor. They were obviously committed to accomplishing a task well—isn't that what independent learners do? When teachers focus their assessment practices on student learning, students are more likely to apply learning to new situations. For example, Jennifer and Steven not only revised their Pet of the Week article for sentence fluency, they began making that a focus of their writing. A month after working with Jennifer and Steven on sentence fluency, Jennifer met with Roxann for a reading conference and they discussed a poetry book she was reading, an anthology entitled *A Pizza the Size of the Sun* (Prelutsky, 1994). Roxann asked Jennifer some questions about the genre of poetry and Jennifer made a very interesting observation while referring to the first poem in the book:

I'm making a pizza the size of the sun,

A pizza that's sure to weigh more than a ton,

A pizza too massive to pick up and toss,

A pizza resplendent with oceans of sauce.

A Pizza the Size of the Sun (p. 7).

Jennifer noticed in this stanza and throughout the book that poetry follows different rules for fluency than nonfiction writing such as persuasive narratives. She noticed how repeating the phrase, "a pizza" brought rhythm and flow to the poem. Roxann asked Jennifer to share this observation with the class. By asking Jennifer to share, the class benefited not only by the discussion about how fluency looks different in various genres but also the students were encouraged to apply learning to new situations—something that independent learners do.

If Roxann had simply focused on assessment of learning, she would have assigned her students to write a persuasive piece of writing and the only audience for the writing would have been her and the only feedback her students would have received would have been on a rubric that they never saw during their writing process. The feedback would have been given to the students and nothing would have been done to improve their writing. The rubric would have simply been used to score the work. How can that develop independent learners? Teachers must use assessment tools carefully. Misusing rubrics and other assessment tools by focusing on assessment of learning results in students who are dependent on teacher control because they see no other reason for their learning except to earn a grade or to please the teacher.

ASSESSMENT THAT ENCOURAGES INDEPENDENCE AND CREATIVITY

One common concern with rubrics is that they can stifle creativity, which may indicate a lack of motivation and independent thinking. When the focus is on assessment for learning; that is less likely to occur. For example, when Roxann's students created and used a rubric (Figure 7.6) for their poetry recital, many went beyond what the rubric outlined as a quality performance. Many students used props and costumes even though the rubric did not mention the use of such materials. The focus of their performance was on entertaining their audience, both during the afternoon and evening poetry recitals. And the rubric helped learners fine-tune their performances. Although students did receive a score for their performance, that was not what they were worried about—they were consumed with doing their best for their audience. For weeks prior to the recital, students were motivated to select and memorize a poem and interested in learning how to portray moods, meaning, and feelings through their performance. They understood and bought into why memorization and public-speaking skills were important. If the poetry recital had been only about earning a grade, it is less likely that students would have gone beyond what the rubric outlined as exceptional and attendance would not have been as high. As a result of student passion for this project, 100 percent of the learners' families were in attendance—in a school where parent involvement was typically low. The students were so motivated to do their best that they came up with the idea of videotaping themselves on stage prior to each of the two performances and watching the video to aid in their self-assessment. When students are independent learners, teachers do not have to coerce them to participate in learning activities: The audience and purpose are so clear to students that they are highly motivated to do their very best. Students simply see a scoring guide as a tool to help them perform.

ASSESSING WITH PURPOSE

Look again at the Poetry Recital Rubric (Figure 7.6). Notice how the criterion for accuracy is described. A strong performance is described as having "no noticeable errors." Some might say that a strong performance in the area of accuracy would be "no errors." But is that what is really important at the recital? Is the student performing for the teacher or for the audience? If the student is performing for the audience, then the assessment

Figure 7.6 Poetry Recital Rubric

Poetry Recital Rubric for _____

Criteria	Quality: Does Not Meet Standards (2)	Quality: Meets Standards (3)	Quality: Exceeds Standards (4)
Did the student introduce the poem?	No introduction	Introduction shared title and author	Introduction got the audience's attention
How did the student sound?	Hard to understand speaker	Showed some confidence	Clear, loud, fluent, expressive voice
How did the student look?	Body language interfered with audience's appreciation of poem	Showed some confidence	Posture and body motions showed confidence and preparation
How accurate was the recital?	Some noticeable errors and/or needed some prompts to continue	A few noticeable errors or pauses to remember	No noticeable errors
How challenging was the poem	The chosen poem(s) is less than the requirement of 100 words	The chosen poem(s) is considered appropriate for this recital	The chosen poem(s) is considered challenging to memorize and recite

Total rubric score: Total the rubric points and divide by 5 to come up with the average rubric score.

Overall rubric evalaution: _____

(A rubric is a scoring tool that lists the criteria for a piece of work. It also articulates gradations of quality for each criterion. This rubric was developed by the students of Ms. Rose's class so that "quality" poetry recital performances were clearly defined. Rubrics are powerful tools for both teaching and assessment. This rubric's quality choices match our district's report card.)

should reflect that. Roxann's students learned about how to deal with mistakes or a lapse of memory. Aren't those important public-speaking skills? Students were assessed with this rubric during both the daytime and the evening performances, and it was their choice which rubric would go into their portfolio. They used feedback from their daytime performance, via the rubric, to help them improve their evening performance. Some teachers would have had a copy of the poem at the recital, checking each word for accuracy. But Roxann paid more attention to whether the students had "noticeable errors"—and that makes a world of difference when it comes to creating independent learners. It was very clear that their learning was not about satisfying their teacher, but it was about performing well for an audience that mattered—their peers, friends, and families. This is what independent learners do—they have a clear sense of purpose.

REFLECT ON YOUR USE OF RUBRICS

If you use rubrics as a form of assessment in your classroom, ask yourself how often students go beyond the expectations outlined in the rubric. Do you find that all of the work students complete tend to look the same? Do you find that students will only do something if "it counts" for their grade? Do students participate in formal and informal assessment opportunities? Can students articulate the importance of assessment to their learning? Reflect on how you are using assessment in your classroom. Are your students consumed with assessment of learning, rather than assessment for learning? Are your assessment practices helping students focus on what they know and can do? Are students able to clearly articulate what they are working on as a reader, writer, mathematician, scientist, artist, etc.? Your students' attitudes and perceptions about assessment will be influenced by their previous educational experiences, but that doesn't mean you can't positively influence these beliefs and attitudes. The decisions you make as a teacher will greatly impact how your students perceive the purpose of assessment and the reason for learning. These will dramatically affect how independent your students are as learners.

THE BENEFITS OF ASSESSMENT FOR LEARNING

Effective teachers strive to create an atmosphere where value is placed on reflection, critique, and collaboration. High expectations and best effort are things that students strive for not because they want to earn a particular score but because they see true value in what they do and what they are learning. Whether a teacher is using rubrics, checklists, observational notes, or written tests, the assessment practices must encourage students to reflect, critique, and collaborate, thus improving student independence. Even with the standardized state tests that students are required to take, the focus can and should remain on assessment for learning. Although the reality of assessment of learning is a part of every classroom, it should not stand alone. Students are motivated to do their best when they see the benefits of reflecting on and of refining their products, processes, and performances.

Assessment of learning plays a role in education. We will continue to give scores and grades as a way of reporting to families and of monitoring student progress. In addition, these scores will be given to the school, district, and state in order to influence programs and funding. We will continue to participate in district and state mandated standardized tests and performance tasks as a means of accountability. There is value in both assessment of and assessment for learning; but it's the daily classroom assessment practices that will impact the success of our students and the degree to which our students will become independent learners. Take a minute to self-assess your teaching and assessment with the questions below. If you tend to use mostly assessment for learning, you will answer "yes" to the following questions:

- Am I assessing student work to give feedback to the student and to help with my daily instructional planning?
- Do my students see purpose in what they are doing in our classroom? Do they "buy into" learning?
- Do my students receive feedback throughout the learning process?
- Do my students receive feedback from a variety of people?
- Do my students get feedback in a timely fashion, immediately if possible?

All assessment tasks could be placed on a continuum of assessment of learning to assessment for learning. Knowing this, we encourage you to reflect on your current assessment strategies and focus on promoting levels of student independence and accountability.

CONCLUSION

There are two main ways a teacher might collect data on student strengths and understandings: assessment of learning or assessment for learning. Whereas in the end both forms of assessment reflect student's strengths and challenges, it is assessment for learning that truly works to shape habits of independence. Whether we use district or state mandated assessments or student generated rubrics, teachers have an opportunity to foster habits of independence in learners. It is how we approach assessment and what we intend to do with it that result in just another paper to grade or a tool for building on student strengths. As a result of analyzing the difference between assessment of learning and assessment for learning, we hope to have prompted an internal dialogue that will help you to reflect on your assessment practices and understandings. Take some time to reflect on the questions that we posed to you at the beginning of the chapter.

A TIME TO REFLECT

Within every classroom, assessment takes place. Perhaps it is formal or informal, documented or not. However testing is employed in the classroom, it is important to use assessment as an opportunity to further learning, not simply measure what has occurred.

To help you reflect on your assessment practices, isolate one test that you currently administer—maybe it is a weekly spelling test, a monthly history quiz, or a district reading assessment. What information are you able to gather once you have analyzed the assessment sample? How could learners benefit from this knowledge, instead of just knowing their score? Talk with a colleague and discuss what is appropriate to share with learners and which aspects of the evaluated assessment can be used to guide teaching decisions.

A VISIT TO OUR CLASSROOMS

Grades K–3: A Primary Perspective by Karin Ramer

When I first began teaching young learners, I compartmentalized teaching, learning, assessment, evaluation, and planning. These were not reciprocal processes, but instead steps that were linear toward the goal of meeting curricular, state, district, and grade-level requirements. As my understandings grew and I participated in more professional development opportunities, I began to see how my thinking was disjointed and ineffective. Over time, with experience and careful coaching by colleagues, I started to see how all of these pieces fit together and in fact were cyclical and interdependent upon one another.

My biggest challenge came as a result of participating in a study group where we looked at providing feedback to students. Together we read literature, reflected on our practices, and challenged our understandings when working with students. Instead of grading papers for the sake of a score and then returning assignments hours, if not days later, I started to ask students to grade a few of their own papers. It was my hope that my young students would have the opportunity to fix errors and confirm or correct understandings, rather than assign themselves a number. I knew that if learners just gave themselves a score without the opportunity to fix errors, we were participating in assessment of learning.

As we began looking at assignments together, we started with simple fact sheets. Once students had a sufficient amount of time to complete their work, I guided them through correcting the assignment. While interacting with learners in this conversation, I walked around the room, glancing at student scoring and supporting the students when appropriate. Here is an excerpt from our conversation when I was working with second and third graders on fact fluency:

Teacher: When you are grading your math today it is very important that you have a chance to fix any error you might find. This is not about a score, but learning. If I correct your work, you don't have the opportunity to fix a confusion that you might have. So that I can best understand your thinking, do not erase your first answer, just cross it out with a line or two and write the correct answer next to your first answer. Let's begin. What is the answer to number one, 12 + 7?

Students: 19. I got 18!

Teacher: Okay. We have 19 and 18 as answers. Are there any other possibilities? If not, let's take a look at our thinking. Does anyone want to explain how they arrived at an answer?

Student: I have 19 because I knew that 2 + 7 was 9 and then I added 10.

Student: Oh. I added up like this: 12, 13, 14, 15, 16, 17, 18. (Showing fingers and using the counting up method.)

Teacher: When you counted up, did you hold up a finger for 12?

Student: Yeah.

Teacher: When we count up we don't hold up a finger for the starting number. You count up like this: 12, and then hold up your seven fingers 13, 14, 15, 16, 17, 18, 19.

Student: Oh! I get it now.

Teacher: Just cross 18 out and write 19. How about number two, 20 − 9?

Students: 11

This encounter may sound laborious, but look at the insight gained by having a conversation about one problem. In reality, this interaction took about two minutes, and grading the entire sheet took no more than five minutes. The time spent in class was more informative to my teaching than just sitting with a stack of papers and giving out a score. In fact, it served to solidify understandings and clarify confusions for learners, along with providing me with insight to student thinking.

It is not a reality to grade everything as a class—some assignments require more teacher support—but spending time reflecting on student work enhances learner understandings and in turn, levels of independence. While I still glance at student work, once it is scored I am now relieved of piles of papers to grade. In addition, students have immediate feedback that is so necessary to building understandings.

In the process of involving students in self-assessment, it was essential to inform families of the student and teacher role in grading particular assignments. You don't want families to think that you have relinquished your responsibility as a teacher, but instead they need to understand the purpose behind this immediate student feedback. I have found that I am more confident with my practice when parents are well informed, and they trust me once they are knowledgeable about what goes on in the classroom. When I move into other classrooms to support teachers, I now sample how this form of immediate feedback might work with all learners. My experience has shown that even preschool-aged students are capable of rethinking a problem as a result of conflicting answers; and after all, isn't it really the students who need to do the learning and growing toward independence, not the teacher?

Grades 4–6: An Intermediate Perspective by Roxann Rose-Duckworth

Each day, I would write a daily fact on our whiteboard. This daily fact would highlight a day in our history. For example, it might read "On this day in 1820, Susan B. Anthony was born. Later in her life, she was a pivotal leader in American women gaining the right to vote." Each day, we would have a short discussion about the daily fact. Oftentimes, students would raise questions such as "When did women get the right to vote?" Very early in my career, I would have answered the question as the "distributor of knowledge" or feeling guilty if I didn't know the answer, I would have run to a book to seek the answer. Then I moved to posting the question(s) to my students. We called these questions "mind movers." These student-generated questions were listed on the board. Students were encouraged to find the answers to these ponderings. When I first began recording the mind mover questions, the focus was on finding the right answer. Students would report their findings to the class and I would evaluate the accuracy of their answers. But as I moved toward assessment for learning, I began to change this practice. At this point, students not only reported their answer, but even more importantly they shared HOW they came up with the answer. We began to keep a list of strategies people used to find answers to our mind mover questions. This list became a great resource when students needed to do research on a topic. Almost daily, we were answering questions and talking about the processes we used. We discussed successes and dead ends. I kept the same practice of using daily facts and mind movers over the years, but continued to refine the practice as my understandings about student learning and independence grew. Mind movers became a favorite time of day for our class where "right answers" were valued, but the learning process that enhanced student independence was valued even more.

Classroom visitors would sometimes ask "Do the students get extra credit for answering mind mover questions?" When I would explain that the students were not receiving any kind of reward for finding the answers to the questions, they would be amazed. It is amazing how a classroom culture can be impacted by focusing on assessment for learning.

8

Evaluation and Analysis That Develops Independence

When students are involved in the assessment process . . . they can come to see themselves as competent learners. We need to involve students by making the targets clear to them and having them help design assessments that reflect those targets. Then we involve them again in the process of keeping track over time of their learning so they can watch themselves improving. That's where motivation comes from.

—Rick Stiggins (as quoted in Sparks, 1999, "Assessment With Victims")

Have you ever had that overwhelming sense that by administering a particular test, you just created hours of grading for yourself that will impact neither teaching nor learning? You stuff the tests and grade book into your bag to take home, only to return with numbers that are the end result. If you test just for the sake of testing, you are not only creating piles of work for yourself but a prime benefit is overlooked: evaluated assessment profoundly informs our teaching. When we analyze student work and reflect on our teaching practice in tandem, we can begin to understand why learners respond to an assessment sample in a particular manner.

Perhaps you have heard the terms *assessment* and *evaluation* used synonymously. Although the semantics of data collection may be interchangeable, in pedagogy assessment and evaluation have different meanings. There may be a fine line separating assessment and evaluation, yet both of these terms work in conjunction; assessment and evaluation are in fact two interdependent parts of the same process. Assessment is the collection of data to identify the occurrences of learning. Evaluation is analyzing the data, aiming to identify the student's strengths, approximations, and challenges. This supports learner independence because when the teachers acutely know their students, they are able to provide students with the appropriate levels of support.

Chapter 8 is specifically designed to focus on how evaluated assessment helps a teacher plan for instruction that enhances skills of independence for individual learners. Prior to reading this chapter, reflect on your current understandings as you answer the following questions:

- How does evaluation of student work help you make instructional decisions that will encourage independence?
- What does assessment and evaluation look like in a classroom where student independence is valued?
- What does it mean to be data rich and analysis poor? How does this impact student learning and independence?
- What assessment and evaluation practices help teachers meet their students' needs?

SUPPORTING STUDENTS THROUGH EVALUATION

Independent learning is supported when the teacher makes instructional decisions based on the cutting edge of students' understandings. According to Lev Vygotsky, "With assistance every child can do more than he can himself. . . . What the child can do in cooperation today, he can do alone tomorrow. Therefore, the only good kind of instruction is that which marches ahead of development and leads it, it must be aimed not so much at the ripe as at the ripening functions"(1962, pp. 103–104).

This is a complex undertaking to orchestrate in the ebb and flow of daily life in the classroom; especially when combined with the myriad of decisions a teacher continuously makes when striving to provide sound instruction.

When making these instructional decisions based on student understandings, learning is enhanced. Let's take a look at how Maylee Turner, a second-grade teacher, supported a writer's ability to proofread his own written work. Joshua was a competent writer in the area of ideas and content, yet his message became tangled due to many errors in his writing. Instead of telling Joshua that he had to proofread his work for spelling and conventions before publishing it on the computer, Maylee worked to help

Joshua understand the significance of proofreading—proofreading is a skill that shows respect for a reader. In order to support Joshua in proofreading, Maylee brainstormed a list of conventions that were evidenced in Joshua's writing. These she documented on a sheet in his writing journal that would remind Joshua of his strengths as a writer and of the responsibility he has to implement them in his writing on a daily basis. Figure 8.1 is an example of such a record that supports a writer as he holds himself accountable for skills that he has already mastered. After documenting his strengths, Maylee focused on one teaching point that would allow Joshua to proofread his writing with competence. Since Joshua often spent more time recording his ideas than carefully spelling, Maylee used explicit instruction to help Joshua check his writing for correct spelling. She taught him to check each line for words that he knew were spelled correctly. This meant that Joshua would read each word carefully and check to make sure that it was accurate. He underlined any word that was in question. Once he had proofread a portion of his writing, Maylee showed Joshua some strategies for spelling words correctly: Try three different ways to spell a word and circle the one that looks correct, check in a dictionary or on the computer dictionary for the correct spelling, or ask a friend for assistance. Maylee noticed that as Joshua read his writing word by word, he caught many of his spelling errors and was able to fix them without using one of the strategies they talked about. This then led to a quick conversation about accountability and the significance of spelling correctly the first time in writing. Before their conference ended, both Joshua and Maylee agreed that in future writing, Joshua needed to hold himself accountable for spelling in his writing. This goal was then written on the top of the next day's writing page as a reminder. As Joshua continues to add to his writing each day, Maylee will briefly monitor Joshua during writing time in order to support him in implementing his strengths and new strategies as he progresses toward independence. These focused and intentional conversations support students to take more responsibility for their own learning and enable the teacher to foster independence that will permeate daily work within the classroom and beyond.

A similar model of this is provided in Chapter 1 in Figure 1.3 with the "I'm Learning/I Can Chart" (adapted from Campbell Hill, 2001; Graves, 1983). As you may recall from Chapter 1, this list is created based on evidence of strengths and challenges in student writing. Skills approximated or nearly correct are recorded as goals for the individual to focus on until competency is demonstrated in daily work. This goal relates to the learner's cutting edge of knowledge and is a skill that can be learned with a small amount of support by the teacher. For example, in Colton Harrison's first-grade class, Maggie is beginning to understand that sentences end with some form of punctuation as evidenced by her random use of periods within a piece of writing. During a writing conference, Colton draws Maggie's attention to her use of periods and highlights the examples where she correctly placed a period. Through a brief conversation, Maggie is able to articulate that "periods are inserted at the end of a thought and sometimes you can decide that by reading your writing out loud." Under the column "I am learning to . . ." Colton records "use periods at the end of a thought" so that Maggie has documentation of her current writing goal. As a level of support, Colton demonstrates how to "read like a writer" by examining how published authors use periods to show ends of sentences. Colton will continue to monitor Maggie's writing for the correct use of periods and he will frequently engage Maggie in brief conversations about her use of periods in her writing. When she has consistently used periods at the end of sentences, Colton will document this growth on the "I can" side of Maggie's goal sheet. With the help of this personalized proofreading list, Maggie will be supported to work toward a goal that is attainable and appropriate, with guidance that moves her quickly toward independence.

The degree of student independence directly links to the teacher's knowledge of the individual student. When teachers know what their students can do and what they need to know next, the orchestration of the learning is based not on tasks that fill time, but rather on tasks that require time to further student's learning. To illustrate this concept, let's look at Delaney Baker's third-grade classroom. While monitoring learners during a social studies project, Delaney notices that Darren is off task and encouraging others to join him as he crafts a paper airplane out of construction paper. Delaney has two choices in this particular scenario: to take control of the situation, or to empower the learner toward independence. If Delaney

Figure 8.1   Writing Skills List

Conventions	Word Choice	Organization	Sentence Fluency	Voice	Ideas	Presentation
• Caps on names • Periods at ends of sentences • Quotation marks for dialogue (talking) • Exclamation points to show emphasis and excitement • Proofreading for spelling	• Other writing skills could be listed for each trait of effective writing					

SOURCE: Adapted from Donald Graves's book, *Writing: Teachers and Children at Work*, 1983, page 298, and Northwest Regional Educational Laboratory's *Six + 1 Traits of Writing*.

decides to intervene and redirect Darren to the given assignment, she might say: "I see that you are busy making airplanes instead of researching how our Constitution was written. Since you are choosing to play now, you can stay in from recess and work on your project then." Although Darren would likely refocus on the task at hand and complete his work, he does not grow in independent behaviors that will help him in the future. On the other hand, if Delaney intervenes in a different manner by encouraging Darren to reflect on his behavior, she is working to foster habits of independence. She might say to Darren: "Talk to me about why you chose to construct paper airplanes instead of working on the Constitution project." Perhaps Darren shares that he couldn't find the information he needed right away and so he wanted to show his friend how to make a cool plane. As a result Delaney is able to help Darren find a solution: "Tell me a little bit about how you tried to research the Constitution. What resources did you use?" Based on Darren's answers, Delaney can support him to accomplish the task at hand and gain a strategy for the next time he is unable to find information quickly. As Delaney leaves Darren's workspace she helps him reflect on their interaction: "So the next time you are unable to find information right away, what is something you can try?" followed by "How do you think that might help you as an independent learner?" When a teacher empowers learners through conversations and self-reflection, she ultimately provides students with modeling that enhances independent behaviors. Providing this kind of support and structure for students will promote habits of independence, whereas making choices for learners takes away control from students and encourages teacher dependency.

An example of how a teacher uses assessment and evaluation to develop independence can be found by looking at Cierra Tromoski's fourth-grade classroom. Cierra worked with her students at the beginning of the year to develop a common understanding of independent reading. Although some would argue that fourth-grade students should be competent independent readers, Cierra understood that her students came to their learning community with diverse reading experiences and attitudes. Cierra began each year demonstrating independent reading expectations. She provided support to her students to help them understand the elements of quiet reading—from book selection, time allotment, use of physical space, as well as what it means to be engaged in a book. After modeling, Cierra monitored the class while students practiced independent reading under her guidance. When she evaluated that students were proficient, she began to use independent reading time for one-on-one reading conferences. The data that were collected from these conferences helped to form future teaching points for her reading demonstrations. For example, when talking with students about their independent reading, Cierra noticed that students were choosing to read only books from the fiction genre. In order to encourage a wider breadth of text selection, Cierra gave book talks on new nonfiction books recently added to the classroom library, along with small group instruction that taught students how to access and understand text features unique to nonfiction genre. Some teachers who struggle with their students reading independently look at this as simply a management issue, and they make a plan for how they will coerce students into reading quietly by using rewards or punishment. This approach tends to make the students more dependent on the teacher and also does not meet student needs. Cierra, instead, focused on how she would teach her students about independent reading. She did not look at this as a deficit her students had as readers; she approached this as a next step in their development as readers. She gathered data on her students' behaviors as independent readers, analyzed that information, and then used the data to inform her planning for future teaching. Her assessment and evaluation greatly impacted the independence of her students and furthered their reading skills by broadening their interests and increasing their levels of engagement.

USING EVALUATION IN PLANNING

When a teacher focuses on student strengths, approximations, and challenges, he utilizes the following guiding questions while planning for instruction (Owen, 2007):

- What is it the student is able to do?
- What is the student attempting to do?
- What does the student need to know next?

He provides instruction and learning experiences aimed at the frontier of learning for an individual, small group, or whole group of students. This understanding supports independence because students are actively engaged in tasks that support their learning needs. These questions assist a teacher in identifying instructional goals aimed at the ripening, rather than the already ripe. A common teaching error is focusing only on identifying student strengths, approximations, and needs. When we fail to actually use this data to inform teaching, we then tend to focus only on teaching content, instead of remembering that we are teaching students. With this in mind, it is important to avoid becoming data rich and analysis poor. Stacks of data, coupled with a lack of analysis, fail to enhance teaching or learning. When we have piles of information, yet no decisions are made as a result, this paper trail is useless and essentially a waste of time. And although we have a wide array of assessment tools, we are often in a quandary as to what to do with the data once they are collected. We know that gathering data for the mere sake of testing students does nothing to enhance teaching and learning if left unexamined. But consider the information that can be gained from carefully selected assessment samples that are scrutinized, analyzed, and evaluated in a timely fashion.

When striving to become analysis rich, Kaleah Jackson, a sixth-grade math teacher, revised her homework assessment practices. After becoming overwhelmed with the hours it took to grade stacks of papers, and ending up with a gradebook full of scores that did little to inform her instruction, she realized that a change was needed. She did not modify student homework—instead she changed what she did with the homework once it came back into the classroom. Students formed homework groups where they shared not only answers, but also processes and strategies used in their problem solving. Kaleah provided each group with a cover sheet that would guide learners in documenting their thinking and work accomplished. Each cover sheet had the following prompts:

1. List the names of people in your group.

2. What problem-solving strategies did your group members use, or attempt to use, when solving problems for this homework assignment? For example, did you use a table to analyze information, draw a picture, use a formula, etc.?

3. What problem did your group find the most challenging?

4. As a group, what is your answer to that problem? In the space below, show with words, pictures, and numbers how you solved the problem. Did all people solve the problem in the same way? Explain.

5. Each person should rate him/herself in the group using the following class-generated scoring guide:
   A—prepared with homework assignment, contributed to group
   B—prepared with homework assignment
   C—contributed to group, even though homework was missing or incomplete
   D—did not have homework, did not contribute
   F—did not have homework, distracted peers from learning

Previously, to gather this information, Kaleah would have needed to analyze all homework during a grading period or at the end of the day. With her new approach, she was able to examine seven cover sheets and get a comprehensive look at what her students struggle with and where they demonstrate competence. Implementing the use of a cover sheet during group time provided Kaleah with time to sit and analyze student work for strengths, approximations, and needs. In addition, these data provided the necessary information to discover the impact her teaching has on learners. For example, Kaleah noticed that five out of seven groups had difficulty on a problem that would have been solved easily when looking for patterns within a chart. When reflecting on her recent instruction, she realized that she had neglected the use of charts when modeling problem solving. Prior to creating this homework cover sheet, Kaleah would have spent her planning period grading papers that may or may not have led her to this conclusion. With this new method, she could glance at the cover sheets while monitoring students working in groups and make a teaching decision that very day. As a result, students were given the opportunity to revise their homework assignments with this new focus and to clarify misunderstandings in a timely fashion. Along with enhancing Kaleah's instruction, students became more responsible and independent as a result of peer accountability and collaboration.

Notice how Kaleah did not abandon the use of grades—she still collected this data. But now instead of focusing only on accurate answers, her grading system recognized complete work, effective strategies, and contributions to group discussions. By having students discuss homework in groups, they spent time focusing on learning and understanding mathematical concepts. Students began to demonstrate accountability and a higher level of engagement as compared to when they simply turned in their homework and waited for a score. Kaleah shortened the time it took to review student homework, yet the information she gathered from the homework assignments informed daily planning. As a result of using current data to inform her teaching, learners had a greater level of instructional support on work that was challenging, and this support from peers and the teacher helped to build behaviors of independence.

CONCLUSION

Most of us have collected an excessive amount of student data at one time or another, just to be overwhelmed in the end at the pile of paper that resulted in no more than student grades and scores. As we discussed in this chapter, isolating assessment from evaluation is just that . . . a test. When we take time to analyze the data we collect, not only is our teaching enhanced but also our efficiency and effectiveness. Regardless of the age or stage of development of their learners, teachers can improve their pedagogy as a result of reflecting on how they assess and evaluate. It is this analyzed data that foster independence and give the teacher time to focus on what is really important—student learning. Take some time to review the questions at the start of the chapter. How has your thinking changed or been confirmed as a result of reading this chapter?

A TIME TO REFLECT

Often when we create lesson plans we hold state, district, and grade-level expectations at the forefront of our minds. It can be easy to leave out the most essential component in planning for instruction—the student factor. If we keep in mind these external expectations and gather information about our learners' strengths and challenges, it is then that we are able to appropriately plan for instruction.

Consider if you have ever prepared for a lesson only to have it be too easy or far more difficult than you expected. These experiences are frustrating to the teacher, and they do not appropriately make use of student engagement time. Take some time to think about a future lesson or unit that you are planning to teach. Ask yourself these essential questions that will assist you in the creation of your plan (Owen, 2007):

- What are the students able to do? What do they know?
- What are the students attempting to do?
- What do the students need to know next?

Discovering learners' prior knowledge, skills, and strategies will help you design a lesson that will not only be effective and efficient, but will foster habits of learner independence. Gathering this type of data will mean that teacher expectations may be altered and the lesson that we had intended requires adjustment, but if the authentic intent is to teach, we will be much more satisfied with a lesson that indeed accomplishes that.

A VISIT TO OUR CLASSROOMS

Grades K–2: A Primary Perspective by Karin Ramer

I shudder when I remember the learning curve I experienced my first year of teaching first grade—I quickly became overwhelmed by the amount of writing first graders could produce as compared to my kindergarteners the year before. I felt responsible for reading each student's writing from the day, along with all of the other student work, so each night I faithfully packed all Draftbooks in my bag to take home. Somewhere after eight o'clock at night I began delving into student writing. With colored pen in hand, I documented each student's strengths, challenges, and spelling approximations in my monitoring notebook. By analyzing student writing each night, my monitoring notebook was bursting with rich data but nothing in my teaching practice changed and I was gradually becoming weary.

Sometime around December I began to dread the time students spent in writing because that meant more work for me. With such an overwhelming list of strengths, challenges, and spelling approximations, I hardly used a tenth of the data I collected. I was data rich, yet analysis poor. As a result, the extra time I spent looking at writing was futile and I swung to the other end of the pendulum: I stopped looking at student writing with the exception of a quick glance in the classroom. After a couple of months, I noticed that my data from early on was outdated, and I felt confused and uncertain; neither collecting everything, nor collecting nothing worked for me. Throughout the rest of the year I dabbled in how to collect data without spending hours to do so.

A few years later as I was sharing this challenge with my literacy coach, Pam Pottle, she suggested that I do a "quick sort" with student work. A quick sort is intended to give the teacher an immediate look at students' strengths and challenges, while at the same time organizing students for small group instruction. After students have written in their Draftbooks, they leave their writing open to their most current sample and I sort their work based on common strengths and needs. This way I form three or four small groups that I can meet with the following day for specific instruction, and by examining all student writing at a glance, I am able to select an appropriate teaching point for my modeled writing lesson the next day.

In order to document learner strengths, challenges, and spelling approximations, I analyze each student's writing once a week. On Monday I closely examine one-fifth of my students' writing, on Tuesday I look at another set of draftbooks, and I continue until I have data on my entire class by the end of the week. Not only is my instruction now based on current evaluated assessment, I am not inundated by piles of student work that weighs me down until the next pile that comes my way. I no longer take bags of student work home and collect data that stays in my monitoring notebook. Now I make teaching decisions for tomorrow after quickly analyzing student work today, and collect data that are not only rich, but impact my daily instruction. My current and specific knowledge of students aids in my teaching and allows me to further students along the continuum of independence as writers. And best of all, this analysis and documentation is done within my work day so that I am able to leave the classroom for today and start fresh when I enter the school doors tomorrow.

Grades 4–6: An Intermediate Perspective by Roxann Rose-Duckworth

Early in my career, I would read students' writing and write revision and editing comments all over the paper. Late one night, as I sat up reading and commenting on papers into the dark hours of the evening, I began to wonder what my students were really learning from my feedback. I came to the conclusion that they were learning "Ms. Rose-Duckworth has all of the answers. She knows how to edit and revise my writing; she knows what is best for my piece of writing." I realized what I wanted my students to understand was "I have the answers and/or I know where to find them. I know how to edit and revise my writing. Others can make suggestions and I hope they do—but only I know what is best for my piece of writing." So, I began to change how I gave feedback to my students.

When I did have students turn in written work as a group, I asked each student to write me a question on their paper. They needed to ask me a question that would guide me as I gave them feedback. So they might ask, "Do you agree with my paragraph breaks?" or "What do you think of the metaphors I used—I modeled them after the book we are reading, do they work?" or "What do you think of the word choice I used? Are my words specific enough?" Now I was responding to the questions they posed as writers and they had ownership of the feedback I gave and how they used it. I also found that students were more likely to use my feedback if they instigated it.

I also began to sort student papers into piles of common teaching needs. So I might make five piles of student papers: The first pile might contain student work where the students needs to work on strong introductions, the second pile might contain student work where the students are attempting to use commas, the third pile might contain student work where the students need to narrow their topic, the fourth pile might contain student work where the students are ready to learn how a planning web can support them as writers, and the fifth pile may be students who have miscellaneous next steps as writers that will require me to meet with them individually. Where I spent hours writing on these kinds of papers before, I now don't write on these papers at all! After doing quick reads and sorting them into their needs-based piles, I simply set them aside until I meet with the students. I meet with the students in their needs-based groups and do a quick, focused minilesson. I then ask students to do some revision work right there on the spot as I hand them back their writing. After recording this new learning onto their ILIC chart (see Figure 1.3 in Chapter 1) and discussing how they can use their new learning as a writer (not just on this piece of writing), they are set free to continue their revision and/or editing. With these new strategies, I was doing less work and my student were doing more learning . . . and my students were being challenged to grow in their independence!

9

Information That Fosters Learner Independence

Teachers should strive to provide feedback that will help students answer three questions about their learning: Where am I going? Where am I now? And how can I close the gap between the two?

—J. Chappius ("Helping Students Understand Assessment" in
Educational Leadership, 63(3), 2005, pp. 39–43)

When we consider that we are teaching children, it is ironic that most of our teacher education has us planning for lessons prior to meeting our learners. Although teachers must be able to construct a sound lesson plan, this type of daily planning can be highly ineffective when we only focus on curriculum, standards, and content. When planning without considering the student factor, three crucial elements are missing: the observations of student behaviors, conversations with learners, and student work (Davies, 2000). Void of these three essential elements, a lesson or unit may match standards and curricular expectations, yet may miss the mark when educating learners and enhancing levels of independence.

In this chapter, we will examine how using a variety of assessment samples aides the teacher in understanding learners and planning accordingly. Meshing observations of student behavior, conversations with learners, and analysis of student work with curriculum standards and guidelines will help a teacher plan to impact student learning. When evidence is collected from these sources over time, trends and patterns become evident, making students' next steps in the learning process apparent. By aiming to triangulate the data, you not only increase the reliability and validity of classroom assessment, but also the likelihood that students embrace independence. Prior to reading Chapter 9, reflect on the following questions and jot down some of your current understandings to support you as you read:

- From what sources do you gather data about student learning?
- What is the difference between descriptive and evaluative feedback? What role should each play in learning?
- What does feedback look like in a classroom where student independence is valued?
- How do your assessment practices communicate that you value independent learning?

OBSERVATIONS AS ASSESSMENT

"Teaching can be likened to a conversation in which you listen to the speaker carefully before you reply" (Clay, 1985, p. 3). Consider evaluation being likened to a conversation in which the skillful teacher listens carefully before intentionally planning for instruction. What does it mean to listen carefully using both your eyes and ears as a tool for evaluation? It means observing the behaviors learners explicitly demonstrate: the body language, the eyes that seek affirmation from the teacher, and the fidgeting that comes as a result of facing a challenge. It is the mind's ear listening to the learner as he approaches learning. It is hearing the learner say, "Wait, I don't get that," or "Can you help me with this?" Hearing what the learner articulates about what she knows and needs to know next will help to inform instruction. It takes an observant teacher to notice and use the subtle and not so subtle nuances that a learner's behavior and attitudes provide. It is when the teacher listens carefully to the learner that she can provide a skillful and responsive reply that furthers the learner's knowledge, skills, and attitudes toward what it means to be an independent learner.

When we assess learners, there are certain outcomes that we expect to discover from each particular test. Perhaps the assessment is designed to evaluate content knowledge, skill, or use of strategies, and the results aid the teacher in making instructional decisions. There are more formal tests that are constructed to provide accuracy, reliability, and validity; the results from these assessments serve to inform programs, policies, and possibly instruction. Regardless of the assessment administered, relying on the test score alone will not provide enough information to impact instruction. If we rely solely on the product or answer and neglect the human factor, we miss a vital piece of assessment.

CONVERSATIONS AS ASSESSMENT

In addition to evaluating students with assessments and observations, engaging in dialogue with learners can enrich what we know and understand about individual learners. Combining student performance with focused conversations helps the teacher to make acute observations of both student understandings and challenges. Whether exchanges occur during one-on-one conferences, group instruction, or through the use of dialogue journals (see Figure 9.1), learner response aides the teacher in shaping instruction and support.

Teachers who focus on encouraging independence are intentional about the kinds of conversations they have with students. Prompting writers to discuss their thinking encourages independence and critical thinking skills, such as "Talk a little about the beginning of your story. Why did you choose to start with a question?" At the other end of the spectrum, prompts such as "I like the way you started this story," are merely comments that draw attention to pleasing the teacher rather than on developing the writer and her understanding about how to impact an audience and fulfill a purpose. As another example, "Tell me about how you solved that math problem," allows a student to share and analyze his thinking, while "You need to solve the problem this way" tells the student that there is one right way to solve the math problem. These brief conversations are significant opportunities to foster habits of independent thinking or to develop a sense of dependence where learners rely on external feedback for approval and correction.

When we engage learners in dialogue, information is revealed that is not otherwise evident. Prompting students with open-ended statements encourages learners to chat about their thinking and understandings, and this has the potential to reveal understandings, strengths, and challenges that may not be readily apparent when glancing at student work or behavior. Consider for a moment the kinds of prompts that can persuade an emergent writer to think about the use of periods within a piece of writing:

- Talk a bit about why authors use periods in their writing.
- As a reader, what do you think when you come to a period in the story you are reading?
- How might using periods in your writing help your readers?
- How do you know where to place a period?
- Is there a part of your writing where you used a period to help your reader? Can you read that section for us?

Focusing on a learner's understanding about the use of periods, for example, allows the teacher to plan for explicit instruction that develops the writer, along with the writing. James Whitmeyer, a third-grade teacher,

Figure 9.1   Reading Dialogue Journal Hints

Reading Dialogue Journal Helpful Hints

Purpose of Reading Dialogue Journal

The Reading Dialogue Journal is a place for you, your teachers, and your friends to talk about books, reading, authors, and writing. It is a place for you to show your understanding of what you have read. The RDJ also provides a place for you to reflect on the process that you use while you are reading.

In your letters, write about WHAT you've read.

- Tell what you noticed.

- Tell what you thought and felt and why.

- Tell what you liked and why.

- Tell what you didn't like and why.

- Tell what the book said and meant to you.

- Tell about the characters, plot, setting, mood, or author's style.

In your letters, write about HOW you read.

- Did you meet any difficulties when reading the text? If so, what were they? How did you overcome them?

- Did you read every word? Why or why not?

- Did you anticipate any words or predict what the text was about? What did you predict? How did you make that prediction? What clues from the pictures or text did you use? Was your prediction accurate?

- Did you struggle with the meaning of any words? What did you do to figure out what these words meant?

- Did you reread any sections or spend a longer time on some words than other? Why?

- How important were your past experiences in helping you understand the text? Did some past experience help make the text more meaningful to you?

- How was the text organized? Why do you think the author chose to organize it in this way?

SOURCE: Adapted from Nancie Atwell, 1998, *In the Middle*, p. 296.

observed that one of his students was experimenting with the use of periods in his writing. Matt often included a period after a sentence fragment, yet would leave a run-on sentence without any punctuation at all. After evaluating his writing, James dialogued with Matt about the use of periods. Although Matt understood the purpose of periods in published work, he did not come up with a strategy for placing periods in his own writing. With this information, James was able to explicitly instruct Matt and guide him through revising a section of writing that required periods. After this guided practice, James prompted Matt by saying, "Consider what you now understand about periods. Take a minute to carefully re-read this section of your writing. Is there a place where you might need a period that you didn't have before?" Then, "Talk to me about why you included a period here." When Matt demonstrates an understanding of the use of periods in his own writing, James could prompt him to reflect on his new learning by saying, "As a result of the work we did here together on your writing, tell me what you understand now about using periods. How will that help you when you write today and in the future?" When we interact with learners in this manner, we are taking the opportunity to structure learning, rather than simply providing a rule for the use of periods. It is this structuring that moves students one step further toward independence.

In contrast to structuring for independence through dialogue with learners, conversations controlled by the teacher potentially promote dependence: "Look here where I marked your work. You forgot a period. Using periods in writing help your reader, so be certain to fix up your piece here where I showed you that a period would be helpful. Yes, you are right. Good job." This conversation demonstrates to students that a teacher is the one with the knowledge and confidence to fix writing. While both interactions focused on the same teaching point, the first promotes reflection, learning, and independence, whereas the second provides feedback that encourages dependence on the teacher's ability to edit. In order to foster learner independence, it is essential to listen to understandings and confusions and to support students as they gain proficiency and competency through focused dialogue.

These intentional conversations with learners will increase habits of independence as the focus is on teaching the learner, not just the skill or content. Let's take a look at Piper Anderson's fifth-grade classroom where learners write a variety of poetry throughout the year. Each time Piper conferences with a student, her focus is on developing the writer, not just the piece of writing. Piper examines student writing in order to select appropriate teaching points, but her goal is to deepen students' understanding of the writing process, not simply teach a formula for poetry. This intentional and explicit teaching will apply to writing beyond poetry as seen in the following example. Upon completing a haiku poem about polar regions, Addison is ready for a writing conference. Within the poem, Piper recognizes that Addison demonstrates strengths and challenges.

After briefly acknowledging Addison's strengths, Piper has the opportunity to select between two instructional points: teaching the correct format for haiku poetry, or demonstrating how to use capital letters appropriately. While either would enhance this specific poem, Piper decides to focus on the latter skill that can be applied to a variety of genres that Addison is responsible for learning. Perhaps at the end of their writing conference, Piper redirects Addison to read published haiku and coaches her to revisit her current poem and make revisions where needed. With the right level of support, Addison's understanding of capitalization is enhanced and she is directed to resources that will help her independently revise the format of her haiku poem. It is this intentional instruction that will enhance the writer's toolbox while developing a piece of writing.

By providing quick feedback on student strengths, explicit instruction that develops the learner, and redirecting the learner to enhance writing, students gain habits of independence that can be applied to future learning.

FEEDBACK: DESCRIPTIVE AND EVALUATIVE

All learners crave a response to their work, either in the form of a grade, a comment, or some kind of verbal reaction. When we strive to enhance learner independence, the response needs to be more than a score or some other form of evaluative feedback. According to Ann Davies (2000), students benefit from descriptive feedback rather than from just evaluative feedback in the form of a grade. Descriptive feedback opens up a discussion between the teacher and the student, whereas evaluative feedback encourages the teacher to provide information to the student as an end result. Davies defines these characteristics of descriptive feedback:

- comes during as well as after learning
- is easily understood and relates directly to the learning
- is specific, so performance can improve
- involves choice on the part of the learner as to the type of feedback and how to receive it
- is part of an ongoing conversation about the learning
- is in comparison to models, exemplars, samples, or descriptions

In her book *Making Classroom Assessment Work*, Davies refers to research that shows student learning improves when the amount of evaluative feedback reduces and the amount of descriptive feedback increases. With this focus, students are able to concentrate on assessment for learning instead of assessment of learning. As a result, students practice habits of independent learning and gain experience being reflective in their daily work.

Effective feedback is not limited to dialogue between students and teachers. Some of the best responses that students can get are responses that we play no part in. These responses might include the response of an authentic audience, the findings of a science experiment, the response of building something based on measurements, the response of hearing a piece of music played, feedback from a peer, or the response of computer software responding to a particular command. The more we can establish genuine responses for our students' efforts, the more honest and meaningful the feedback our students will receive. Too often, the only response a student receives is an evaluative response from his teacher, but there are so many other responses that will teach, encourage, and motivate our students. The responses need to be timely, specific, honest, and developmentally appropriate in order to foster habits of independence.

FEEDBACK THAT INFORMS INSTRUCTION

In addition to building on student strengths and challenges, data gathered from assessments, observations, and conversations with learners should directly impact instruction. The feedback we provide to students needs to reflect the fact that we have carefully analyzed and evaluated their work and this information directly impacts instruction. For example, Remington Walters, a fourth-grade teacher, might say, "While looking at your reading response journals, I noticed that many of you are having difficulty finding the right book for independent reading. Although you wrote about what you read, I saw little evidence of passion, interest, or wonder as you filled the pages of your journals. Our goal as readers is to find texts that make us feel, question, laugh, and desire to read beyond the time we have in class; that is a good book. Today I am going to model how I choose something to read. I want you to listen to what I am thinking so you can see how I select a book that is truly engaging to me as a reader." By providing his fourth graders with feedback about their reading selections as evidenced in their response journals and how these data influenced his teaching, students are held accountable for learning.

In order for students to feel a sense of ownership and control, it needs to be abundantly clear to students that what they do, or don't do, matters. Learners need to see that our teaching decisions are based on their learning attempts, struggles, and successes. In his book, *Starting From Scratch* (1996), Stephen Levy writes:

> Our goal is for the children to be self-motivated . . . this goal is more likely to be realized for each child when they can see the purpose of the work they are given. For example, whereas a child may not see the purpose for filling out worksheets, he or she would see the purpose for estimating how many pencils the class would need for the year, if in fact we were going to actually buy the amount they determine. (p. 183)

When we ask learners to complete a worksheet and return the assignment the next day with an evaluative comment such as "Great work!" or "Try again," how does this feedback shape learning and independence? But the response of buying the number of pencils students predict truly motivates them to be accurate with their mathematical figuring. It is this type of feedback that fosters learner independence and student ownership. While working to foster habits of independence there are endless possibilities for genuine responses to student learning. We must look for a variety of ways that students can solicit responses for performance. In addition, students need their teachers to clearly articulate learning goals and to provide descriptive feedback that helps them move toward independence.

ANALYZING STUDENT WORK FOR EVIDENCE OF INSTRUCTION

In order to fairly evaluate student work and provide appropriate feedback, a teacher must analyze observations, assessments, or assignments for evidence of specific teaching. In order to do this, teaching must be explicit with a clear objective, so clear in fact that the objective could be restated as measurable evidence in student work or thinking. If the teaching objective is for students to write a scientific hypothesis, then student work should be evaluated for that exact element: a scientific hypothesis using the criteria the teacher explicitly demonstrated. For example, second-grade teacher Judy Osten examines student writing in math following a demonstration of how to write about mathematical thinking. In her demonstration, Judy models how to write about her mathematical thinking, "This problem is asking me to put fifty cookies in two boxes. I know that the number of cookies is larger than the number of boxes, and I need to share the cookies as evenly as possible. I know that the word share tells me to divide. I understand that you use division to break a larger number into smaller groups. I also know that fifty cents is two quarters and a quarter is twenty-five cents. That means if I have fifty cookies I can make two boxes of twenty-five cookies." Since Judy's writing demonstration in math included modeling how to articulate mathematical understandings, not the steps it takes to solve a problem, student work should be examined for evidence of mathematical understandings. Writing about thinking in this manner is opposed to writing the steps it took to complete a problem. "First, I read the problem and then divided 50 by 2. It equaled twenty-five. I know there are twenty-five cookies per box." If communicating mathematical understandings was the lesson's objective, then that is exactly what student work should be examined for. When the lesson focuses on reading for fluency, evaluate a student's degree of fluency when reading. If you intentionally taught students how to craft smooth transitions between paragraphs, examine their written work for evidence of these smooth transitions, not for conventions, word choice, or voice. When we focus on examining student work for evidence of our teaching, we are not only evaluating student understandings, but we are also analyzing the effectiveness of our own instruction. This is the habit of mind of a teacher who is reflective of her own practice.

When teachers are able to narrow the focus to one teaching point per lesson, this clarity allows for students to concentrate on acquiring very specific skills, strategies, and understandings. Students are not overwhelmed by trying to change all understandings at once, but instead are allowed to focus their attention on one specific learning objective. In addition, evaluating student work or behavior while looking for the impact of one objective, allows teachers to analyze work with clarity and to provide feedback with precision.

When we look at student work, it is important to collect information on strengths and potential learning targets. Instead of looking at approximations as deficits and errors, viewing student responses as attempts and patterns will help to shape instruction and independence. For example, a teacher may look at a student's piece of writing and notice that the student is misusing apostrophes, misspelling common words, and needs to expand paragraphs. But a teacher focusing on creating independence looks at the same piece of writing and notices that the student is attempting to use apostrophes, is using chunking as a strategy to spell unfamiliar words, and is using the transitional phrase "and then" to indicate when a new idea is being introduced. When the teacher notices what is there rather than what is missing, the teaching points become clear and learning can be built on current understandings, as opposed to assuming the child is a "blank slate." Acknowledging approximations as steps toward independence helps the teacher plan appropriate instruction and supports the learner accordingly.

In seeking to understand student thinking, looking for error patterns can reveal learner misconceptions. Some errors that students make are random; the result of a memory lapse, a distraction, carelessness, or fatigue. However, many errors follow a pattern; they are consistent and systematic and noticeably repetitive in student work. Error patterns may help us recognize bad habits our students have developed, misunderstandings our students hold, and skills students are attempting to use. Acknowledging errors and close approximations will provide opportunities for children to learn and allow the teacher to gain insight about student needs. It is these errors and approximations that are building blocks to learning and steps toward independence.

ANALYZING WITH OTHERS

After analyzing student work from within one cohort of learners for a period of time, perception of student work may be skewed. Kindergarten teacher Kelley Aldridge found this out when she met with her grade-level colleagues to discuss student writing. All three teachers brought writing samples that represented beginning, developing, and proficient writers so that the teachers could discuss the spectrum of writing from their students. Kelley believed that her three writing samples represented a typical kindergarten classroom, but after comparing her proficient writer to the other two proficient writers, Kelley noticed that her students had room for growth. This observation then led to a discussion about teaching practices and how to impact student learning. It is this shared collaboration that eliminates the feeling of teaching in isolation, increases teacher awareness of student potential, and allows teachers to share expertise and work together toward a common goal.

Consider the following example of second-grade teacher Isaiah Shockley. Each month Isaiah and his colleagues gathered to dialogue about teaching by reflecting on their instructional practice and presenting a challenge or teaching goal to share with the group. Since Isaiah had been focusing on learner independence with his students, he hoped to examine the impact this had on their daily writing. As a group, the second-grade teachers began to determine what Isaiah's students could do independently as evidenced in their writing and the areas where Isaiah needed to foster a higher level of independence. The teachers identified general strengths and challenges that would inform Isaiah's instruction: Students independently selected topics to write about and included generous ideas and details in their writing, but a large portion of the student samples demonstrated a lack of organization. As a result, Isaiah reflected on his instructional practices and recognized that he was not explicitly teaching planning strategies for organization. He recognized that this was the next piece in fostering habits of independence in his writers that would encourage students to write in an organized fashion. Not only did this collaboration help Isaiah assess student writing for evidence of independence, his teaching practices were refined as he reflected on his instruction and beliefs about student learning.

CONCLUSION

Ultimately it is the triangulation of data and the analysis of that information that drives focused planning and in turn facilitates intentional teaching. It is the role of the teacher to know how assessment and evaluation supports the creation of independent learners within the classroom. The teacher needs to know what the student strengths are and what the next steps are for learning. When a teacher utilizes assessment and evaluation as a foundation for teaching, students cannot help but become responsible for their learning experiences. David Clarke encourages teachers to consider their assessment practices: "It is through our assessment that we communicate most clearly to students which activities and learning outcomes we value" (p. 1).

As a result of thinking about feedback that enhances habits of independence, what are you thinking now? Take some time to review the questions that we addressed at the start of this chapter.

A TIME TO REFLECT

In order to encourage independent habits of mind where we focus on the learner, not so much the learning, it is essential to carefully analyze our role in providing feedback. While we ultimately want students to feel proud of their accomplishments, praise is a short-term solution. If we provide feedback that helps learners to reflect on their work and understandings, we are helping them to practice skills of independence.

Collect a sample of student work and sort it based on student approximations. Limit your piles to approximately four, and place similar approximations together. For example, if you are looking at a scientific process, analyze each write-up for strengths, approximations, and challenges and place it accordingly. Perhaps some students excel in writing a hypothesis while neglecting the conclusion for the experiment. Maybe another pile of work includes samples where materials are clearly identified, yet the hypothesis needs to be expanded or clarified. Possibly a third pile is student work that demonstrates a complete understanding of the entire scientific process and the students appear ready to challenge their understandings. Once you have formed three or four groups using student work, plan to meet with one group where you will clarify understandings and support learners in their next step. If you are meeting with learners who wrote a clear hypothesis, yet demonstrated a lack of understanding about the conclusion, your conversation starter might sound like this: "In looking at your write-up each hypothesis that I examined matched the scientific process exactly. It appears that you clearly understand that portion of the write-up. When I looked at your conclusion about your science experiment I noticed that you might want to expand it for clarity. Let's talk for a moment about what you understand about a conclusion, either in a book, in science, or anywhere else you might find a conclusion." Having a conversation about current understandings and guiding students through this process will support and develop learners as they apply their new skills, strategies, and knowledge to the learning process.

A VISIT TO OUR CLASSROOMS

Grades K–3: A Primary Perspective by Karin Ramer

I can still remember attending teacher meetings where I left with binders that were intended to guide my planning, instruction, and assessment. I was set. On paper everything appeared manageable. I would assess students, evaluate their performance, and report it accordingly. As I implemented my new understandings students were often unaware of their level of achievement because the final grade was in my gradebook and the assessment sample was filed for parent conferences. With no response to their performance, a major piece of the learning process was absent for students. They never really had a measure of their own performance.

After years of teaching this way, I began to work more closely with colleagues regarding feedback in the classroom. I realized that other teachers were informing students about their progress and encouraging learners to revise their thinking as a result of strengths and approximations on tests. The focus was on more than just a score, but also an evaluation of current understandings. Involving students in this manner encouraged learners to see assessment as part of the learning process, not necessarily an end product. With timely feedback and an opportunity to discuss test results, I began to notice the impact assessment for learning was having on learner independence.

Today the assessment scores I collect are still documented, but just because I have a score in my gradebook it does not mean that I am finished with the test itself. We take time to celebrate strengths and examine confusions and errors. Students are given an opportunity to confirm and revise their thinking even if it is in another color pen or on a separate piece of paper. In essence, students practice habits of independent thinking as the assessment sample becomes a working document upon which students reevaluate understandings and revise them accordingly. It is this shift from evaluative feedback to descriptive feedback that influences learning and enhances levels of student independence.

Grades 4–6: An Intermediate Perspective by Roxann Rose-Duckworth

Throughout my teaching career, I have used formal and informal strategies for assessment. It wasn't until later in my teaching career that I realized that I was equating "informal" to often mean "invalid." Somehow, I felt that if assessment could not be broken down into numbers, it somehow wasn't valuable data. I began to realize that I could gather incredibly useful data oftentimes just by sitting next to a student and asking, "How's it going?." I began to ask more questions that would help students become more aware of what they were doing as readers, writers, mathematicians, scientists, or whatever else we were focusing on. I would ask questions such as:

- What were you thinking when you . . . ?
- Which strategy were you using here . . . ?
- What was the most challenging part of this task?
- Why was it challenging and how did you face that challenge?
- What are you trying to do here?
- How can I help you as a reader/writer/thinker?

I took monitoring notes to record our conversations and I began to realize that these data were very helpful for my planning of the next learning steps. Sometimes the planning took place simultaneously and the teaching occurred right there on the spot. Other times the planning took place later to guide a future learning opportunity. When I realized that qualitative as well as quantitative data are valuable, I saw student independence increase as students were learning to talk about their learning and thinking.

10

Planning to Support Independence

Good teachers see the importance of creating the right climate for learning and recognize that students learn in different ways.

—Michael Henniger and Roxann Rose-Duckworth
*(The Teaching Experience: An Introduction
to Reflective Practice*, 2007, p. 27)

For the reflective individual, evaluation and analysis occur naturally on a daily basis. You're getting ready for a full day of teaching when your child slips on a silk scarf, slides down a flight of stairs, topples directly onto his arm, and proceeds to scream in pain. First you evaluate the severity of the situation and then you act accordingly based on your analysis of the circumstances. Is it broken? Do we need to go to the emergency room? Will a simple ice pack ease the pain? This careful plan that you create should remedy the situation. In another scenario, you go out to dinner and order a thick peanut butter brownie and a cup of espresso for dessert. Rarely will one order such a delicacy without commenting on the texture, flavor, and consistency of the delicious morsel. It may even be compared to others you tasted before. Once you have collected the data, namely the taste and quality of the dessert, you will then evaluate the information and analyze whether it was not only worth the money, but also the calories. Planning for future indulgences will then ensue. Will

I order it again or try something different the next time? Planning that is based on analyzed and evaluated data also happens in the teaching world, although planning from academic data can be more precise and challenging than circumstances that occur in everyday life.

Just as we have expectations of how we would like our morning to unfold and what our dessert should taste like, we have learning goals for students. In order to know where our students are in relation to the target objectives, we collect specific data as we observe, monitor, and assess student behavior and learning. When these data have been scrutinized and a judgment and decision have been made, this information has the potential to impact teaching and learning. It is this judgment that is the analysis and evaluation of the collected data. It is the decision that is the planning.

In this chapter, we will address purposeful decisions and examine the *Teaching and Learning Cycle* (Owen, 2007) that helps us to make these educated judgments and decisions. We will look at how this process impacts planning in the classroom, including approaches, grouping, and resources. As you read this chapter ask yourself the following questions about planning:

- How can I plan to enhance independence in my classroom?
- What teaching decisions are made based on student work and behaviors?
- How does evaluated assessment impact planning?
- How are data used for daily and long-term planning?
- How does planning influence teaching?

PURPOSEFUL DECISIONS

Purposeful teaching decisions happen as a result of careful analysis and evaluation of student work and behavior. It benefits no one to test for the sake of testing. An assessment sample may be scored, but if intentional thought is not placed on student understandings or misconceptions evidenced in the work or behavior, future instruction will not be enriched. Consider for a moment a student in Caroline Sway's second-grade classroom. Each Friday, Caroline tests her students on spelling words gathered from their daily writing and uses these assessment data to create an individualized spelling list for each student. Once tested, students receive a score reflecting the number of words spelled correctly and are then given new words. When a word is spelled incorrectly on the test, that word is placed on the next week's list, giving students the opportunity to have more practice with tricky words. Now consider what it would look like if Caroline took her individualized spelling program a bit further. Students are still assessed on their ability to write their spelling words; however when students are given a spelling list, Caroline briefly conferences with each child about the words. She analyzes the misspellings from the writing and points out specifics of the word that are correct and then errors that become a focal point for the child. For example, when Mary writes *liket* in her daily writing, Caroline's instruction focuses on the ending of the word, either in a whole group, small group, or one-on-one. This approximation of 'liked' becomes a specific teaching point for -ed endings. With this focused attention on a specific detail about the word, along with a strategy for understanding how to spell it correctly, Mary not only has a better chance of spelling "liked" correctly on her weekly test, but more importantly in her daily writing. She may even begin to generalize the rule to other words that end in -ed. If she continues to display misconceptions about the -ed ending, Caroline does not stop at a score, as that does nothing to enhance Mary as a writer. Instead, she intentionally teaches this writer about the -ed ending and the different sounds that ending makes. As we shift from merely scoring assignments and tests to planning ways to impact student understandings, the level of student independence shifts to a higher degree.

This is also true when considering student behavior. Student behavior can be judged based on what is observed, but unless a clear evaluation of the entire situation accompanies the judgment, truly informed decisions will not be made about the students we teach. The teacher must take into consideration not only obvious student behaviors, but also her own behaviors that impact students. If a lesson seems to leave children chatty and disengaged, it may mean that the students are squirrelly or ready for the end of the day. It also may imply that the teacher failed to set up clear and appropriate expectations, suitable objectives, interesting concepts, or engaging conversations. It is easy to blame student misbehavior on students because we are watching and analyzing them, but when things are not as successful as planned, it is important to reflect on our role as the teacher and what may have been done to enhance and support undesirable student behavior. Alfie Kohn echoes this sentiment in his book *Beyond Discipline* (1996): "When students are off-task the first question a teacher should ask himself, 'What is the task?'" (p. 19). It is this careful reflection and planning that allow a teacher to design intentional instruction for learners.

THE TEACHING AND LEARNING CYCLE

The essence of teaching is student learning. Whether it is academic, social, or behavioral, educators constantly seek to improve student understandings, behaviors, and performances. These decisions are based on needs that are determined from the triangulation of data and predetermined expectations. Planning for instruction based on evaluated and analyzed data is an essential component of the Teaching and Learning Cycle (Figure 10.1). And it is this process that aids the teacher in fostering learner independence.

Although students of different grade levels will express diverse needs, a skillful teacher expects that within one grade level many needs are

Figure 10.1   The Teaching and Learning Cycle

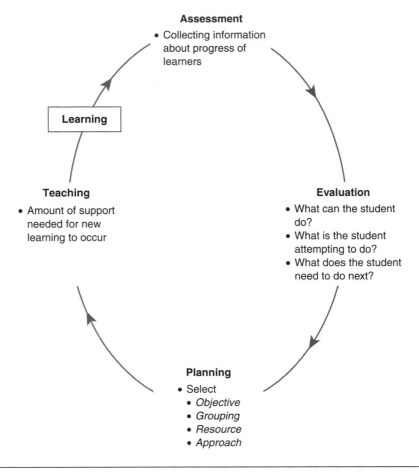

SOURCE: Reprinted with permission from R. C. Owen Publishers, Inc.

present. Understanding that one teaching point will not meet the needs of all students is the first step in planning for this sophisticated and complex job of teaching. Planning for student learning begins as you seek to align the element of students with the expectation of curriculum and content (Wiggins & McTighe, 2005). The state and district within which a teacher is employed mandate that certain curriculum is delivered and specific skills and understandings be attained during a given academic year. These grade-level expectations are the first guidelines to examine when planning for instruction. Consider how this might be done with a mandated content area in the second grade. Bryce Leam is expected to teach his second-grade students about bees. In the past he used to approach the unit with confidence as he pulled down a bee unit from the shelf, not acknowledging student knowledge, understandings, or misconceptions. A variety of books, detailed worksheets, art projects, and minibooks filled the box so full that he had to carefully select appropriate material in order to cover all expected curriculum. After reflecting on how students learn best, Bryce decided that by using the same bee activities and tasks from year to year he was merely covering curriculum. Recognizing that his goal was not to just cover curriculum, Bryce altered how he approached instruction for the bee unit. According to Heidi Hayes Jacobs (*ASCD Education Update*, 1998, p. 1), "the word *cover* also means to *pass over quickly*." The idea of brushing over the curriculum suggests "the teacher's work is appropriate even though the teacher may not know what the students are learning." Now Bryce strives to meet expectations by working from what children already know about bees and planning to teach based on misunderstandings, gaps in knowledge, and authentic questions. After assessing his students, Bryce discovers student understandings and misconceptions about bees. For example, Bryce realizes that two-thirds of his students mistakenly believe that wasps are a type of bee. This evaluated assessment helped to create the following guiding questions:

- What is a bee? Are there other insects that are similar to bees? How are they alike and how are they different?
- How do bees benefit our world? What problems do humans have with bees?
- What are the different types of bees? What are their similarities and differences?

Upon visiting Bryce's second-grade classroom, you might notice students researching questions about bees using a variety of text levels and genres, including Internet sites. Students collaborate and work to develop common understandings while Bryce monitors students, challenging them with probing and encouraging questions. Students are motivated to be independent learners because they work to answer genuine questions for an authentic purpose. As a culminating project, students create brochures for local pediatric waiting rooms in hopes that the information will alleviate other children's fears and misconceptions about bees while alerting them to potential hazards such as severe allergic reactions.

Bryce's new approach to teaching about bees is in sharp contrast to how he taught at the start of his career. While he guided a small group of learners through a Round Robin reading lesson from a science textbook about bees, other students busily worked on the assignments he identified. After students participated in the reading lesson, they returned to their desks to individually answer summary questions about their reading. When this assignment was complete, learners followed a list of tasks on the board; alphabetizing words that pertain to bee life, completing a worksheet that emphasizes the role bees play in pollination, and completing the bee art project started the previous day. Each of these activities presented essential information about bees and allowed the teacher to feel that he taught required curriculum. Students may have even appeared to be working independently because they were kept busy with assigned tasks. The danger in implementing such a unit is when we confuse "covering" curriculum with actual learning: students may learn the same information, yet they miss out on opportunities to think independently.

The way that Bryce changed the bee unit to structured learning allows students to engage in creating deep understandings about bees and their role in the world. Common misconceptions are corrected, while fears are acknowledged and likely dispelled. In addition to learning about bees, students gain skills essential for lifelong learning. When he covered curriculum, students were presented with essential information about bees, but just because learners completed assignments does not mean that learning occurred. By presenting learners with pertinent bee information, students become passive in their learning journey and the teacher is highlighted as the expert; there is no reason for students to think independently. Teaching children, not just content, requires deliberate and intentional planning that occurs as a result of meshing mandated expectations and an understanding of how to foster habits of independence through the everyday thinking that occurs in the classroom.

LONG-RANGE PLANNING

Although intentional teaching decisions are made based on students' strengths, approximations, and needs, planning can occur prior to even meeting students. A teacher can begin planning for the academic year by examining state, district, and school grade-level expectations since there are particular requirements that teachers are expected to address each year. It is essential for teachers to understand and implement these expectations so that students are well prepared to contribute to society with a wide array of knowledge, experiences, and understandings.

When working on a long-range plan for the year, a teacher can ask questions that will help to balance certain expectations with the time allotment for the year.

- Are there certain content areas that work better during a particular part of the year?
- Is there a certain order to the expectations that makes sense for student learning?
- Does the availability of curricular resources dictate when units can be taught?
- Are there skills and strategies that would benefit students at the start of the year and others that should be taught near the end of the year?
- Do certain field trips or learning experiences need to be preceded by particular instruction? Or vice versa?

- Which units require more time and emphasis?
- Are there any content area expectations that can be taught in tandem? (For example, a science unit on space exploration could be taught parallel to a social studies unit on Lewis and Clark's expedition. As students work to answer their questions about exploration, they would meet the literacy expectations as they read nonfiction text, create timelines, and give a PowerPoint presentation. It may also make sense to teach the required unit on measurement at this time as students compare distances traveled as they interpret and develop map keys while gaining new understandings about ratios.)

It is essential that this long-range plan be viewed as a guideline, not a calendar to dictate future teaching decisions. The intended goal of long-range planning is to ensure that time is set aside to incorporate a variety of learning targets within an academic year, not just to check off curriculum that is covered as it is presented to students. It is this intentional teaching based on careful planning that ensures students are well prepared for future learning.

DAILY PLANNING

Once a long-range plan has been set for the year, it is essential to consider the strengths and needs present within your cohort of children. Using grade-level standards will help to guide long-range planning, but individual student strengths, approximations, and needs must determine the day-to-day teaching decisions that ultimately move children along personal learning curves. These strengths, approximations, and needs are found in observations, conversations, work samples, assessment, and behaviors. As data are collected on individual students, the teacher must carefully evaluate and analyze the information to recognize what each student is capable of, what he is approximating, and what skills and strategies he needs to acquire next. As data is contemplated, a specific learning objective can be determined and short-range planning can ensue. Selecting goals for students in this manner will work to scaffold learning and ensure student success. When working on daily planning for instruction, a teacher can ask questions that will foster the alignment of expectations with what students bring to the classroom.

- How can I build on student strengths, approximations, and needs so that each student can function at an increasingly independent level?
- What curriculum and content would the entire class benefit from?
- What strengths and challenges do analyzed and evaluated data highlight?

- Are there particular skills and strategies that would best be taught in a small group?
- Do students demonstrate needs that necessitate individualized instruction?

Long-range and daily planning are essential to ensure that students make gains academically. It is when we analyze how to facilitate learning that students not only learn content, skills, and strategies, but also acquire habits of independence.

APPROACHES, GROUPING, AND RESOURCES

When planning for instruction that fosters independence, it is important to consider how to best support students by asking the following questions:

- Which approach should I use?
- How should I group students?
- What resources are necessary and available?

Approaches

Considering the approach to instruction has the potential to further habits of independent learning. Depending on students' readiness, the teacher will choose from modeling to students, sharing experiences with students, guiding students, or providing opportunities for independent practice. For example, if the goal is for students to learn how to use a protractor the teacher might consider the following approaches:

- Modeling how to use a protractor while verbalizing the thought process.
- Sharing the experience of using a protractor by asking students to offer suggestions during a demonstration.
- Guiding students as they practice using a protractor, steering them according to their responses.
- Providing students independent practice with protractors, allowing them to apply their mathematical understandings.

Based on assessment data, the teacher may decide on one approach for the entire class, or a variety of approaches for small groups and individuals. These approaches do not occur step-by-step; one approach does not beget the next. In fact, a teacher might move in and out of approaches during the course of one lesson depending upon the challenges faced by the students. Each approach supports a different level of student independence as the teacher's role changes. It is critical to include all four approaches because it is with this varied support that students gain new insight into how proficient learners think and function.

Grouping

In addition to considering the approach, a teacher needs to decide how to best group students for instruction. "Groups are created for many different reasons and range in size from one student and the teacher to the whole class. Students may be grouped with others of similar interests or abilities" (New Zealand Ministry of Education, 1997, *Reading for Life*, p. 146). Groups should frequently change based on current and ongoing assessment. When groups are not changed in a timely fashion, they become stagnant, affecting student motivation and esteem. When learners are placed in the same reading groups, for example, over a period of weeks without regrouping based on assessment, it is fair to wonder how appropriate the instruction is for all students in the group. While it is true that assessment may determine that learners will benefit from instruction similar to others in the same reading group, it is important to base this on current and ongoing assessment, not data from the beginning of the year. We have all heard stories or experienced the perpetual reading group where students stayed in the "turtle" group all year long, while the "eagles" were always soaring a book or two ahead. This does nothing to foster habits of independence, but instead categorizes student ability as a result of limited assessment samples. When students are grouped appropriately, teaching time is used efficiently and learners are supported appropriately, enhancing behaviors of independence.

In addition to grouping learners for instruction over a short period of time, teachers may utilize a variety of grouping strategies throughout the day in order to most effectively impact student learning. Here is an example of how one teacher might group students during a literacy block:

- Whole group writing demonstration focusing on an author's thought process when planning a research report.
- Small group instruction on accessing an index in nonfiction texts. Group members represent a wide range of reading abilities.
- Small group instruction for students who have yet to select a research topic. Group membership represents a wide range of writing abilities.
- Small group instruction for tangled readers on determining importance while reading nonfiction text.
- Individualized work with a student who needs support with narrowing his topic.
- Individualized work with a student who is planning an interview with a local expert.

Acutely knowing students allows a teacher to utilize grouping strategies effectively while supporting learners as they become increasingly independent. Consider how grouping for instruction impacted Rylan

Tucker's fourth-grade learners. Although there were times when Rylan grouped students based on assessment samples or similar interests, Rylan also organized learners for instruction based on their daily performance in writing. Once students finished writing for the day, their draftbooks were set in a bin with a sticky note marking the most current writing sample. While his students were at recess, Rylan took fifteen minutes to analyze and evaluate each piece of writing for strengths, approximations, and next learning steps with respect to his whole group writing demonstration for the day. For example, when Rylan focused on organization during his modeled writing, he examined student work for evidence of organization. In addition he carried on an internal dialogue that might sound something like this, "As a result of my writing demonstration today that focused on organizing ideas within a paragraph, what are students able to do? What are they attempting to do? What instruction would they most benefit from next? Is there a change in student understandings regarding organizing ideas within a paragraph, or do I need to be more clear in future instruction?" While answering these questions, Rylan sorted student writing into five different piles that reflected strengths, approximations, and next teaching points (see Figure 10.2). He was able to determine his whole group writing demonstration objective, along with organizing small groups with specific and appropriate teaching points that would further students' levels of independence in the area of writing.

In addition to recording specific teaching points for each group, Rylan systematically documented student learning in his monitoring notebook once a week. As a way of recording teaching and learning, Rylan recorded student strengths, approximations, and next steps as a way to track student progress over time. In order to remain useful over a period of time, Rylan's monitoring notes included the learner's name, date of documentation, behaviors, and understandings. Systematically examining student work for evidence of teaching and learning encourages the teacher to reflect on the impact of instruction, gain a brief but thorough understanding about students, use planning time efficiently, and support students as they gain habits of independence.

Resources

In addition to choosing the appropriate approaches and grouping students systematically, a teacher must give careful consideration to the resources that will support student learning. When choosing resources, it is essential to consider not only what resources to use, but also how to use them. For example, Regie Routman (2003, p. 210) encourages teachers to examine how they are using word walls:

> Many primary classrooms now have word walls, but too few teachers know why they have them or how to use them effectively. You can be an excellent teacher and not have a word wall. The word wall per se is not important; what is important is to have available, easy to access

Figure 10.2   Rylan's Monitoring Notes

Students	Strengths What is the student able to do? What is the student attempting to do?	Next Learning Step What does the student need to do next?
Mark Carrie Conner Tyler Kirsten Jeff	Logical sequence of main ideas Ideas enhanced by specific and relevant details Attempt at organization: writes introduction	Conclusion to satisfy reader and wrap up ideas
Michelle Georgia Olivia Lillian Mack Michael	Clear introduction and satisfying conclusion Sequential ideas with supporting details Paragraphs with limited ideas Attempts to organize writing with some transitional phrases	Transitions to help writing flow between paragraphs
Jenny Taylor Anneli Trinity Aaron Kelley	Plans for ideas and details Provides clear and relevant details to support topic Attempts to organized by using *first, second, third*	Organize information with introduction sentence and then categorize details accordingly
Phoebe McKenna	Talks about ideas to support topic Attempting to plan for writing	Complete plan Begin to write using plan
Conner Mikki Caroline Mary Joey	Writes with concise ideas and content in an organized manner Uses transitional words to make writing flow Includes specific and relevant details Attempts to address reader	Uses the introduction and conclusion sentences to speak to the reader: for example, the first sentence should hook the reader's attention and the conclusion needs to satisfy the reader

resources that foster investigating and solving words on one's own. Unfortunately, in too many classrooms, homogeneous word walls decorate the walls rather than inform the students. . . . Clearly, this is a misuse of a potential resource.

Routman prompts teachers to evaluate whether or not students are using the word walls in everyday reading and writing. This example makes the point that resources are not resourceful if they do not support student independence. When thinking about selecting resources, consider how they can be used to support learners. A text can provide content; however, if carefully selected, it may also support independence. For example, when teaching students about minerals, the teacher should strive to have texts with a variety of reading levels available for student use. Resources can go beyond texts and traditional supplies. Contemplate bringing in menus, bus schedules, newspapers articles, community members, a voter's pamphlet, and other "real world" materials such as owl pellets, bird's nests, and stream water to support your instruction and student growth. Broadening the kinds of resources you provide can have a big impact on engagement, purpose, and independence.

CONCLUSION

When we hope to instill habits of independence in learners, we must plan to teach accordingly. It is how we reflect on our teaching practices and the planning we do that directly impacts how prepared we are to teach students. While we come to students with a plan, the expectation should be that of implementing our plan but always being ready to start over when we encounter the Galileos of this world. Educator Steven Levy (1996) writes:

> I always tell my students about Galileo. When he was in school his teachers told him emphatically that everything there was to know was known. If you wanted to find out what was true, you needed only to look in the books of Aristotle. . . . His teachers taught everything by demonstration, never allowing the pupils to try something for themselves. . . . "But what if Aristotle was wrong?" Galileo would feel compelled to ask. He was expelled from school for his constant questioning. I wonder what happens to the Galileos in our classrooms today. (p. 26)

Now turn to the questions at the start of this chapter and consider how your understandings have shifted or been confirmed a result of your reading.

A TIME TO REFLECT

As you work with students throughout a day, you will notice times where learners are more engaged and other times where you feel like you are just trying to hold the lesson together. Take some time to reflect on your teaching and identify a couple of lessons that were a success and others that left you feeling frustrated and students confused. In order to best reflect on a day with students, you will need to collect some data.

Alfie Kohn writes in *Beyond Discipline* (1996), "When students are off-task the first question a teacher should ask himself, 'What is the task?'" Collect data including the following:

- What is the particular task or activity?
- What is the duration of the task or activity?
- What is evidence of student engagement/lack of engagement?

Once you have isolated a period of time where students were highly engaged, ask yourself what the task was and your role during this time. Next, find the block of time where students are least engaged and analyze it accordingly. What were students asked to do? What was your role during this session? As a result of analyzing your day, what do you notice and how will this impact future instruction?

A VISIT TO OUR CLASSROOMS

Grades K–3: A Primary Perspective by Karin Ramer

Early on in my teaching career, I created an elaborate word wall that I had read and heard so much about. After hours of decorating, selecting the words for the display, and posting the words alphabetically, I was ready to tear the word wall down. It took up so much room, and I really didn't understand the purpose of posting words on a wall as opposed to teaching learners to access a dictionary. Quite honestly I only vaguely referred to its presence in the room. As a result students hardly noticed the word wall, and I began to regret having ever constructed it in the first place.

Later that year students were studying William Steig's writing and the word choice he incorporates into his literature. During my writing demonstrations, I often referred to a particular word William Steig used in a book and incorporated it into my modeled writing. As I demonstrated this writing-reading connection, students began to use his writing as a sort of thesaurus. The popularity of his word choice grew and learners were independently seeking out his books to use as a support in their own daily work. Collectively we determined that posting select words in one place would be a helpful resource for writing. As a class we created a word bank of student-selected words that were identified as unique, unusual, and desirable to use in writing. Learners wrote these words on cards and posted them in one central location for everyone to access. While students basically ignored the previous word wall, the collection of words based on genuine need and interest was continuously added to, revised, and accessed. The difference was not so much in the words that were posted, but more importantly the student interest, need, and ownership. Through this experience I learned the significance of planning to teach based on students, not external expectations or what others choose to do in their classrooms. And as a result, I discovered the impact this type of planning and teaching can have on fostering learner independence. Although word walls may have worked in other classrooms, I discovered the importance of developing resources to meet my students' needs.

Grades 4–6: An Intermediate Perspective by Roxann Rose-Duckworth

As I began to use a problem-based learning focus in my planning for large group and small group instruction, I also began to see opportunities for one-on-one application. This helped me encourage the Galileos in my classroom. For example, one day as I wandered around the lunchroom as my students ate lunch, I heard some students complaining about the straws that came attached to their juice drink boxes. They complained that as they tried to insert the straws, they often broke. I stopped to talk with the students, "Wow, that sounds frustrating! What could you do about this problem?" Some of the students who were not in my class got defensive (maybe they weren't used to solving their own problems) and snapped back, "We are being careful! It's not our fault!" One of the students from my class understood how to be a problem solver and how writing can be used to solve problems. I did not need to lead her with any more questions. She said, "Hey look! The company's name and address is right here on the box! We could write a letter to the company and tell them about our problem!" The students who were not in my class said, "Yeah, like that will make a difference." My student, whom I was quite proud of at that very moment said, "Well, maybe it will."

The next day in literacy block, she began writing a letter to the company. When I met with her for our writing conference, I immediately picked out a teaching point. She had great content—but her format needed work. She was writing a friendly letter when it was appropriate to write a business letter. I helped her distinguish between the two letter formats and I showed her the essential parts of a business letter. By the end of the week, her letter was ready to send in the mail. In just a few weeks, she received a letter back from the company along with some gift certificates for their products. The juice company expressed regret for the difficulties she had encountered with their straws. They made a suggestion of how she might avoid this problem and assured her that they would pass her concern onto their packaging department. This student was so excited to show her letter to the "nay-sayers" she lunched with on a regular basis and they were quite impressed. Months later, these students claimed that the letter really had made an impact because they didn't have the broken straw problem anymore. I'm not sure if the company really changed the straw or if the students just learned how to use the straws correctly—but really, who cares? They felt empowered to solve problems they faced—and what better life lesson is there?

11

Differentiating for Independence

Ultimately, the greatest gift we can give our students is not an isolated, interesting day designed by teachers, but a deep understanding of how they learn. If students walk out of a classroom more empowered to understand the world around them, make healthy decisions, participate in our democracy, then we have succeeded as educators.

—Instructional Differentiation for Student Independence (Southern Maine Partnership, 2007, p. 19)

In recent years, differentiation has become a popular topic among educators. While teachers are attending workshops and conferences that promise secrets to effective differentiation and buying books that give ideas on how to differentiate, school districts around the nation are hiring educational consultants to help their faculty members meet the needs of an ever-diverse student population. Carol Ann Tomlinson (1999) explains that differentiating instruction means adapting what goes on in the classroom so that students have multiple choices for taking in information, making sense of ideas, and expressing what they have learned. A teacher who is differentiating instruction provides different avenues for students to acquire content, process ideas, and develop products.

So what does differentiation have to do with developing independence in students? The Southern Maine Partnership (a school–university collaboration that has linked schools and higher education in support of learning since 1985) recently wrote a report entitled *Instructional Differentiation for Student Independence*. There were ten teachers involved in the study. These teachers represented a wide range of grade levels, student populations, and content areas. Their classroom management strategies and instructional techniques varied tremendously—but they all had common core beliefs including this crucial conviction: The goal of differentiation is that students become independent learners, and the job of educators is to choose appropriate strategies to achieve that end. Each of these teachers held the opinion that the importance of educators has not changed, but the role of the teacher must change from provider of knowledge to supportive coach.

The ten teachers highlighted in the Southern Maine Partnership (2007) held seven core beliefs that influenced the decisions they made about teaching and learning. Teachers who hold these beliefs tend to strive for student independence via differentiation (pp. 15–16):

1. All students can learn.

2. Teaching must be responsive to the differences and similarities among learners.

3. The use of a variety of processes and resources simultaneously or over time allows for greater success in reaching all learners.

4. It is more important that students know things in depth than it is to cover many things superficially.

5. The more students understand about their own learning, the more successful they will be.

6. Students who are able to choose and design their own paths of academic exploration are more engaged and successful.

7. The goal of differentiation is that students become independent learners and choose appropriate strategies to achieve that end.

In this chapter, we will address each of these essential core beliefs related to differentiation. We will look at how these principles can greatly impact student independence. As you read this chapter, ask yourself the following questions about differentiation:

- What evidence is there that I believe all students can learn?
- How can I help my students develop deep understandings related to our curricular goals?
- In what ways am I differentiating instruction to meet the needs of my students?
- How am I encouraging my students to differentiate their own learning?

ALL STUDENTS CAN LEARN

Most, if not all, educators will proclaim that they believe all children can learn—yet their actions and voices often indicate strong doubts about their students. "That student can only. . . ." "This student never. . . ." "That student always. . . ." "This student could never. . . ." Effective teachers must become aware of their own biases. Arends (2000) states:

> Becoming aware of one's expectations for students who are different than oneself is probably the single most important action teachers can take to create classrooms that are free of bias and instructionally effective. (p. 131)

Research has proven that teacher expectations have a big impact on student learning (Brophy & Good, 1974; Claiborn, 1969; Rosenthal & Jacobsen, 1968). As stated in Chapter 4, our words to and about students need to be chosen carefully; they carry much power. In 1987, Good and Brophy shared what they called the "Cyclical Process of Teacher Expectations." The process can be described in this way:

Teachers expect certain behaviors which leads to . . .

Teacher behaves based on expectations which leads to . . .

Teacher's behavior communicates expectations to students which leads to . . .

Teacher's behavior affects students which leads to . . .

Students conform to teacher expectations which leads to . . .

Student behavior reinforces teacher's expectations which leads to . . .

Teacher expects certain behaviors which leads to . . . and the cyclical process continues.

Two nationally recognized educators prove that teacher expectations directly impact student learning. From 1974 to 1991, Jaime Escalante was a teacher of mathematics at Garfield High School in Los Angeles; he gained fame and distinction for his work in teaching calculus to Hispanic students who were poor (Mathews, 1988). Escalante's teaching was honored in the film *Stand and Deliver* (1988). You might remember this movie where Edward James Olmos played the dedicated teacher who aimed to teach his dropout-prone students calculus and ends up doing this so well that the students are accused of cheating on an Advanced Placement Calculus Exam. Thanks to Jaime Escalante and his teaching partner, Ben Jimenez, many Garfield students followed in the footsteps of these students highlighted in the film. In 1990, Escalante shared this in an interview (Dirmann):

> The movie *Stand and Deliver* brought home several important points: First, no one expected severely disadvantaged barrio students to achieve academic excellence. The movie also revealed that some educators hold the false and racist idea that Hispanic students are not as smart as some others, and that they shy away from courses that require hard work. It also showed how an even more insidious prejudice leads to a prevailing opinion that requiring academic excellence from poverty-level students presents a grave risk to their "fragile" self-esteem. . . . If we expect kids to be losers they will be losers; if we expect them to be winners they will be winners. They rise, or fall, to the level of the expectations of those around them, especially their parents and their teachers. (p. 420)

It would have been easy for Escalante to have low expectations for his students—many other educators and administrators did. But Escalante would not give up on his students. This quote from Escalante is something for all educators to ponder, "I may not be solely responsible for their success or failure, but that is the attitude with which I approach my work."

Ron Clark is another example of a teacher who truly embraced the idea that all students can learn. Oprah Winfrey was so impressed by his success with students that she had him as a guest on her show and also chose him to be the first man she honored in her magazine as a Phenomenal Man (2001, http://www.oprah.com/rys/omag/rys_omag_200111_phenom.jhtml). In the Q and A article that documents a conversation between Oprah and Mr. Clark, Oprah asks, "Why does your philosophy work?" and he replies:

> I'm sincere—my students know I mean what I say. They know everything I do is for them and that I'm giving it everything I've got. Some people say I'm crazy because I put so much effort into dealing with the kids. But when the kids see my effort, it makes them put forth more effort. They know I have high expectations for them.

Clark's first year of teaching in Harlem was the focus of a 2006 made-for-TV movie starring Matthew Perry. During his first two years at

Harlem, Clark was able to increase the test scores of his students to such a degree that many of his students were able to attend a prestigious middle school in Manhattan—a school where not one student from the Harlem Public School #83 had ever been admitted before.

How were these two teachers successful with students who had previously been thought of as students who could not accomplish much? These teachers represent the thousands of teachers across our nation who hold the belief that all students can learn. It's easy to say, "I believe all students can learn"—it's quite another thing to actually live these words. Teachers who believe that all students can learn see the potential of their students and when they begin to focus on developing independence in their students, they do not say, "Well, my students can't handle that level of independence"; instead they say, "What could I do to raise the level of independence of my students?" They do not say, "I work with students who are unmotivated," instead they say, "What can I do to motivate my students?"

Educational consultant and author Regie Routman writes about a weeklong school residency she did in a first-grade classroom (2003). On that first Monday morning, she introduced herself to the students by telling them about all of the reading and writing they'd be doing together that week. She was surprised to hear the students share that they didn't know how to read. She writes,

> Realizing I had a crisis on my hands—that is, if I was to teach these children to read—I immediately had to win their trust and convince them they were readers. So right on the spot, I boasted "I'm a magician of sorts. I guarantee by the end of this week every single one of you will be able to read. I'm a terrific reading teacher, I've never had a student I couldn't teach how to read. I promise you by Friday you will be able to read. I never make a promise I can't keep." They looked back at me with wide, astonished eyes, and I scrapped my lesson plan and started afresh. "Here's what we're going to do. We're going to write a book together right now. And by the end of the week, you'll be able to read it all by yourself." (p. 12)

Regie Routman writes about how she is always looking for ways for her students to shine. She emphasizes the importance of finding ways to have students experience success and then building on those positive experiences. She reminds us of something we must never forget as educators, "Success breeds more success; repeated failure leads to the feeling, 'I can't do this.' Often students just give up" (p. 15). Our students' evidence of independence will increase as we believe and then they believe that they can and will learn.

TEACHING RESPONSIVELY ENCOURAGES INDEPENDENCE

Prior to the standards movement, school curriculum goals used to focus on what educators were responsible for teaching. Thankfully, curriculum is no longer defined by what a teacher will teach but instead on what students will learn. A real estate agent may work on selling houses, but she is only recognized as being successful when people actually buy the homes she is selling. The same can be said for effective teachers—they are only successful when their students have learned what they have taught. This seems obvious but it is easy to get caught up in the job of teaching and forget that our students' learning must be at the forefront of what we do.

Teachers must believe that all students can learn but they also need to understand that all learners do not learn in the same way. John R. Passarini, Disney's 2003 Outstanding Teacher of the Year, is a special educator who lives by this mantra: "Nobody is disabled, we are all differently abled" (2007, online). Howard Gardner's theory of multiple intelligences (1983) encourages teachers to assess all learners in a way so that instead of finding out "who is smart," the teacher aims to find out "how are my students smart?" Carol Ann Tomlinson points out that differentiated instruction is proactive when teachers assume that different learners have differing needs and unique life experiences. New learning must be built on prior understandings and experiences and teachers who aim to differentiate instruction acknowledge that not all students possess the same understandings and experiences at the outset of a particular learning experience. These teachers focus on what students can do. For example, instead of describing the student with this statement, "Tyrel has not learned to read yet." The teacher would state what Tyrel does do:

> Tyrel shows a lot of interest in listening to books. He particularly enjoys listening to adults read to him. He eagerly joins in choral reading experiences when the class is reading books with patterned text such as "Brown Bear, Brown Bear, What Do You See?" by Eric Carle and "I'm Going on a Bear Hunt" by Michael Rosen and Helen Oxenbury. When choosing books for his enjoyment, he usually chooses nonfiction books about wild animals and dinosaurs and frequently points to the pictures to ask questions. He is often found playing with magnetic letters and letter rubber stamps at the writing center while singing the alphabet song. He is able to identify the names of all capital letters and some lower case letters and calls attention to signs and labels that have letters. His favorite class game is one that requires word rhyming. (adapted example, Campbell Hill, 1999, p. 40)

By focusing on our students' abilities, we are focusing on their strengths, approximations, and needs. It becomes clearer to us what they are ready to learn next and the developmental steps they are making. So rather than focusing on what they are lacking, these teachers observe what students are doing.

One way that some teachers try to differentiate, as a way of being responsive to student needs, is to focus on quantitative strategies. This means they give some students more work to do and others less. Rather than adjusting the quantity of assignments, the focus for effective differentiation uses qualitative strategies. This means that the teacher varies the nature of assignments to meet students' needs. Refer back to the spelling example given on page 22. The teacher did not differentiate simply by giving a different amount of spelling words to students—the teacher met the students' needs by assessing students' spelling development and applications. If we are to be responsible for what a child learns, then it is essential that we understand what he knew at the beginning and how to move him forward from that point in a successful manner. This means we need to understand how each student learns best. It also means that we need to build on what learners already know.

We believe every student deserves work that is focused on the essential knowledge, skills, and attitudes necessary to move them forward in the learning process. Every student ought to find their work interesting and powerful, not too easy and not overwhelming but at the zone of proximal development (as discussed on pages 34–37). Tomlinson (2003) points out that "good instruction stretches learners" (p. 16). She goes on to explain that the best tasks are those that students find a little too difficult to complete comfortably. Some teachers are differentiating unintentionally, but in order to enhance habits of independence, it is essential for teachers to make intentional instructional decisions that are responsive to learners' similarities and differences.

USING A VARIETY OF PROCESSES AND RESOURCES TO ENCOURAGE INDEPENDENCE

Teachers who aim to differentiate encourage independence in their learners by using a mixture of whole class, small group, and individual instruction. Teachers who use this kind of model usually have the whole class come together for a focus lesson and then they facilitate learning in small groups and/or individually, coming back together for reflection and goal setting. Kathleen Fay and Suzanne Whaley (2004) share what writing workshop looks like in their classroom:

> We have students with varying levels of language proficiency and literacy backgrounds in our classrooms. During writing workshop,

our goal is to treat them all the same: every student is included in all aspects of the writing workshop—read-aloud discussions, writing, conferring, sharing, and reflecting. They all have writers' notebooks, folders, and journals, regardless of their level of English language proficiency. We do, however, differentiate instruction by providing the students with different opportunities and different kinds of support in order to challenge each of them. We adjust our instruction based on what we have learned through conferences and assessments to meet the varying needs of language learners in the writing workshop setting. (p. 157)

Teachers are discovering that informally grouping and regrouping students in a variety of ways throughout the school day can make teachers more effective and students more productive. This planning sheet, displayed as Figure 11.1 from Marilyn Duncan's *The Kindergarten Book: A Guide to Literacy Instruction* (2005), shows how she uses flexible grouping based on her ongoing assessment data. Notice how she uses a variety of processes and resources to meet her students' needs. Although this is a kindergarten classroom, teachers at all grade levels could use a similar planning sheet.

GO DEEP, AVOID COVERAGE

LaShondra Haywood, a well respected third-grade teacher in a rural school district, used to spend a great deal of time planning interesting, fun, and hands-on lessons around the topic of pioneers. She earned a reputation for the culminating activity she used in her pioneer unit and students looked forward to the annual Pioneer Day she ran in her classroom. She recruited parents to help run various centers where students explored pioneer life:

- Center One: Students created cornhusk dolls.
- Center Two: Students churned butter.
- Center Three: Students rolled bread dough into thin sheets to make flat bread.
- Center Four: They listened to lively fiddle music performed by someone dressed in clothing to emulate the pioneer era.
- Center Five: They created table centerpieces out of pine boughs, pinecones, and dried flowers.
- Center Six: They observed a woman who was a member of a local spinning and weaving club spin wool into yarn.

The students and parent volunteers ended the day eating the bread and butter they prepared while sitting at tables decorated with their handmade centerpieces. The children enjoyed the day immensely. The parents were pleased and showed appreciation to LaShondra for the

Figure 11.1   Planning Sheet

Literacy Planning for Date: _Oct. 5_____   **DAILY PLAN**

WRITING DEMONSTRATION	READING DEMONSTRATION	SONGS/POETRY
Obj: To match writing with planning sketch Topic: Burnt Toast	Obj: To use pictures to anticipate. Text: I Went Walking (Sue Williams)	If you're Happy and you Know It Head, Shoulders, Knees, Toes Down By the Station

Small Group Instruction

READING	READING	WRITING	ALPHABET
Obj: Word-by word matching Group: Alberto, Keisha, Jazz, Julio, Marcy Resource: So Sleepy	Obj: Directionality (L to R) Group: Celia, Jaren, Kyle, Maria Resource: The Pond	Obj: Using plan to tell story Group: Anna, Paul, Colin Resource: Draft Book	Obj: Match pictures to letters Group: Janisha, Caleb, Beau Jasmine, Quenton Resource:

Publishing

NAME	TEACHING POINT
*Celia	→ add to plan
*Jaren	→ L to R
*Maria	→ talk about plan
*Kyle	→ plan matches story
*Janisha	→ plan matches story
*Caleb	→ plan matches story
*Jasmine	→ oral language / L to R
*Quenton	→ L to R
Jazz	→ use of "t", word "my"
Keisha	→ ending sounds
Celeste	→ end sounds
• Daily Sophie	→ reinforce "I"

Spelling
José
Keisha

Oral Reading
Paul
Jaren
Celia

Monitoring Learning
Focus: Story structure - classroom library puppets
Who? Julio, Dani, Jasmine, Janisha, Kyle

NOTES

SOURCE: From Duncan, M. (2005). *The kindergarten book: A guide to literacy instruction*. Katonah, NY: Richard C. Owen Publishers (page 124).

effort and time it took her to plan this special day. As the school community gave accolades to this teacher, no one stopped to think about the hidden curriculum woven into the day's events. What have children really learned about pioneer life? When LaShondra asked the students what they learned, student after student said, "Pioneer life was fun!" This was clearly not the understanding LaShondra was shooting for with her students.

As teachers work to align their curriculum with state and national standards, many are turning toward an approach that takes learning beyond the facts. Teachers using a concept-based curriculum (Erickson, 2002) work to help students develop and deepen their understandings. A common approach educators use when developing a concept-based curriculum is a framework called Understanding by Design (UbD). UbD, developed by Grant Wiggins and Jay McTighe in the late 1990s, utilizes a three-stage "backward planning" curriculum design process (2005). UbD advocates that teachers begin with the end in mind. Educators work through a curriculum design process that includes three stages that encourage independence in learners:

- Stage One: Identify the desired results (goals and standards).
- Stage Two: Figure out how students will show evidence of learning the identified desired results (performance and assessment).
- Stage Three: Design learning opportunities that will promote understandings and equip students to perform successfully (lessons and instruction).

During Stage One, teachers identify the enduring understandings that they want their students to have developed at the completion of the learning sequence. Enduring understandings go beyond facts and skills and instead focus on larger concepts, principles, or processes. When LaShondra aimed to improve her pioneer curriculum, she decided to use the Understanding by Design framework. Accepting that she could not go into depth on everything, LaShondra chose these big ideas that have enduring value for her learners:

- Many lives were lost and hardships endured to settle the West.
- Many pioneers had naïve ideas about the opportunities and difficulties out west and on the trail.
- The settlements of the West threatened the lifestyle and culture of Native American tribes.
- Pioneers display great ingenuity and courage in overcoming obstacles to realize their dreams.
- People migrate for a variety of reasons.

LaShondra then developed essential questions that helped students come to these identified understandings. These questions helped students make meaning from the activities geared toward these understandings as well as providing guidance for her as the teacher as she devised assessment tasks that required students to answer these questions:

- How does your life compare to the life of a pioneer?
- How would you feel if your family decided to move West in a covered wagon?
- How would you and your family prepare for the trip?
- If you lived during this time, would you have chosen to move West? Why or why not?
- How did the pioneers affect the land and people of the West?
- If your family was moving West and you were looking for a person to join your wagon train, what skills and characteristics would you look for in a traveling companion?

During Stage Two, LaShondra developed performance tasks based on the six facets of understanding (Wiggins & McTighe, 2000). These tasks included:

- Explaining: Students will imagine they are a pioneer and write a letter to relatives who stayed behind, describing what pioneer life is really like and how the life differs from what they expected.
- Interpreting: Students will read and discuss stories of pioneers, learning about westward expansion from biographies, journals, informational, and historical fiction texts.
- Applying: Given a list of items and their weight and a weight limit for their wagon, students will create a list of what they will pack into their wagon for the trip westward. They will include a rationale for what they packed.
- Perspective: Students will perform role plays from various perspectives including Native American children, women settlers, and pioneer children.
- Empathy: Students will create a list of a typical pioneer child's chores, evaluating each chore for effort and time.
- Self-Knowledge: Students will create a Venn diagram, comparing their own daily life to the daily life of a pioneer child.

During Stage Three, LaShondra needs to plan lessons that will help her students accomplish the performance tasks she has chosen. For example, she chose to have students read *Dandelions* (Bunting, 2001), a picture book about a girl and her family that move west to Nebraska in the 1800s. The family faces many challenges, including when their mother battles depression, as they build their sod house and settle into a new life. As students read the book, LaShondra had students compare their own life to the life of the main character in the book. She also had the students list the challenges faced by the family and then items that they packed or could have packed that would help them with these challenges. Teachers using a concept-based approach to curriculum tend to use an interdisciplinary approach to learning, weaving subject areas together. Steven Levy, an award winning elementary educator and educational consultant and author, writes in his book *Starting From Scratch* (1996):

> Compartmentalized learning does not help children reach our highest educational goals because it does not correspond to the way human beings experience life . . . presenting the world broken up into subjects puts it into a form already abstracted and shaped—predigested, if you will. It's like giving the children a coloring book or a paint-by-number set rather than a blank piece of paper. . . . How do we learn naturally about the world? In reality, we experience the world whole, not broken into discrete chunks. (pp. 19–20)

Teachers who are using a concept-based approach to curriculum are careful to go beyond facts, helping students to grasp transferable concepts (Erickson, 2002).

LaShondra did not scrap her pioneer day, but she definitely altered it. Consider how students previously made cornhusk dolls—they thought it was so much fun. Now she still has the students create the dolls but now they discuss these questions:

- Why do you think the pioneers made dolls out of cornhusks?
- What other toys did pioneer children have?
- What if this was the only toy you had?

Now this activity may still be fun, but the children are walking away with accurate and deep understandings of pioneer life.

It is important to understand that UbD is not a prescriptive program or specific curriculum; it is simply a design process that helps educators teach for understanding. It is a framework for curriculum development that an increasing number of teachers are finding helps them to focus on "uncovering" the content rather than "covering" the information. Teachers who are using concept-based curriculums are constantly reflecting on what it truly means to understand and what is worthy of understanding. For example, when teaching students about poetry, many educators focus on teaching students a variety of poetry formats. A search on the Internet brought up a poetry unit which recommended that the teacher teach students the basic formats of a list poem, a cinquain poem, and a haiku. Along with writing the poems, students learned how to create glitter-glue butterflies, poem kites, and watercolor sketches as a means of illustrating their poetry. Consider how this poetry unit would improve if the teacher first identified the enduring understandings she wants her students to develop about poetry. There is not one correct list of enduring understandings about poetry, but the list of understandings might look something like this:

1. Poetry is not easily defined; various people define poetry in a variety of ways.

2. A lot of poetry uses rhyming words, rhythm, and/or word patterns. Poets choose the words for their sound and the images and ideas they suggest, not just for their obvious meaning.

3. Poems do not always follow the conventions (e.g., capitalization and punctuation rules) of other forms of writing.

4. When people talk about poetry, they often use poetry terms such as *lines, stanzas, alliteration, hyperboles, onomatopoeia, metaphors,* and *similes,* all of which refer to how words are used and organized.

5. There are various forms of poetry, including narrative, limericks, cinquain, haiku, and couplets.

6. People write poetry to express emotions and opinions and to convey ideas.

The teacher might still teach the same poetry formats, but now she would be doing this with a focus on these enduring understandings. So when learning about haiku poetry, the teacher would no longer just teach "the rules" of the format but also help students see how haiku poetry uses rhythm and word patterns. When reading various haiku poems, the class would predict what led the poet to write these poems—was the author aiming to express emotions, share an opinion, or convey an idea? They may also discuss how some people would not identify haiku poems as poetry because many people think that rhyming is a requirement for the genre of poetry. Five or ten years from now, the students may not remember the exact rules for writing a haiku poem—but they are not likely to forget these enduring understandings about poetry.

The teacher writes these enduring understandings to help with planning and assessment, and she establishes essential questions based on the enduring understandings. Rather than having access to the list of understandings, her students have repetitive access to the questions. These questions are referred to over and over again throughout the study of poetry. The questions will help lead the students to the enduring understandings. The questions also help focus the teacher's planning. For example, if the teacher taught a lesson that outlined the haiku format, how would students respond to these essential questions?

1. What is poetry? What is a poem?

2. What kinds of poetry do you prefer to read? What kinds of poetry do you prefer to write?

3. What advice do you have for someone who is just learning how to read and/or write poetry?

4. If you were asked to choose a few poems to be published and you were given dozens of poems to choose from, what criteria would you use to choose the poems for publication? Do you think your criteria should be used for publishing all poems? Why or why not?

5. If you were asked to write a review on "[*poem title*]," how would you describe, analyze, and review the poem? What if the poet was asking you for advice on how to improve that poem; what feedback would you offer?

The teacher would quickly realize, "I need to go beyond just teaching the format. By just learning the haiku format, they aren't able to answer these questions." The questions, when referred to on a regular basis, help the teacher stay accountable to the enduring understandings. Everything the students learn should help them develop these big understandings. These questions help guide students as they work independently. As students are writing poetry, reading poetry, and discussing poetry, they have guiding questions to steer their thinking and interactions. These essential questions become the fundamental queries that direct students in their search for understanding. Everything in the curriculum is studied for the purpose of answering these questions. Effective essential questions meet these criteria:

1. Written in an open-ended fashion.

2. Focused on topic.

3. Require high level cognitive thinking.

4. Have emotive force or intellectual bite.

5. Written in a succinct and clear manner.

6. Do not lead.

7. Use student-friendly language.

8. Ask students to use information they learn and skills they develop.

9. Relate back to the enduring understandings.

When teachers create their enduring understandings, they often struggle with writing statements that will give them the necessary guidance. For example, Josh Duckworth is planning a unit about occupational choices. These are the enduring understandings he began with:

1. The reasons that people take jobs.

2. The skills and knowledge needed for jobs.

3. The idea that hard work = more opportunities.

These statements do not clarify what students will actually come to understand. When revised, Josh found much more guidance with these enduring understandings:

1. There are a variety of things that influence the jobs that people take (i.e., location, pay, benefits, enjoyment, coworkers, challenge, advancement, hours, opportunities, prior experience, and education).

2. All jobs require skills and knowledge related to what we learn in school.

3. People have many choices when it comes to jobs and careers. The harder you work, the more opportunities you'll have.

4. In years past and currently in some locations, some people unfairly have limited opportunities due to their race, gender, or other characteristics.

5. Not everyone can be good at every job. We all have characteristics that make us more likely to succeed in certain jobs than in others.

Josh had taught this unit for many years prior to developing these enduring understandings. Now he had to use these understandings to help filter the lessons he had planned. If the lessons helped students reach these big understandings, he kept them. If they did not relate to these enduring understandings, he had to make changes or delete the lesson all together. For example, one of his favorite lessons for this unit was bringing in various items and having the students brainstorm what occupations were necessary for that item to get into consumer's hands. For example, a gallon of milk requires a dairy farmer, truck driver, and store manager just to name a few. Now, although students had fun with this lesson in the past, Josh came to realize that this activity was not leading students to any of the enduring understandings he had written for this unit. But he realized he could simply tweak this lesson and it would fit with the understandings he was aiming for. He still brought items in and he still had students work in groups to identify the various jobs required. But now the second enduring understanding for this unit led Josh to help his students investigate these jobs to figure out what school-related skills (e.g., math, reading, writing) these people used on the job. Students were interviewing, researching, and inviting community members to be guest speakers in their classroom. Josh wrote these questions to guide his students as they learned about occupational choices:

1. What are some possible reasons that one person might quit one job for another job?

2. If you were offered a job, what questions would you have for the employer offering you the job?

3. What can you do to increase the likelihood of getting the job you want in the (near and far) future?

4. How does school prepare you for jobs in the workplace?

5. What can we do to improve work conditions and opportunities for people working in unsafe and/or unfair working conditions?

6. What advice would you give to someone who is trying to make a career choice?

Josh found that applying the UbD curriculum format enabled struggling learners to grasp and use powerful ideas and, at the same time, encouraged advanced learners to expand their understanding and application of the key concepts and principles. His instruction moved from lessons and assessment opportunities that stressed regurgitation of fragmented bits of information to instruction and assessment opportunities that emphasized deep understandings, higher level thinking skills, and independence. Upon reflection, he realized that the "coverage-based" curriculum he used before led his students to all do the same work in the same way. When he moved toward this concept-based approach, he was inspired to introduce varied learning options. He saw the difference it made for his students when they had the opportunity to explore meaningful ideas in a variety of ways. His students that once showed little independence were now displaying many qualities of independent learners. He had moved from students being "on task" to students being truly engaged in their learning. As a result of increased student independence, he will never return to just "covering" the curriculum.

What would happen if teachers stopped using the phrase, "covering the curriculum"? What does that phrase imply? Heidi Hayes Jacobs, an educational consultant, has encouraged teachers to ban this phrase (as cited in *ASCD Education Update*, 1998). Jacobs contends that when teachers state, "I am covering the curriculum," they imply that they are passing over the content quickly. It also implies that the focus is on teaching the curriculum, rather than teaching the students. The expression encourages teachers and students to think of learning as a passive activity. Chapter 10's example of Bryce Leam teaching students about bees emphasizes this point (see pages 154–156).

We suspect that some kindergarten and first- and second-grade teachers may be reading about concept-based curriculums and figuring that this does not apply to them. We challenge you to think differently. Regie Routman (1994) points out that teachers of young learners often use superficial units or themes with topics such as bears, kites, and dragons. Teachers gather a variety of books on the subject and then implement a lot of activities related to the topic. She acknowledges that the activities may be fun, creative, and interesting but she questions whether these activities have substance or are related to major concepts worth the amount of time put into teacher planning and preparation—not to mention the amount of class time these activities use. She advocates that teachers invest their time in curriculum development around themes that go beyond the literal level. So a teacher who once led a unit on bears where students got to make bear cookies, create bear puppets, and write stories about bears would make drastic changes to this unit. Regie Routman (1994) shares how teacher, Loretta Martin, developed a unit on bears with these enduring understandings:

1. Bears are not the gentle creatures we think they are.

2. Bears are a family unit with definite nurturing patterns.

Routman also shares how teacher Elaine Weiner implemented a unit on the topic of trees with these enduring understandings:

1. We cannot live on earth without trees.

2. Trees provide shade, beauty, paper, homes for animals, and more.

Routman goes on to share how Elaine led her students in learning about trees:

> Students observed trees at the school throughout the year and noted changes, growth, and animal life in and around trees through the seasons. The class also identified the trees on school property. Each student then adopted one tree and kept a year-long observational record. With the help of parents, students also counted and identified the trees in their own yards. The class then did a tally and prepared a group graph that included over ninety different kinds of trees found in students' yards. Students read books and poems about trees and did bark and leaf rubbings of some of the school's trees. A parent who is an arborist also shared what he does in his work. (p. 278)

All grade levels can benefit from concept-based curriculums. Units of study that are designed to develop important concepts and provide opportunities for skill development in meaningful contexts benefit all learners.

There are four types of curriculum (Henniger &Rose-Duckworth, 2007):

1. Formal Curriculum: content that schools intend to teach students. This formal curriculum is often identified at the national level via professional organizations, defined more specifically within individual states, and further refined at the district, school, and classroom levels.

2. Informal Curriculum: extracurricular activities such as sports, clubs, special classes. Extracurricular activities promote citizenship and sportsmanship, teach lessons about teamwork and self-discipline,

and facilitate the physical and emotional development of students while instilling a sense of school and community pride. These activities can also provide opportunities for students to build helpful and supportive relationships with staff members. The informal curriculum increases the likelihood of students going beyond a high school education.

3. Null Curriculum: topics not included in the classroom due to fear of controversy or perceived low value.

4. Hidden Curriculum: everything that the educational system indirectly teaches students through the attitudes and behaviors of teachers and staff. Sometimes our instruction can unintentionally have hidden curriculum that leads to misunderstandings that affect students' current and future understandings about the formal curriculum.

By creating enduring understandings and essential questions, it is less likely that you will have a hidden curriculum that leads students to major misunderstandings you didn't intend to teach. Teachers who use the UbD model know it is more important that students know things in depth than it is to cover many things superficially. The concept-based curriculum model directs educators to continually ask themselves if they are addressing what is truly vital for each child to learn and when educators do this, student independence is increased.

STUDENTS NEED TO KNOW THEMSELVES AS LEARNERS

Mel Levine (2007) shares the importance of students knowing themselves as learners:

> We must help them look backward and forward, review their recurring autobiographical themes, and uncover the consistent assets and proclivities that could blossom into fulfillment for them. . . . Schools should help students pose the right questions about themselves. Throughout their education, children and adolescents should be working on their autobiographies, sifting through earlier pages and pondering implications for the next several chapters. (p. 20)

The more students understand about their own learning, the more successful they will be. Students benefit from teachers using differentiation in the classroom—but the ultimate goal should be for students to differentiate for themselves. Isn't this what we do in the adult world? When playing Scrabble with a friend, do you ever make reference to a dictionary? When working on a big project at your school, do you ever ask for an extension on the due date? When driving to a friend's home, do you ever call on a cell phone to get verbal directions because the written directions are too confusing to follow? We need to not only teach our students how to think critically and creatively, but we need to help them learn how to think about their thinking—educators refer to this as metacognition. Metacognition consists of two processes that occur hand in hand:

1. Students monitor their progress as they learn.

2. Students make changes and adapt their strategies if they perceive they are not getting the desired results.

Metacognition is about self-reflection, self-responsibility, initiative, goal setting, and time management—all critical aspects on independent learning (Winn & Snyder, 1996). Students who possess a strong knowledge of self are more likely to make wiser decisions within and beyond the classroom. By modeling metacognition in think-alouds as we read aloud, demonstrate writing, perform science experiments, solve math problems, and so forth, we are developing learner autonomy, learner independence, and learner self-regulation.

Metacognition consists of three basic elements: developing a plan of action, maintaining/monitoring the plan, and evaluating the plan. As teachers model metacognition and encourage the use of metacognitive reflection, they may find it helpful to use the questions outlined in Kujawa and Huske's *Strategic Teaching and Reading Project Guidebook* (1995):

Before—When you are developing the plan of action, ask yourself:

- What in my prior knowledge will help me with this particular task?
- In what direction do I want my thinking to take me?
- What should I do first?
- Why am I reading this selection?
- How much time do I have to complete the task?

During—When you are maintaining/monitoring the plan of action, ask yourself:

- How am I doing?
- Am I on the right track?
- How should I proceed?
- What information is important to remember?
- Should I move in a different direction?
- Should I adjust the pace depending on the difficulty?
- What do I need to do if I do not understand?

After—When you are evaluating the plan of action ask yourself:

- How well did I do?
- Did my particular course of thinking produce more or less than I had expected?
- What could I have done differently?

- How might I apply this line of thinking to other problems?
- Do I need to go back through the task to fill in any "blanks" in my understanding?

STUDENT CHOICE IS CRITICAL

Many teachers fear that when students are given choices, the teacher must abandon rules, requirements, and expectations—yet this is simply not so. Choices provide opportunities for meaningful conversations where students are taught how to prioritize and take ownership of their own learning. For independent learning to proceed, student choice must become a regular part of the classroom environment, including the structuring of assignments, topics, problem solving, group processes, and timelines. Take some time to reflect on the types of choices students make in your classroom. What are some areas where student choice could be introduced or increased? Alfie Kohn (1993) shares a troubling trend in American schools:

> Several years ago, a group of teachers from Florida traveled to what was then the USSR to exchange information and ideas with their Russian-speaking counterparts. What the Soviet teachers most wanted from their guests was guidance on setting up and running democratic schools. Their questions on this topic were based on the assumption that a country like the United States, so committed to the idea of democracy, surely must involve children in decision-making processes from their earliest years. The irony is enough to make us wince. As one survey of American schools after another has confirmed, students are rarely invited to become active participants in their own education. Schooling is typically about doing things *to* children, not working *with* them. (p. 10)

Many educators have been up in arms recently as states and districts have become more prescriptive with school curriculums. Recently, Bellevue School District in Washington State began standardizing its curriculum in every classroom, requiring teachers to log in to see what pages and subjects they must teach each day (Shaw, 2007). To many teachers, this is alarming. Not only is this seen as a professional offense, many teachers claim that a prescriptive school curriculum like this affects their motivation and creativity. But yet, many of these teachers do the same thing to their students each day. If we are motivated by choices within our school day, why should it be any different for our students? Just as we do not have free reign of what to teach (we have standards we must help our students accomplish), our students do not need to be given free reign within our classrooms. But student choice does not need to be black or white—there are many shades of gray.

DIFFERENTIATION LEADS
TO INDEPENDENT LEARNERS

Some educators are troubled by this trend to differentiate instruction for students. They are worried that we are making education too easy for students. They are concerned that teachers are being asked to create a separate education plan for each student. They also have concerns that differentiated instruction tends to be chaotic. Teachers who differentiate instruction effectively do not see differentiation in these ways. To them, differentiation is not a teaching strategy, but it's a way of thinking about teaching and learning. They don't look for a recipe to follow. Instead they continually reflect on their own professional understandings, beliefs, and practices—aiming to do whatever it takes to reach and teach each learner. When teachers begin to differentiate, we recommend that you look for small changes to make in your teaching. Aim to differentiate just one part of your day; then as your comfort and confidence grows, begin to differentiate more.

If you are thinking that differentiated instruction is a crutch for students, Rick Wormeli (2006) agrees with you! Rick explains in his book, *Fair Isn't Always Equal:*

> Some educators and parents still see differentiated instruction and assessment as a crutch. In truth, they are correct—but not in the negative sense they intend. In their minds, a crutch refers to something leaned on too much. Students limp around, never really growing autonomous, always dependent because things are made easier for them when the teacher differentiates. Nothing could be farther from the truth. In the last few decades, we've witnessed amazing heroes of our time . . . who've achieved greatness through the use of prosthetic legs, crutches and wheelchairs. These objects (and their analogous applications to the classroom) allow individuals to rise, be held accountable and soar. We wouldn't dream of limiting them by removing these support devices. Because of the differentiated approaches, they become full individuals, identified first for who they are inside, and labeled only much farther down the road with an almost incidental comment that they happen to be in a wheelchair or have a fake leg. This is what can happen when we differentiate instruction and assessment for students. . . . (pp. 4–5)

When we differentiate correctly, then both teachers and students transform their relationships and amend their expectations. The student is expected to take a more active role in his learning. This means that the teacher sometimes has to allow the student to struggle if the challenging experience will lead to improved learning and is in the learner's zone of proximal development. The teacher's role changes from the one who dispenses knowledge to a coach who supports and guides learning.

Differentiation requires an ongoing collaboration between students and teachers. Carol Ann Tomlinson (2006) points out that differentiation is a great approach to use when aiming to meet academic standards. She reminds us that standards guide WHAT we teach and differentiation guides HOW we teach. No matter what we are teaching, it will be learned better if we teach in a way that is responsive to students' needs. Differentiation simply makes standards accessible to a wider array of students—all the while encouraging independent learning habits.

CONCLUSION

Put quite simply, differentiation is acknowledging that our students learn in different ways, and responding by doing something about that through curriculum, instruction, and assessment. Differentiated instruction has a direct impact on the independence our students show as learners. Students who were once unmotivated and showed little independence tend to become highly motivated and independent when put in an educational setting that focuses on their needs and interests in a flexible way. To help you apply the recommendations from this chapter, we encourage you to take some time to reflect on the questions that we posed on page 162.

A TIME TO REFLECT

Early on in this chapter we talked about quantitative strategies for differentiating (where the amount of work varies) as compared to qualitative methods (where the nature of the assignment varies) as a way to meet students' needs. Perhaps altering the quantity of a particular assignment will help some learners, but when a student is truly struggling, how do fewer problems enhance understanding? And for the student who is in need of a challenge, how does increasing the same level of work build core concepts?

Analyze a current expectation you have for all learners: writing a poem, testing chemical reactions, researching marine life, solving logic problems, balancing and weighing in science, etc. Identify enduring understandings that you plan for students to take away from the lesson or unit. Keeping these goals in mind, consider three different ways to accomplish the same outcome. Construct a continuum of sorts that highlights how a tangled learner, an average learner, and a highly capable learner might gain enduring understandings during the unit or topic of study. Instead of altering the workload for students, what can you do to differentiate instruction? Consider differentiating the process, content, and products. Share your thinking with a colleague and consider how you might be able to generalize your strategies for differentiation to other lessons or units.

A VISIT TO OUR CLASSROOMS

Grades K–3: A Primary Perspective by Karin Ramer

Just recently I moved classrooms and came across a variety of binders and colorful tubs. Each was labeled neatly with a variety of topics: apples, pumpkins, colors, seasons, etc. Books were labeled and stored in the tubs, along with activities that would be ceremoniously brought out during the appropriate time of the year. In looking at the activities, I was disappointed to realize that early on in my career, I had been keeping students busy with tasks that I determined to be of value. Although it is true that some of the activities focused on learning, such as estimating and measuring a variety of pumpkins and their seeds, many of the paper-and-pencil tasks and premade books required students to make few decisions and demanded no independence. Instead the jobs focused on conformity.

After many years of reflecting on best practices, I no longer have a need for binders full of crafts or bins that hold sacred activities and books for a special time of the year. These tubs now line my garage walls with heavy ink marking out the labels, filled with winter clothes, sewing materials, and kids' toys, and the binders too have found new purpose. In the classroom I now make decisions based on student interest, curriculum expectations, standards, and developing independent habits of mind. Students are more engaged and leave at the end of the day with skills and strategies, rather than facts and snippets of information. Not only is teaching more rewarding, student learning is more effective and efficient. After all, just how did that apple coloring activity foster independence and develop higher thinking skills? I, for one, am certain that I could not tell you.

Recently, I read about a kindergarten teacher, Melanie Fry, who had a similar epiphany that she shared in Regie Routman's *Reading Essentials* (2003):

> This school year I stopped doing worksheets to start the day, and I will never go back! I was wasting thirty-five minutes of class time each day. Now my children spend that time reading. Each day they prepare one or two books to take home and read to their parents instead of a handful of papers that will eventually end up in a trash can. What a wonderful change the reading has made! I have watched these children gain so much confidence in their abilities and the pride they have as readers is just amazing! (p. 90)

Grades 4–6: An Intermediate Perspective by Roxann Rose-Duckworth

I have used literature circles in my classroom throughout all of my years of teaching but the way I did this changed dramatically when I began aiming to differentiate instruction for my students. There are three different ways that educators can differentiate: they can adapt the content, the process, and/or the product, and I adjusted all three as I worked to meet my students' needs via the use of literature circles.

Early on in my teaching, all students would read the same book for literature circles. For example, in the early 90s, my students all read the biography about Martin Luther King entitled *I Have a Dream: The Story of Martin Luther King* by Margaret Davidson (1986). For some students, this chapter book was too challenging; for others it was neglecting to stretch them as readers; and for some it was a "just-right" fit. As I began to *differentiate the content* of my literature circles, I realized that our entire class could all be reading books about Martin Luther King and the Civil Rights time period—and each group could read a different book depending upon their interest, skills, and needs as a reader. So, my students were placed in literature circles with the following books:

1. A group was reading the chapter book (Davidson, 1986) I had used for years.

2. A group was reading *A Picture Book of Martin Luther King, Jr.* by David Adler (1989).

3. A group was reading *The Day Martin Luther King, Jr. Was Shot: A Photo History of the Civil Rights Movement* by Jim Haskins (1992).

4. A group was reading a picture book entitled *Martin's Big Words: The Life of Dr. Martin Luther King, Jr.* by Dorren Rappaport (2001).

5. A group was reading *Martin Luther King* by Rae Bains (1985).

6. A group was reading *If You Lived at the Time of Martin Luther King* by Ellen Levine (1990).

In addition to students reading the books listed above in their literature circles, I also provided background knowledge for them by sharing these books as my read-alouds:

1. *Martin Luther King, Jr.: A Big Biography* by J. C. Reed (1994)

2. *If a Bus Could Talk: The Story of Rosa Parks* by Faith Ringgold (1999)

3. *The Story of Ruby Bridges* by Robert Coles (1995)

4. *Rosa* by Nikki Giovanni (2005)

5. *This Is the Dream* by Diane Z. Shore and Jessica Alexander (2006)

All students were learning about Dr. King and the changes that occurred in our country during the Civil Rights Movement, but students were able to gain that information using a text that met them at their zone of proximal development and using a text that they had some input on choosing. We were able to have class discussions based on our essential questions (Figure 11.2) where students were able to share with one another what they were learning from their readings and small group discussions.

Figure 11.2   Enduring Understandings and Essential Questions

Enduring Understandings (for my eyes only—guides my planning, teaching, and assessment)	Essential Questions (posted in room to guide literature circles, class lessons, and read-aloud discussions)
1. Prejudice and racism have been present in the past and still exist today.	1. How was prejudice and racism evident in our country back in the days of Martin Luther King?
2. The civil rights movement was a grassroots movement that began in the 1950s. The movement, led by Dr. King, included people from every walk of life, who through their commitment and determination, redirected the nation's understanding of the creed "all men are created equal." Because of this movement, blacks gained rights in a variety of arenas including voting, court system, schools, housing, and public accommodations.	2. How are prejudice and racism evident in our school, community, country, and/or world today? What can you do to make our school, community, country, and/or world more accepting of differences among people?
3. People involved in the movement used a variety of strategies including the courts, civil disobedience, the use of media, drafting legislation and public awareness campaigns to achieve their goals.	3. If you could choose only 3 words to describe Dr. King, what words would you choose and why?

4. How has life for African Americans changed since Dr. King was living? How did these changes come about? Who influenced these changes? |
| 4. Leaders play a key role in stopping discrimination against groups of people but it's important to remember that the civil rights movement is a story of common men and women who struggled and persevered to make positive changes in our nation. | 5. What advice would you give someone who is trying to make an improvement for a group of people who are being treated unfairly? |
| 5. If we want to make big, important changes, we may need to struggle, sacrifice, and persevere. | |

In addition to differentiating the content that students were reading, I began to *differentiate the products* that students created to show their understanding and appreciation of the books they were reading. I used to have all students do the same response of their reading. We might all create book posters or we might all create a timeline or we might all use a Venn diagram to compare characters. But I found that if I introduced a variety of options to students, they would take more interest and students were able to show me what they comprehended in a variety of ways. For example:

1. The group reading *I Have a Dream: The Story of Martin Luther King* (Davidson, 1986) created a polar opposite chart (Yopp & Yopp, 2001) where they analyzed various people represented in the book by rating their characteristics on a five-point scale (e.g., kind—mean, happy—sad, brave—fearful) and found text evidence to support their ratings.

2. The group reading *A Picture Book of Martin Luther King, Jr.* by David Adler (1989) chose to do a quotation share (Yopp & Yopp, 2001) where each student shared excerpts they found compelling or interesting. After sharing these in their small group, they decided which passages to share with the entire class.

3. The group reading *The Day Martin Luther King, Jr. Was Shot: A Photo History of the Civil Rights Movement* by Jim Haskins (1992) decided to create a timeline of events that led up to and followed the assassination of Dr. King.

4. The group reading a picture book entitled *Martin's Big Words: The Life of Dr. Martin Luther King, Jr.* by Dorren Rappaport (2001) chose to create a feelings chart (Yopp & Yopp, 2001) by identifying several events that occurred in the book, then listing the people mentioned in the book, and then predicting and recording feelings that the various people had about each of the events, looking for text evidence to back up their conclusions.

5. The group reading *Martin Luther King* by Rae Bains (1985) asked if they could create a readers' theatre performance based on key events in Dr. King's life. They performed this for their classmates and at the school assembly that preceded the three-day weekend to commemorate Dr. King's birthday.

6. The group reading *If You Lived at the Time of Martin Luther King* by Ellen Levine (1990) were excited to create a PowerPoint slide show to compare and contrast life now and life then. They used quotes from the text throughout their presentation.

There were some products that were universal. For example, we created a class chart where we recorded the titles of the books we were reading, the authors and illustrators, the genres, and the lessons we could learn from these books. This chart helped us focus on the enduring understandings we were all aiming for, even though we were using different texts. I also had each student complete an anticipation guide (Yopp & Yopp, 2001) where students were asked to take a stand on statements such as "It's fun to be different" or "Sometimes one person can make a difference in the world." Then after our literature circles were completed, I asked students to respond to these statements again and share how their opinions had changed and what had influenced these changes and what opinions were reinforced and what class experiences supported their original judgments.

I also began to *differentiate the process* by helping students develop as readers and writers based on their strengths and needs as readers and writers. So for example, over the course of one week, these were my teaching points with each literature circle:

1. The group reading *I Have a Dream: The Story of Martin Luther King* (Davidson, 1986) learned about the use of italics. The author used italics throughout the text, and we discussed how this text feature could help us understand the text better. Students were also encouraged to consider where they could use italics in something they were currently writing or something they wrote in the past.

2. The group reading *A Picture Book of Martin Luther King, Jr.* by David Adler (1989) learned how illustrations can help readers understand the text. They looked for details in the illustrations that connected the text in the book. They also brainstormed questions and predictions the illustrations gave them and then talked about where they could find text evidence to answer those questions or support those predictions. They were also encouraged to consider how they use illustrations as a writer.

3. The group reading *The Day Martin Luther King, Jr. Was Shot: A Photo History of the Civil Rights Movement* by Jim Haskins (1992) learned about the difference between primary and secondary resources. The book includes pictures of actual newspaper articles, copies of flyers, and copies of documents. The group discussed how the author used primary and secondary resources in his research. The students were encouraged to look back at a recent research project they completed and identify the types of resources they used, all of which they identified as secondary resources. The group then brainstormed how they could have used primary resources in that research and why that would be a good idea.

4. The group reading a picture book entitled *Martin's Big Words: The Life of Dr. Martin Luther King, Jr.* by Dorren Rappaport (2001) learned about inferences. They were shown how to and encouraged to make inferences as they found text evidence for their feelings chart. We discussed how authors can "show" rather "tell" and how this can improve a piece of writing. They were encouraged to look back on their own writing to "show" rather than "tell"—which will lead their audience to infer as they read.

5. The group reading *Martin Luther King* by Rae Bains (1985) learned about reading fluency as they practiced and performed their readers' theatre. They focused on expression, rate, and phrasing as they rehearsed and performed.

6. The group reading *If You Lived at the Time of Martin Luther King* by Ellen Levine (1990) learned about various graphic organizers that help when comparing and contrasting information. They then chose the graphic organizer(s) that would best help them organize the information for their presentation. Figure 11.2 shows the enduring understandings and essential questions that I developed to guide our literature circles and read-aloud conversations.

Bonnie Campbell Hill, Katherine Schlick-Noe, and Nancy J. Johnson provide a chart in their book *Literature Circles Resource Guide* (2001) that is a good description of how I changed the way I facilitated literature circles in my classroom. The chart (Figure 11.3) shows how teachers can move from very teacher-dependent strategies to student-independent strategies. As I changed the way I implemented literature circles in my classroom, I found that my students' motivation increased and their independence as learners soared to an unbelievable realm!

Figure 11.3 Literature Circles: Change Over Time

Literature Circles: Change Over Time

Component	Some First Steps	Some Next Steps	Some Later Steps
Teacher Beliefs	• There is only one "right" way to do literature circles	• There are many options for literature circles • I'll try out some, refine them, try others	• This is what works in my classroom • My students and I are constantly learning and changing how we do things
Goals	• Learning the structure and surviving • Choosing one component to focus on	• Refining structure • Learning how to discuss • Deepening meaning and engagement	• Developing meaningful response, higher levels of thinking • Using themes, nonfiction, poetry
Timeline: K–1	• 1–2 weeks; no response project • 1–2 literature circle cycles, then other literacy activities	• 1–2 weeks, including simple response project	• ~ 1–3 weeks with more elaborate response projects
2–8	• ~ 3–6 weeks • Emphasis on learning the process	• ~ 3–6 weeks • Emphasis on developing response	• ~ 3–6 weeks • Emphasis on deepening response
Schedule: K–1	• Teacher sets schedule • Groups discuss once a week	• Teacher sets schedule or with student participation • Groups may discuss more than once a week	• Teacher sets schedule or with student participation • Groups may discuss more than once a week
2–8	• Teacher sets schedule • Groups discuss once a week	• Teacher and students set schedule together • Groups may discuss more often	• Groups decide how long entire book + extension will take and set own schedule
Choosing Books	• Whole class reads same book • Books chosen by teacher • Read from anthology/basal or whatever is available	• Two or three book choices • Books selected because they are engaging and meaningful	• Four or five book choices • Books selected because they relate to a theme, topic, genre, author, *and* represent good literature
Forming Groups	• Teacher gives book talks • Groups formed by student choice	• Teacher or students give book talks • Groups formed by student choice	• Teacher or students give book talks • Groups formed by student choice

Component	Some First Steps	Some Next Steps	Some Later Steps
Preparing for Discussion	• Teacher assigns response prompts • Students read alone, in pairs, with audio taped book, or with support	• Teacher offers choice of a few response prompts • Students/teacher generate responses	• Students choose from a menu of ideas or develop their own
Discussion	• Teacher sets discussion schedule • Teacher facilitates group; *or* teacher participates as group member; *or* teacher sits near group and observes; *or* students facilitate own groups, teacher roams • Use roles and forms	• Groups meet on a rotating basis • Students generate discussion guidelines • Modify/adapt forms	• Groups set their own schedule • Adapt forms or give them up entirely
Written Response	• Teacher assigns response prompts • Required response to each chapter/book • Try out a few forms	• Teacher offers choice of responses • Given number of responses required per week; written only • Modify/adapt forms	• Students choose from menu of ideas or develop their own • Flexible number of responses per week in variety of forms (e.g., written and art) • Modify or dispense with forms
Focus Lessons	• How to do literature circles • Literacy strategies, literary elements • Anything the teacher notices	• Refining literature circles • Literacy strategies, literary elements • Anything teacher/students notice	• Perfecting literature circles • Literacy strategies, literary elements • Anything teacher/students notice
Extension Projects	• Teacher assigns one option • Teacher decides: group or individual	• Teacher offers choice of options • Students decide: group or individual	• Students select from menu of options or develop their own • Students decide: group or individual
Assessment	• What assessment?	• Use one or two forms • Try out limited student self-assessment • Students choose a few responses to be graded; begin to evaluate discussion	• Modify forms and develop own instruments • Take and use anecdotal notes • Extensive student self-assessment • Students choose a few responses to be graded

SOURCE: Used with permission of Nancy Johnson, Western Washington University.

12

Conclusion

Changing and Reflecting

I often ask, "If you were ever accused of being a good teacher, would there be enough evidence to convict you?" My continuing hope is that I stand in the ranks of the guilty.

—David Funk (2002, *Love and Logic,* p. 191)

It is our hope that after reading this book and reflecting on your experiences, we have helped you define what an independent learner is and how to foster independence in your students. It is critical that we end this book by making the point that independent learning must not be something teachers want just for their students, but it is crucial that this is something they seek for themselves as well. Art Costa and Robert Garmston (1996) draw these four assumptions about self-directed learning:

1. All behavior is produced by thought and perception.

2. Teaching is constant decision making.

3. To learn something new requires engagement and alteration in thought.

4. Humans continue to grow cognitively.

As you reflect on what you are currently doing to impact student independence and what you plan to do to increase student independence, we ask you to consider these four assumptions.

In the conclusion to this book, we will address each of these assumptions about self-directed learning. We will help you reflect and make changes that will positively influence your students' levels of independence. As you read, ask yourself the following questions:

- If someone visited my classroom and observed my teaching, what would they assume I value as an educator?
- What decisions have I made recently that impact student independence? How did I make these decisions?
- What are some changes I have made in my teaching that have required me to alter my thinking about teaching and learning? How have these changes impacted student independence?
- As a teacher, how do I continue to challenge myself to grow and change?

OUR BEHAVIORS ARE INFLUENCED BY THOUGHT AND PERCEPTION

In Chapter 11, we emphasized the importance teacher expectations have on student success. In this final chapter, we want you to consider the effect that your own expectations can have on your teaching and leadership in the classroom. In a study of peak performers (Costa & Garmston, 1994), Charles Garfield found that top performers have a nearly indisputable belief in the likelihood of their own success. We too have noticed this trend in classrooms we visit. The most successful teachers whose students exude independence tend to take a very optimistic approach to challenges. They do not look at a lack of student independence as a situation that cannot be changed. In his book on peak performers, Garfield (1987) identifies these two key beliefs of peak performers:

1. I believe I can successfully execute the behavior required to influence outcomes.

2. I believe in my own coping abilities.

We encourage you to be open to new ideas and creative solutions. Costa and Garmston (1996) share a story about NASA that makes a point about how important it is to remain flexible:

When NASA was developing the Apollo and Mercury space capsules, it needed to deal with the tremendous heat of reentry.

A capsule literally glows cherry red as it encounters friction within the earth's atmosphere, and the scientists needed to develop a material that would withstand the heat. Finally, one scientist observed "You know, we're doing it all wrong. Rather than trying to develop a material that would withstand the heat, we need to conduct the heat away from the space capsule." And to this day, ships like the space shuttle are lined with tiles that burn up on reentry, conducting heat away from the spacecraft's surface. (p. 14)

According to John Dewey (Roe & Ross, 2002) reflective teaching is behavior that relates to active and persistent consideration of beliefs or practices in view of supporting evidence. Brian Cambourne (as cited in Taylor, 2001) explains it this way:

For me reflective learning is what happens when one has a discussion with one's self and clarifies one's conceptual confusions. It is a form of discussion—except it occurs within the same nervous system not between different nervous systems—it's a form of soliloquy and it serves the same function Hamlet's famous soliloquy served: to address and resolve the big questions of life and/or learning. (p. 185)

It is our hope that this text has encouraged you to reflect on your teaching practices and that your inner dialogue helps you clarify your conceptions about teaching, learning, and student independence. Our goal with this book has not been to tell you what to believe, but to help you consider what you believe and to nudge you to evaluate if these beliefs encourage or hinder student independence in your classroom.

TEACHING IS CONSTANT DECISION MAKING

Ron Ritchhart (2002) uses the metaphor of a red thread to help teachers identify the ideas and values that are the core of their teaching. He purports that every teacher has a "red thread," whether he or she is aware of it or not. He encourages teachers to become aware of their "red thread" as a way of taking more control of their teaching, reminding us that it's hard to change or modify something we are not fully aware of:

I often tell teachers that I can identify their red threads quickly by just asking their class one question: "What is it that your teacher says over and over again?" Our speech reveals us. What we harp on and bring up repeatedly is what we care about. (p. 238)

He goes on to share how one teacher realized that her students would probably answer that question with "Where's your pencil?" and after some reflection, she decided to change that question to "What's your responsibility as a learner?"

As teachers, we are constantly making decisions: big and small. The more we can be conscious of the decisions we make, the more we can positively impact student independence. Dawn Christiana, a second-grade teacher who recently gained national board certification in the area of literacy, is accutely aware of the decisions she is making in her classroom. She decided to make a change to how she concludes her literacy focus lessons. At the end of a guided writing lesson, she used to say "So, today in your writing, I want you to. . . ." and then she would refer back to her teaching point. After continuing to learn about effective minilessons, she has changed this concluding sentence to "So remember, today and everyday one strategy you can use as a writer is. . . ." Consider how this teaching decision will impact student independence.

Mary Haymond and Linda Lee, two multiage teachers in Spokane, Washington, made a small change in how they organized their literacy block that had a great impact on student writing performance. This is the order they used to use:

1. Students met on the community rug for a writing minilesson.

2. Students were excused to get their writing utensils and notebooks.

3. Students began writing.

Mary and Linda made this slight change in the order:

1. Students place their writing utensils and notebooks at their tables.

2. Students meet on the community rug for a writing minilesson.

3. Students return to seats and begin writing.

Linda and Mary shared how this decision greatly impacted the amount of writing time their students had, which in turn impacted the growth they made as writers. When students had to get their writing tools out after the minilesson, this delayed their writing and also lowered the application of the lesson's teaching point. This small change in their management of writing time made their writing time calmer, increased student independence, and proved to have a huge impact on students applying the strategies emphasized in the minilessons.

All of these teachers have something in common—they were willing to reflect on the decisions they were making as facilitators of learning. It would have been easy to just complain about a lack of independence in their students: "My students are never prepared for learning," or "My students don't apply prior teaching points to their writing," or "Our students take forever to get started with their writing, obviously they don't care." But instead these teachers were willing to reflect and look at their own decisions and how those actions impact student behaviors; because of their willingness to do so, they saw increased student independence and learning.

LEARNING REQUIRES ENGAGEMENT AND ALTERATION IN THOUGHT

Leah Mermelstein, a literacy consultant and author, has helped many teachers rethink the role of sharing in a writers' workshop. For years, many teachers have attempted to use "the author's chair" where a student would read a piece of writing to the class and then take questions from classmates. We know of teachers who stopped incorporating this as part of writers' workshop because they felt it was just a glorified "show and tell." They did not see this classroom routine improving their students' writing. Apparently, Leah agreed with these concerns about sharing time—but rather than scrapping this practice, she wrote *Don't Forget to Share: The Crucial Last Step in the Writing Workshop* (2007) where she helps teachers alter their thoughts about the role of sharing in a writers' workshop. She encourages teachers to see that there can be different kinds of conversations in share sessions:

1. In a *content share*, one or two (perhaps three) students read their writing aloud. After each kid reads, the teacher asks the rest of the students to retell what they heard to make sure everyone understood it. Then the kids ask for more information. Finally, the writer decides which part of the discussion (if any) will help him revise the writing (p. 33).

2. In a *process share*, the teacher poses a question that pertains to the writing process: e.g., What do you do when you don't know how to spell a word? What do you do when you don't know what to write about? Then the kids explore the question, using all of their prior writing experiences to help them (p. 59).

3. In a *progress share*, the teacher poses a question such as "How has your writing improved in this unit of study?" The students then discuss the questions and set goals for their future writing (p. 70).

Are you a classroom teacher who scraps an idea because it is not working or are you willing to be engaged in reading professional books and journals, talk with colleagues, and attend conferences seeking ideas of how you might alter some thoughts and practices? Effective teachers do put some teaching practices aside, but this is only after careful consideration—not simply because "it didn't work for me."

HUMANS CONTINUE TO GROW COGNITIVELY

Whether you are a rookie teacher, a teacher-in-training, or a veteran educator, you can surely fill in these blanks: I used to _____, but now I _____.

Sometimes as we do this, we cringe with memories of things we did to and with our students. We did them then because we believed that we were making the best decisions for our students but now we know better. Assessment practices, instructional strategies, homework procedures, behavior management techniques, parent communication routines—all of these change as we grow as teachers. We do better when we know better.

This book was six years in the making, and our understandings of teaching and learning changed during these six years, requiring us to alter the content as we went through our extensive writing and research process. We know that there will be content in our book that a few years from now we will have rethought. Some might call this our disclaimer. Maybe we all need a disclaimer hanging in our classrooms: "I am doing the best I can as your teacher. In the future, I will learn ways to teach better. Please do not hold that against me, for I am doing the best I know how to do right now." We have found, and this seems to be echoed by many of our colleagues, the more experience we get as teachers, the more we want to learn about teaching and learning. Amy Krouse Rosenthal's picture book *Cookies: Bite Size Life Lessons* (Rosenthal & Dyer, 2006) shares some essential life lessons that can be connected to a life of teaching. She ends her book with a "cookie definition" of what it means to be wise:

> I used to think I knew everything about cookies, but now I realize
> I know about one teeny chip's worth. (p. 25)

Most teachers can relate to this sentiment. We have found that the most effective teachers we meet remain open to learning and actively seek to improve their teaching practices and understandings about best practices in education. We hope you are not only feeling wise, but that you are also willing to be open-minded. Rosenthal gives this "cookie definition":

> Open-minded means I've never seen cookies like that before, but,
> uh, sure, I'll try one. (p. 30)

We hope that after reading this book you are feeling ready to try some things you had never considered before. So, if you are looking at making changes in your classroom based on your reading of this book, we ask you to choose carefully. It can seem overwhelming when aiming to develop independence with students—where do we start? When deciding what changes to make, we encourage you to minimize the ratio of effort to effect (adapted from Beck, 2007). Consider a change and rate it using the following rubrics.

Effort Rubric

1. I love doing this; it takes hardly any time and doesn't require much energy.

2. I enjoy doing this; it does take some time but not much brain or muscle energy.

3. I don't mind doing this; it does take some time and some energy.

4. I can do this; it takes a large amount of time and energy.

5. I really don't like doing this; it takes a lot of time and brain/muscle power. This is something I dread doing.

Effect Rubric

1. Students will not learn independence.

2. Some students may gain some independence.

3. Student independence will be impacted.

4. Student independence will be greatly impacted on an ongoing basis. My teaching job will be made easier. Student learning could improve.

5. Student independence will be greatly impacted on an ongoing basis. Student learning will improve based on this.

After figuring the effort and effect score for the change you are considering, set the numbers side by side to determine the effort to effect ratio. For example, a change with an effort score of 1 and an effect score of 4 (minimum effort for maximum effect) will be a change that you can easily implement. Sophia Alexander, a third-grade teacher, made a change with this kind of effort: effect ratio recently. As we observed her working with small groups in her classroom, we noticed that as groups finished, she would announce this to the class. "One of the groups has finished," or "Two groups are still working." Sometimes she might get busy helping one group and then need to shout, "How many groups are still working?" She seemed to be frantically moving from group to group checking on progress. Her interactions with students did not seem to focus on the quality of their work, but more so on the quantity of the work they had left to complete. She appeared to be consumed with keeping track of where each group was in the completion of the task. She was acting as the "task master" more so than the "learning facilitator." We suggested a small change that would have a low effort and a high effect. Sophia introduced a new routine to her students. Before sending them off to work in groups, she wrote a number on the board in large print. The number represented the number of groups that were working. So if six groups were working, she wrote a number six on the board. She instructed students that as they finished their group task, they should send a group member to the board to change the number. So after one group finished, the number would read five, and so on until one would turn to zero when all groups were finished. Then she brainstormed a small list of choices for what groups should do when they complete the task. Sometimes she would also create a list to complete the phrase "We will know we are done when . . ." as a way of reminding students about what makes quality work in the particular task they were engaged in. After implementing this low effort-high effect change, she was able to monitor each group, focusing on the content, thinking, and communication. She found that student groups paced themselves better when they saw that other groups were finishing work. She was amazed at how much less stressed she was during group time and how this impacted student behavior. Her students were showing a lot more independence than before.

There will be some changes that require a five in effort, but they are still worth it because they score high in effect. Taking the time to analyze the effort and effect of changes you are thinking about making may help you prioritize the changes you will make first and those that can wait. We also want to encourage you to choose only one high effort change to make at a time. For example, starting an individualized spelling program is a high effort practice with high effects. Starting writing conferences in a writers' workshop is another high effort/high effect alteration to your literacy program. Both are worthy endeavors that will increase student independence but we would not recommend making both transformations at the same time. Take some time to analyze both tasks using the effort-effect rubrics to help you decide which one you will do first. Changes that are low effort and high effect can be done many at a time, but do be realistic, since our educational experiences most likely did not value independence.

As we work to increase independence in students, we must realize the incredible challenge we are taking on. This is a difficult task. Doing something that you have never seen demonstrated is a huge undertaking. This is not an excuse to neglect student independence in our classrooms but it is a reminder that we must go in with the expectation that this will be a challenging endeavor. No matter what grade level you work with, no matter what special needs your students have, all of your students have the potential to grow in their independence. This is the greatest gift you can give your students, and it is the greatest gift you will ever give yourself as a teacher. This is why we call independence the ultimate reciprocal gift and as cliché as it sounds, it truly is the gift that keeps on giving.

Resource A

Task Analysis

	Highly Independent	Somewhat Independent	Dependent
EXAMPLE **Impact on homework**	Takes home any necessary homework, gathers needed resources and supplies, seeks help when needed, turns in homework on time, makes connections to other learning or extends assignment, seeks genuine feedback—not just a score or grade. Learners plan ahead by setting up systems for success—routine, location, resources, etc. This is not necessarily the gifted student: it has to do with ownership, not just ability or learning success.	Are able to meet homework standards when the task is simple. When they meet any challenge, the result is incomplete or missing homework, or the assignment becomes a parent task instead of a student task. Learners may wait until the last minute to complete homework.	Needs teacher and parent support for all parts of the homework process. If support is not available, homework will not get done. Students do not express a sense of ownership, often blaming others or circumstances for missing or incomplete homework. Learners don't remember homework without support. This could be a student who exceeds the standards, but they rely on the adults around them to experience success.
Impact on math problem solving			
Impact on independent reading			
Impact on independent writing			
Impact on peer interactions			

NOTE: See page 15 for directions.

204

Resource B

Moving From
Controlling Learning

Structure, Procedure, or Protocol	Controlled Activity	Structured Activity
Penguin Art	The teacher provides templates for each part of the penguin body for students to trace. Each child takes turns tracing shapes onto black, white, and orange construction paper per the teacher's directions. All students use the same materials when adding details to the penguin and follow specified criteria during the entire activity. When complete, all children have a penguin that resembles the teacher's example of a penguin. Student understandings about penguins have not been furthered.	Students have read books of a variety of genres about penguins. They have researched penguins using a multitude of technology resources and learners understand the characteristics of a penguin. The teacher supports students as they work to create penguins using a variety of materials. As a result, student products vary while understandings are formed and expressed.

NOTE: See pages 27–28 for directions.

Resource C

Responses That Encourage Independence

Student Comment or Action	Affirmative Response That Encourages Dependence	Supportive Response That Encourages Independence
Student shows you her assignment saying, "I'm done."	"I like the way you finished your writing."	
Students clean up the floor after a messy art project.	"Thank you for cleaning up the floor."	
"Suzie told me that I couldn't play with her."	"Oh, you're lots of fun to play with. Suzie, make sure you include everyone."	
"I'm bored."	"Let me show what you can do . . ."	
Student shows you his science hypothesis.	"Wow. That is perfect!"	

NOTE: See page 63 for directions.

References

Adler, D. A. (1989). *A picture book of Martin Luther King, Jr.* New York: Scholastic.

Allington, R. L., & Cunningham, P. M. (1996). *Schools that work: Where all children read and write.* New York: HarperCollins.

Arends, R. I. (2000). *Learning to teach.* Boston, MA: McGraw-Hill.

Atwell, N. (1998). *In the middle: Writing, reading, and learning with adolescents* (2nd ed.). Portsmouth, NH: Heinemann.

Bains, R. (1985). *Martin Luther King.* New York: Troll Associates.

Beck, M. (2007). Avoid the Holidaze. *O at Home, 4*(4), 47–50.

Black, P., & Wiliam, D. (1998). Inside the black box: Raising standards through classroom assessment. *Phi Delta Kappan, 80*(2), 139–148.

Boushey, G., & Moser, J. (2006). *The daily five: Fostering literacy independence in the elementary grades.* Portland, ME: Stenhouse.

Brooks, J. G., & Brooks, M. G. (1999). *In search of understanding: The case for constructivist classrooms.* Alexandria, VA: ASCD.

Brophy, J. E., & Good, T. L. (1974). *Teacher–student relationships: Causes and consequences.* New York: Holt, Rinehart & Winston.

Bunting, E. (2001). *Dandelions.* San Diego: Voyager Books.

Cambourne, B. (2008, February 4–7). *An online discussion revisiting the conditions of learning.* Available: http://www.rcowen.com/DiscussionTranscriptBrianC.htm

Campbell Hill, B. (2001). *Developmental continuums: A framework for literacy instruction and assessment K–8.* Norwood, MA: Christopher Gordon.

Campbell Hill, B., Schlick-Noe, K. L., & Johnson, N. J. (2001). *Literature circles resource guide: Teaching suggestions, forms, samples book lists and database.* Norwood, MA: Christopher-Gordon.

Chappius, J. (2005). Helping students understand assessment. *Educational Leadership, 63*(3), 39–43.

Chappius, S., & Stiggins, R. J. (2002). Classrooms assessment for learning. *Educational Leadership, 60*(1), 40–43.

Charney, R. (1991). *Teaching children to care: Management in the responsive classroom.* Greenfield, MA: Northeast Foundation for Children.

Claiborn, W. L. (1969). Expectancy effects in the classroom: A failure to replicate. *Journal of Educational Psychology, 60,* 377–383.

Clark, D. J. (1989). *Assessment alternatives in mathematics.* Canberra, Australia: Curriculum Development Centre.

Clark, R. (2001) Phenomenal man: Mr. Clark's opus. [online article]. *O Magazine.* Retrieved June 29, 2007, from http://www.oprah.com/rys/omag/rys_omag_200111_phenom.jhtml

Clay, M. M. (1985). *Recording of oral language and biks and gutches.* Portsmouth, NH: Heinemann.

Coles, R. (1995). *The story of Ruby Bridges.* New York: Scholastic.

Coloroso, B. (1994). *Kids are worth it! Giving your child the gift of inner discipline.* New York: Avon.

Coskie, T., Hornof, M., & Trudel, H. (2007). A natural integration: Student-created field guides seamlessly combine science and writing. *Science and Children, 44*(8), 26–31.

Costa, A., & Garmston, R. (1994). *Cognitive coaching: A foundation for renaissance schools.* Norwood, MA: Christopher Gordon.

Costa, A., & Garmston, R. (1996). *Cognitive coaching: A syllabus for the foundation for renaissance schools.* Highlands Ranch, CO: Center for Cognitive Coaching.

Cummings, C. (2000). *Winning strategies for classroom management.* Alexandria, VA: ASCD.

Davidson, M. (1986). *I have a dream: The story of Martin Luther King.* New York: Scholastic.

Davies, A. (2000). *Making classroom assessment work.* Courtenay, BC Canada: Connections Publishing.

Dewey, J. (1897). My pedagogic creed. *The School Journal, 54*(3), 77–80.

"Differentiation myths and realities." (2006, January). *Education Update, 48*(1). Alexandria, VA: ASCD. Retrieved on December 18, 2006 from http://www.ascd.org/portal/site/ascd/menuitem.ab1d8e6fc42e2ffcdeb3ffdb62108a0c

Dirmann, J. (1990). The Jaime Escalante math program. *The Journal of Negro Education, 59*(3), 407–423.

Drew, N. (2000). *Peaceful parents, peaceful kids: Practical ways to build a happy home.* New York: Kensington Publishing.

Duncan, M. (2005). *The kindergarten book: A guide to literacy instruction.* Katonah, NY: Richard C. Owens.

Duke, N. K., Purcell-Gates, V., Hall, L. A., & Tower, C. (2006). Authentic literacy activities for developing comprehension and writing. *The Reading Teacher, 60,* 344–355.

Erickson, L. (2002). *Concept-based curriculum and instruction: Teaching beyond the facts.* Thousand Oaks, CA: Corwin Press.

Fay, J., & Funk, D. (1995). *Teaching with love and logic: Taking control of the classroom.* Golden, CO: Love and Logic Press.

Fay, K., & Whaley, S. (2004). *Becoming one community: Reading and writing with English language learners.* Portland, ME: Stenhouse.

Fisher, B. (1995). *Thinking and learning together: Curriculum and community in a primary classroom.* Portsmouth, NH: Heinemann.

Fountas, I., & Pinnell, G. S. (2001). *Guiding readers and writers: Grades 3–6, teaching comprehension, genre and content literacy.* Portsmouth, NH: Heinemann.

Funk, D. (2002). *Love and logic solutions for kids with special needs.* Golden, CO: Love and Logic Press.

Gagné, R., Yekovich, C. W., & Yekovich, F. R. (1993). *The cognitive psychology of school learning* (2nd ed.). New York: HarperCollins.

Gallagher, D. (2006, January 22). Refinery jobs: One of whatcom's best kept secrets. *Bellingham Herald,* p. 1E.

Gardner, H. (1983). *Frames of mind: The theory of multiple intelligences.* New York: Basic Books.

Garfield, C. (1987). *Peak performers: The new heroes of American business.* New York: Avon.

Ginott, H. G. (1965). *Between parent and child.* New York: Avon.

Giovanni, N. (2005). *Rosa.* New York: Holt and Company.

Glasser, W. (1986). *Control theory in the classroom.* New York: Perennial Library.

Glasser, W. (1993). *The quality school teacher.* New York: HarperCollins.

Good, T. L., & Brophy, J. E. (1987). Looking in classrooms (4th ed.). New York: Harper & Row.

Graves, D. H. (1983). *Writing: Teachers and children at work.* Portsmouth, NH: Heinemann.

Graves, D. H. (2001). *The energy to teach.* Portsmouth, NH: Heinemann.

Graves, D. H., & Kittle, P. (2005). *Inside writing: How to teach the details of craft.* Portsmouth, NH: Heinemann.

Haskins, J. (1992). *The day Martin Luther King, Jr. was shot: A photo history of the civil rights movement.* New York: Scholastic.

Henniger, M., & Rose-Duckworth, R. (2007). *The teaching experience: An introduction to reflective practice.* Boston: Pearson.

Hodgkinson, H. (2007). [Quote]. Retrieved March 30, 2007, from http://www.sedl.org/pubs/t105/intro.html

Independent. (2007). In *Merriam-Webster Dictionary.* Retrieved April 30, 2007, from http://www.m-w.com/dictionary/independent

Jacobs, Heidi Hayes. (1998, December). Playing hardball with curriculum. *ASCD Education Update, 40*(8), 1.

Johnston, P. H. (2004). *Choice words: How our language affects children's learning.* Portland, ME: Stenhouse.

Keene, E. O. (2008). *Reading writing thinking strategies.* Retrieved January 25, 2008, from http://www.readinglady.com/mosaic/tools/Ellin%20Keene%27s%20Reading-Writing.doc

King, M. L. (1961). *The American dream* [Martin Luther King]. Retrieved March 18, 2007, from http://www.africa.upenn.edu/Articles-Gen/Letter-Birmingham.html

Kohn, A. (1993). Choices for children: Why and how to let students decide. *Phi Delta Kappan, 75*(1), 9–20.

Kohn, A. (1996). *Beyond discipline: From compliance to community.* Alexandria, VA: ASCD.

Kohn, A. (1997). Students don't "work," they learn. *Education Week* [online]. Retrieved March 23, 2006, from http://www.edweek.org/ew/articles/1997/09/03/01kohn.h17.html?print=1

Kohn, A. (1999). *The schools our children deserve: Moving beyond traditional classrooms and "tougher standards."* Boston: Houghton Mifflin.

Kohn, A. (2003). Almost there, but not quite. *Educational Leadership, 60*(6), 26–29.

Kostelnik, M. J., Whiren, A. P., Soderman, A. K., Stein, L. C., & Gregory, K. (2002). *Guiding children's social development: Theory to practice.* Clifton Park, NY: Delmar.

Kujawa, S., & Huske, L. (1995). *The strategic teaching and reading project guidebook* (Rev. ed.). Oak Brook, IL: North Central Regional Educational Laboratory.

Levine, D., Beck, M. W., Naylor, M., & Rose, R. (2006). *Puzzlewise for growing minds: Math, level 5.* Bellingham, WA: Puzzlewise.

Levine, E. (1990). *If you lived at the time of Martin Luther King.* New York: Scholastic.

Levine, M. (2007). The essential cognitive backpack. *Educational Leadership, 64*(7), 16–22.

Levy, S. (1996). *Starting from scratch: One classroom builds its own curriculum.* Portsmouth, NH: Heinemann.

Marzano, R. J., Marzano, J. S., & Pickering, D. J. (2003). *Classroom management that works: Research-based strategies for every teacher.* Alexandria, VA: ASCD.

Mathews, J. (1988). *Jaime Escalante: The best teacher in America.* New York: Holt.

Mathews, J. (2000, October 24). Writing by the rules no easy task: Rubrics can help students focus on basics, but some teachers and parents say they squelch creativity. *Washington Post* (section A). Retrieved March 16, 2007, from http://pqasb.pqarchiver.com/washingtonpost/access/62847774.html?dids=62847774:62847774&FMT=ABS&FMTS=ABS:FT&date=Oct+24%2C+2000&author=Jay+Mathews&pub=The+Washington+Post&edition=&startpage=A.13&desc=Writing+by+the+Rules+No+Easy+Task

Menendez, R. (Director). (1988). *Stand and Deliver* [Film]. (Available from American Playhouse)

Mermelstein, L. (2007). *Don't forget to share: The crucial last step in the writing workshop.* Portsmouth, NH: Heinemann.

Mooney, M. (2000, October 14). Keynote address for Washington Organization of Reading Development Conference: *How much can you get from a book?* Richland, WA.

New Zealand Ministry of Education. (1997). *Reading for life.* Katonah, NY: Richard C. Owens.

Owen, R. C. (2007). *The teaching and learning cycle.* Katonah, NY: Richard C. Owens.

Palmer, P. (1998). *The courage to teach.* San Francisco: Jossey-Bass.

Passarini, J. R. (2007). *Dr. John R. Passarini's homepage.* Retrieved June 15, 2007, from http://www.johnpassarini.com

Pearson, P., & Gallagher, M. (1983). The instruction of reading comprehension. *Contemporary Educational Psychology, 8,* 317–344.

Perkins, D. (1999). The many faces of constructivism. *Educational Leadership, 57*(3), 6–11.

Piaget, J. (1950). *The psychology of intelligence* (M. Piercy & D. Berlyn, Trans.). New York: Harcourt, Brace.

Prelutsky, J. (1994). *A pizza the size of the sun.* New York: HarperCollins.

Rappaport, D. (2001). *Martin's big words: The life of Dr. Martin Luther King, Jr.* New York: Scholastic.

Reed, J. C. (1994). *Martin Luther King, Jr.: A big biography.* New York: Newbridge Communications.

Rich, D. (1988). *Megaskills.* Boston: Houghton Mifflin.

Ringgold, F. (1999). *If a bus could talk: The story of Rosa Parks.* New York: Scholastic.

Ritchhart, R. (2002). *Intellectual character: What it is, why it matters, how to get it.* San Francisco: Jossey-Bass.

Ritchhart, R., Moran, S., Blythe, T., & Reese, J. (2002). *Teaching in the creative classroom: An educator's guide for exploring creative teaching and learning.* Burbank: Disney Learning Partnership & Project Zero, Harvard Graduate School of Education.

Roe, B. D., & Ross, E. P. (2002). *Student teaching and field experiences handbook.* Upper Saddle River, NJ: Merrill-Prentice Hall.

Rose, R., & Rathjen, D. (2001). Motion of visionary education. Change is a constant. *Primary Voices K–6, 9*(3), 22–30.

Rosenberg, M. B. (2003). *Life-enriching education: Nonviolent communication helps schools improve performance, reduce conflict, and enhance relationships.* Encinitas, CA: Puddle Dance Press.

Rosenthal, A. K., & Dyer, J. (2006). *Cookies: Bite size life lessons.* New York: HarperCollins.

Rosenthal, R., & Jacobson, L. (1968). *Pygmalion in the classroom.* New York: Holt, Rinehart & Winston.

Routman, R. (1994*). Invitations: Changing as teachers and learners K–12.* Portsmouth, NH: Heinemann.

Routman, R. (2003). *Reading essentials: The specifics you need to teach reading well.* Portsmouth, NH: Heinemann.

School-survival.net. (2007). Retrieved July 20, 2007, from www.school-survival.net.

Shaw, L. (2007, June 24) "Set lesson plans stir controversy." *Seattle Times.* Retrieved June 25, 2007, from http://seattletimes.nwsource.com/cgi-bin/PrintStory.pl?document_id=2003760509&slug=curriculum24m&date=20070624

Shore, D. Z., & Alexander, J. (2006). *This is the dream.* New York: HarperCollins.

Sitton, R. (1996). *Increasing student spelling achievement.* Scottsdale, AZ: Egger Publishing.

Southern Maine Partnership. (2007). Instructional differentiation for student independence. Retrieved on June 20, 2007, from http://www.usm.maine.edu/smp/Files/usmDiffFinal.pdf

Sparks, D. (1999). Assessment with victims: An interview with Rick Stiggins. *Journal of Staff Development, 20*(2). Retrieved February 27, 2005, from http://www.nsdc.org/library/publications/jsd/stiggins202.cfm

Stiggins, R. J. (1999). Assessment, student confidence, and school success. *Phi Delta Kappan, 81*(3), 191–198.

Stiggins, R. J. (2002). Assessment crisis: The absence of assessment FOR learning. *Phi Delta Kappan, 83*(10), 758–765.

Taylor, D. (2001). A day in the life of Brian Cambourne: Teacher, activist, scholar. *Language Arts, 79*(2), 178–187.

Tomlinson, C. A. (1999). Mapping a route toward differentiated instruction. *Educational Leadership, 57*(1), 12–16.

Tomlinson, C. A. (2001). *How to differentiate instruction in mixed-ability classrooms.* Alexandria, VA: ASCD.

Tomlinson, C. A. (2003). Deciding to teach them all. *Educational Leadership, 61*(2), 6–11.

Udall, A. J., & Daniels, J. E. (1991). *Creating the thoughtful classroom: Strategies to promote student thinking.* Tucson, AZ: Zephyr Press.

Vygotsky, L. (1962). *Thought and language.* (E. Hanfmann & G. Vakar, Trans.). Cambridge, MA: MIT Press.

Vygotsky, L. (1978). *Mind in society: The development of higher psychological processes.* Cambridge, MA: Harvard University Press.

Wiggins, G., & McTighe, J. (2000). *Understanding by design study guide.* Alexandria, VA: ASCD.

Wiggins, G., & McTighe, J. (2005). *Understanding by design* (2nd ed.). Upper Saddle River, NJ: Prentice Hall.

Winn, W., & Snyder, D. (1996). Cognitive perspectives in psychology. In D. H. Jonassen (Ed.), *Handbook of research for educational communications and technology* (pp. 112–142). New York: Macmillan.

Wong, H. K., & Wong, R. T. (1998). *The first days of school: How to be an effective teacher.* Mountain View, CA: Harry K. Wong Publications.

Wormeli, R. (2006). *Fair isn't always equal: Assessing and grading in the differentiated classroom.* Portland, ME: Stenhouse.

Wood Ray, K., & Cleaveland, L. B. (2004). *About the authors: Writing workshop with our youngest writers.* Portsmouth, NH: Heinemann.

Yopp, R. H., & Yopp, H. K. (2001). *Literature-based reading activities* (3rd ed.). Boston: Allyn & Bacon.

Index

CORWIN PRESS

The Corwin Press logo—a raven striding across an open book—represents the union of courage and learning. Corwin Press is committed to improving education for all learners by publishing books and other professional development resources for those serving the field of PreK–12 education. By providing practical, hands-on materials, Corwin Press continues to carry out the promise of its motto: **"Helping Educators Do Their Work Better."**